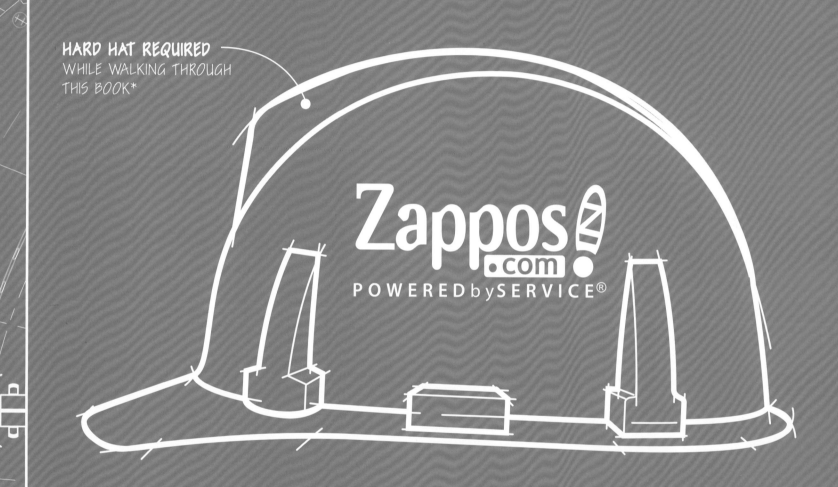

HARD HAT REQUIRED
WHILE WALKING THROUGH
THIS BOOK*

*HARD HAT NOT INCLUDED

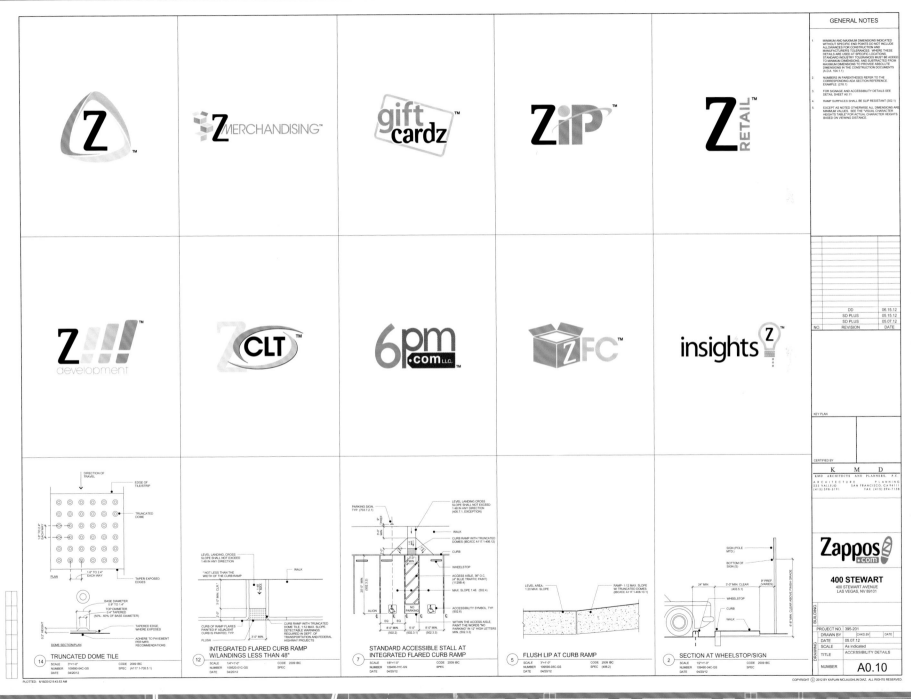

GENERAL NOTES

1. MINIMUM AND MAXIMUM DIMENSIONS INDICATED WITHOUT SPECIFIC END POINTS DO NOT INCLUDE ALLOWANCES FOR CONSTRUCTION AND MANUFACTURER'S TOLERANCES. WHERE THESE DETAILS ARE USED AT SPECIFIC LOCATIONS, STANDARD INDUSTRY TOLERANCES MUST BE ADDED TO MINIMUM DIMENSIONS, AND SUBTRACTED FROM MAXIMUM DIMENSIONS TO PROVIDE ABSOLUTE DIMENSIONS IN THE CONSTRUCTION DOCUMENTS (A.D.A. 104.1.1)

2. NUMBERS IN PARENTHESES REFER TO THE CORRESPONDING ADA SECTION REFERENCE. EXAMPLE: (216.1)

3. FOR SIGNAGE AND ACCESSIBILITY DETAILS SEE DETAIL SHEET A0.11

4. RAMP SURFACES SHALL BE SLIP RESISTANT (302.1)

5. EXCEPT AS NOTED OTHERWISE, ALL DIMENSIONS ARE MINIMUM VALUES. SEE THE "VISUAL CHARACTER HEIGHTS TABLE" FOR ACTUAL CHARACTER HEIGHTS BASED ON VIEWING DISTANCE.

NO.	REVISION	DATE
	DD	06.15.12
	SD PLUS	05.15.12
	SD PLUS	05.07.12

KEY PLAN

CERTIFIED BY

K M D
KMD ARCHITECTS AND PLANNERS, P.C.
ARCHITECTURE   PLANNING
222 VALLEJO   SAN FRANCISCO, CA 94111
(415) 398-5191   FAX (415) 394-7158

Zappos.com

400 STEWART
400 STEWART AVENUE
LAS VEGAS, NV 89101

PROJECT NO. 395-201
DRAWN BY   CHKD.BY   DATE
DATE 05.07.12
SCALE As indicated
TITLE ACCESSIBILITY DETAILS
NUMBER A0.10

14. TRUNCATED DOME TILE
SCALE 3"=1'-0" CODE 2009 IBC
NUMBER 109520-04C-GS SPEC (A117.1-705.5.1)
DATE 04/20/12

12. INTEGRATED FLARED CURB RAMP W/LANDINGS LESS THAN 48"
SCALE 1/4"=1'-0" CODE 2009 IBC
NUMBER 109520-01C-GS SPEC
DATE 04/20/12

7. STANDARD ACCESSIBLE STALL AT INTEGRATED FLARED CURB RAMP
SCALE 1/8"=1'-0" CODE 2009 IBC
NUMBER 109400-01C-GS SPEC
DATE 04/20/12

5. FLUSH LIP AT CURB RAMP
SCALE 3"=1'-0" CODE 2009 IBC
NUMBER 109580-03C-GS SPEC (406.2)
DATE 04/20/12

2. SECTION AT WHEELSTOP/SIGN
SCALE 1/2"=1'-0" CODE 2009 IBC
NUMBER 109480-04C-GS SPEC
DATE 04/20/12

PLOTTED: 6/18/2012 9:43:53 AM

2012-2013

CULTURE BOOK

AS DEFINED BY OUR EMPLOYEES,
PARTNERS AND CUSTOMERS

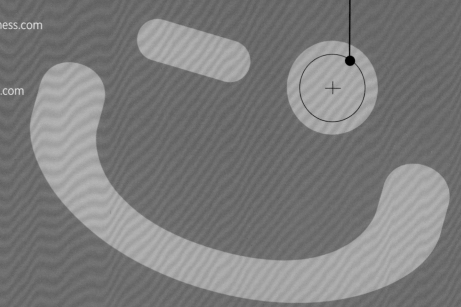

SINGLE OPEN
OCULAR
FRONT VIEW

Editor in Chief and Aperitifs

Jenn Lim facebook.com/byjennlim | @DHMovementCEO | jenn@deliveringhappiness.com

Designers, Producers and Flair Inducers

Fadhly Bey facebook.com/fadhlybey | @fadhlybey | fadhly@deliveringhappiness.com

Roger Erik Tinch facebook.com/retinch | @tinch | ret@retinch.com

Copy (So We're Not Sloppy) Editors

Kathleen Winkler

Iris Zinck purrformer@gmail.com

Created in cahoots with Delivering Happiness, LLC
www.deliveringhappiness.com

facebook.com/deliveringhappiness

@DHMovement

Printed by Fanny Chen, Orbitel International LLC | fanny@orbitelinternational.com

2012-2013 CULTURE BOOK IS
BREAKING DOWN WALLS...LITERALLY

CONTENTS

ZAPPOS
FAMILY CORE VALUES

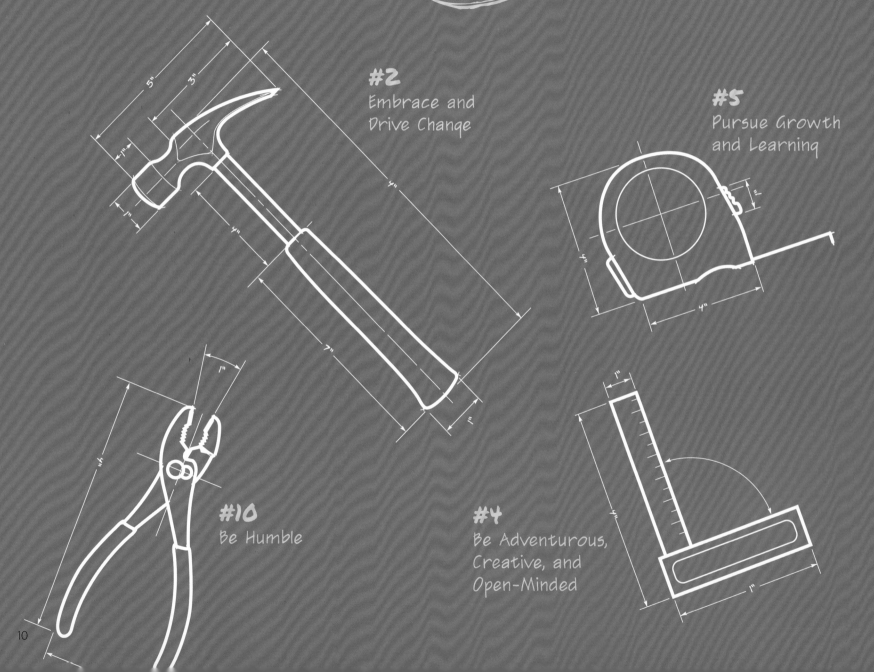

#2
Embrace and
Drive Change

#5
Pursue Growth
and Learning

#10
Be Humble

#4
Be Adventurous,
Creative, and
Open-Minded

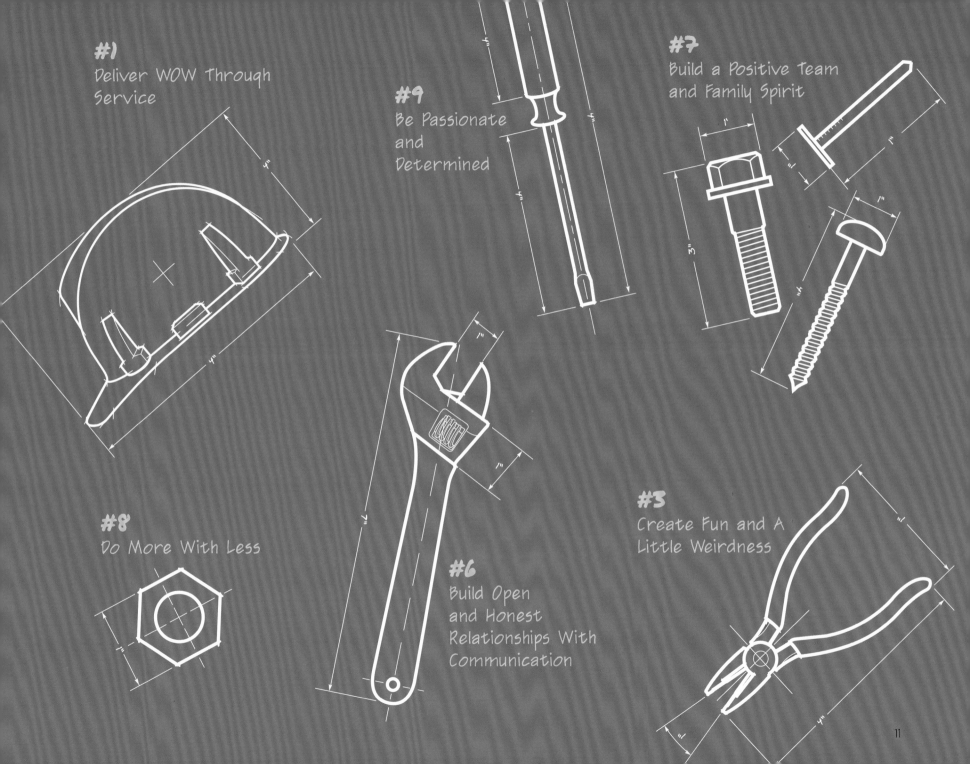

#1
Deliver WOW Through Service

#9
Be Passionate
and
Determined

#7
Build a Positive Team
and Family Spirit

#8
Do More With Less

#6
Build Open
and Honest
Relationships With
Communication

#3
Create Fun and A
Little Weirdness

11

FOREWORD →

The culture book is an annual tradition for the Zappos Family. Every year, I send an email to our employees asking people to write a few paragraphs about what the Zappos culture means to them. Except for typos, it's unedited, because one of our core values is to Build Open and Honest Relationships With Communication.

For us, our #1 priority is company culture. Our belief is that if we get the culture right, most of the other stuff -- like delivering great customer service, or building a long-term enduring brand and business -- will happen naturally on its own.

In my book "Delivering Happiness: A Path to Profits, Passion, and Purpose", I write about how a company's culture and a company's brand are really just two sides of the same coin. The brand is simply a lagging indicator of the culture.

Over the past 13+ years, we've continuously experienced rapid growth. As we continue to grow and hire new people, we need to make sure that they understand and become a part of our culture. That is the purpose of this culture book -- to provide a glimpse of what the Zappos culture is all about to new hires, prospective new hires, our vendors and partners, and anyone else who might be interested.

So what is the Zappos culture? To me, the Zappos culture embodies many different elements. It's about always looking for new ways to WOW everyone we come in contact with. It's about building relationships where we treat each other like family. It's about teamwork and having fun and not taking ourselves too seriously. It's about growth, both personal and professional. It's about achieving the impossible with fewer people. It's about openness, taking risks, and not being afraid to make mistakes. It's about being part of a story that never stops unfolding. And it's about having faith that if we do the right thing, then in the long run we will be a part of building something great.

Our culture is based on our 10 core values:
1) Deliver WOW Through Service
2) Embrace and Drive Change
3) Create Fun and A Little Weirdness
4) Be Adventurous, Creative, and Open-Minded
5) Pursue Growth and Learning
6) Build Open and Honest Relationships With Communication
7) Build a Positive Team and Family Spirit
8) Do More With Less
9) Be Passionate and Determined
10) Be Humble

Unlike most companies, where core values are just a plaque on the wall, our core values play a big part in how we hire, train, and develop our employees.

In addition to trying to WOW our customers, we also try to WOW our employees and the vendors and business partners that we work with. We believe that it creates a virtuous cycle, and in our own way, we're making the world a better place and improving people's lives. It's all part of our long term vision to deliver happiness to the world.

Of course, the Zappos culture means different things to different people, so I thought the best way for people to learn what the Zappos culture was all about was to hear from our employees directly. Below is the email that I sent to our employees in 2012:

From: Tony Hsieh
Subject: 2012 Culture Book!

It's time to put together a new edition of the Zappos Culture Book, to be distributed to employees, prospective employees, business partners, tour guests, and even some customers!

Our culture is the combination of all of our employees' ideas about the culture, so we would like to include everyone's thoughts in this book.

Please write a few sentences about what the Zappos culture means to you. (What is the Zappos culture? What's different about it compared to other company cultures? What do you like about our culture?) We will compile everyone's contribution into the book.

When writing your response, please do not refer to any previous culture books, any training/orientation material, the company handbook, or any other

company-published material. We want to hear YOUR thoughts about the company culture.

Also, please do not talk to anyone about what you will be writing or what anyone else wrote. And finally, if you contributed to last year's Culture Book, please do not look at what you wrote last year until after you've written and submitted this year's entry.

Remember, there are no wrong answers. We want to know what the Zappos culture means to you specifically at this point in time, and we expect different responses from different people.

...

Thanks everyone!

We hope you enjoy the 2012-2013 edition of the Zappos culture book!

-Tony Hsieh
CEO - Zappos.com, Inc.
ceo@zappos.com
twitter.com/zappos

PS: If you'd like to learn more about our culture, check out our blogs at:
http://blogs.zappos.com

Learn more about the Zappos Family at:
http://about.zappos.com

Our job openings are available online at:
http://jobs.zappos.com

Also, we offer free tours of our offices in Las Vegas. You can schedule a tour at:
http://tours.zappos.com

We hope you enjoy
the 2012 edition of the

ZAPPOS CULTURE BOOK

If you'd like to learn more about
our culture, check out our blogs at:
http://blogs.zappos.com

You can also learn more about the
Zappos Family at:
http://about.zappos.com

Our job openings are available online at:
http://jobs.zappos.com

Also, we offer tours of our offices in Las Vegas.
You can schedule a tour at:
http://tours.zapppos.com

ZAPPOS ZAPPER
T2000
PROFILE VIEW

2011 RANDOM FUN

MERCH VS. FINANCE WATER FIGHT

ZAPPOS DERBY

WOODEN CARS GO FAST

THE TWO PISTOL
POINTEE FREEZE
FRONT VIEW

2011 8000 METER CHALLENGE

MOUNT CHARLESTON

THE TWO COOL
FOR SCHOOL
DAYTIME MODEL

INSERT COIN(S)
VIDEOLOUNGE GAMEBAR

nom-nom nom

BOTTLES OF
GOOD TIME
GROUPED FORMAT

2011 RANDOM FUN

INSERT COINS

THE
DOUBLE-FIST
NIGHTTIME MODEL

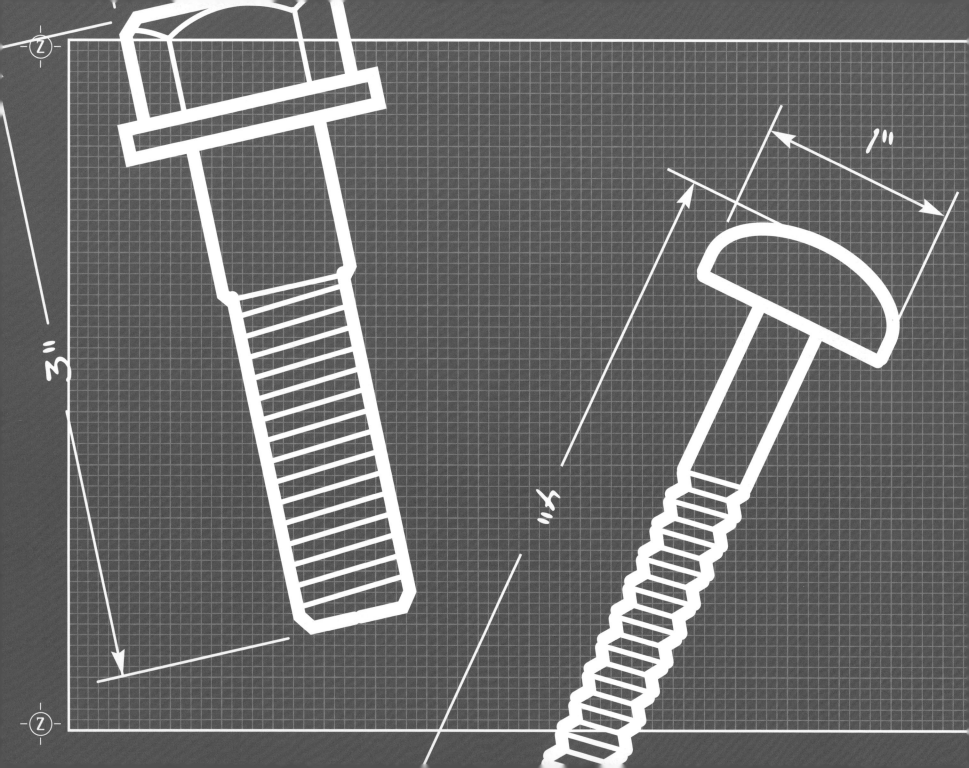

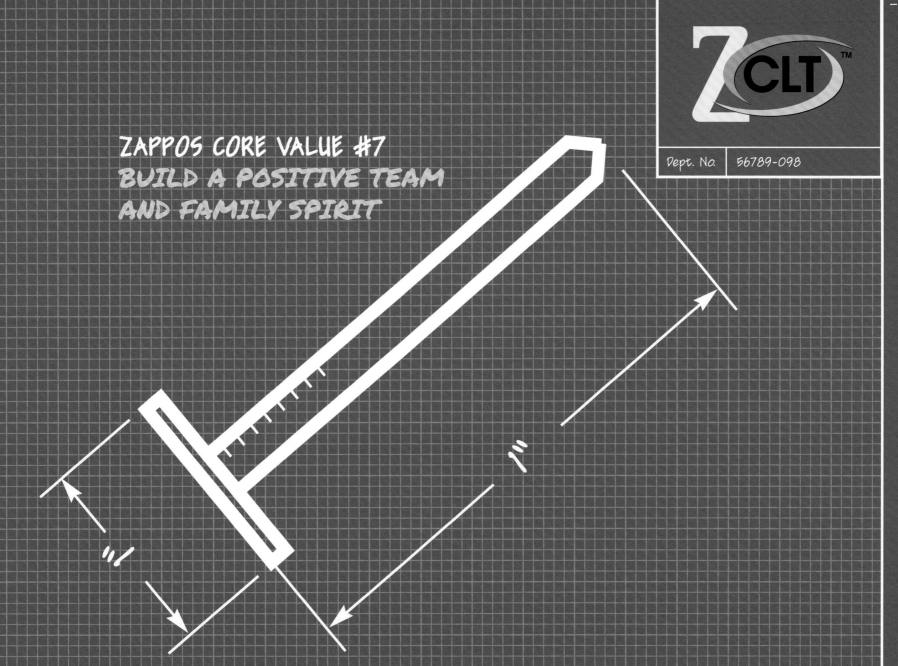

ZAPPOS CORE VALUE #7
BUILD A POSITIVE TEAM
AND FAMILY SPIRIT

Dept. No. | 56789-098

ANONYMOUS
employee since 2003

I walk through the doors with a smile on my face every day. I love this company and our Zappos Culture. From day one, I knew this was the job for me. Just being able to walk in every day and be 100% myself means that I will be here for a very long time. I love all the fun things we do to keep our culture going. Celebrating team membersĺ birthdays, parades, picnics, happy hours, parties, team buildings and much, much more. I am very happy and proud to work for a company that cares for their employees. This is why it's very important that we always support, participate, and protect our culture. It's up to us to make it what is and keep it alive.

ANONYMOUS
employee since 2010

The Zappos Culture has gone from being office conduct to a way of life. Every day now I bring a little Zappos home with me! I'm excited to be a part of an amazing group of people who live to put a smile on the faces of others.

ANONYMOUS
employee since 2011

I love Zappos!

ANONYMOUS
employee since 2010

Working at Zappos is not for everyone. If you don't like free food, meeting life-long friends, having fun, random Nerf» gun wars, free food, people in penguin suits roaming the halls, free food, celebrations almost every day, free food, parties, meeting celebrities (Aaron Sanchez!), freedom, your very own coffee shop, using the free gym, laughing, and getting paid for all of that, then this is not the place for you. (Did I mention free food?) I love this company and I'm happy to call myself a Zapponian!

ANONYMOUS
employee since 2009

I have been at Zappos nearly three years. I have never had more of a family then I do here. This company has brought me so much joy in my time here. I love that we are able to ñPursue Growth and Learningî and have all the possibilities in the world. I am very grateful to have the friends and the job that I do.

ANONYMOUS
employee since 2012

When I first read Zappos' Ten Core Values, they were everything that I thought a company should stay true to and aspire to, every single day _ which is not limited just to companies, but to people in general. They are words to live by.

Coming into Zappos and actually seeing how much these values play a role in everyday situations is tremendously inspiring. After all, it is always easier said than done, but that is not the case here. Zappos came at just the right time for me, when I'd finally come to a point of questioning exactly who I am and knowing who I want to be and what I want to give to the world. Prior to this, the thoughts were there, but now I am pushing myself forward, pursuing change for the better for all, and am surrounded by people who feel the same way.

Zappos is a family. Zappos understands pushing the boundaries, doing the best you can with what you have, learning, and having fun along the way since you cannot always be serious. The Zappos Culture is its people and I want to give it a huge thanks for everything that it has done for me, everyone it has touched, and how it has influenced all around me. Thank you.

ANONYMOUS
employee since 2011

Zappos is a reason to push myself to try harder than I ever have before.

Zappos reminds me that I can be better.

ANONYMOUS
employee since 2007

Zappos means having an extended family that always has your back. Doing for others while expecting nothing in return. EVERYONE coming together in a time of need. Giving back.

ANONYMOUS
employee since 2010

Friends, family and fun. The three Fs that make my life awesome, all of which have something to do with the Zappos Culture. Who would've known that an F could be so good?!

ANONYMOUS
employee since 2010

Zappos is simply awesome.

When I set off on my journey to be happy, I knew that I needed to find a job where the people were great and the job was enjoyable. I found both of these at Zappos.

I've now been here for over a year, I've made some great friends and I love what I'm doing. Zappos has provided me with the opportunity to make great things happen.

Thank you all!

ANONYMOUS
employee since 2008

My favorite thing about Zappos is the "come as you are" aspect of our culture. Not only are our personalities allowed to shine, but being yourself is totally encouraged. The Zappos family is widely diverse and very accepting of others. My next favorite thing is wearing whatever you want to work. I love being casual. If I am at a loss for what to wear, I can always don a Zappos T-shirt or pajamas.

ANONYMOUS
employee since 2010

To me, the Zappos Culture means an individual opportunity, and responsibility, to act/work towards an environment that is conducive to personal and sustainable company growth. It means seeking to make the sum of the whole greater than the sum of the parts, while keeping an open mind to what we can do better without sacrificing what we have accomplished.

ANONYMOUS
employee since 2011

Wow, Zappos!!!! What is there to say about a company that really values its employees and lets them express themselves any way they want? I had come from a company that didn't care about its employees, and to come here was a big change. I love the fact that we are in charge of our own destiny here and that we are encouraged to pursue our dreams. I hope that more companies will treat their employees the way we are treated here, really value them, and help them grow and achieve their dreams.

ANONYMOUS
employee since 2012

The Zappos Culture is a unique creature. It's multifaceted and far-reaching. Once you're fully enveloped by it, it inevitably begins to seep into other aspects of your life. However, this isn't really a bad thing, as it's a culture that's passionate about fostering kindness.

ANONYMOUS
employee since 2011

The Zappos Culture is certainly different from what I was used to at my previous job. I was with my last employer for over seven years and after my first month with Zappos, I was more aware of what the company is all about and what we do outside of sales than I had been in all my seven years at the last job.

Another thing I had to get used to was the level of trust and understanding from other employees ƒ not just from my department but all over the company. We can easily talk to higher-ups in the company and even build friendships with them. The switch between the two jobs was like going from the Dust Bowl to the Jetsons ƒ from being in a daily grind of just carrying on to zipping around in a flying car that turns into a suitcase to carry around.

That is the Zappos Culture to me — a magic flying car I can carry around wherever I go. Becoming a member of the Zappos family has been liberating, challenging and downright enchanting. I am grateful to be a part of the Zappos Culture.

ANONYMOUS
employee since 2010

The Zappos Culture, to me, means becoming a better person, not just in my job, but in my life outside of work as well. Whenever I think about the Ten Core Values, I am reminded that I need to apply them to every aspect of my life, and in turn I will become a better person.

ANONYMOUS
employee since 2010

The Zappos Culture means high-fives through the hall, smiling faces everywhere, and having that sense of family.

ANONYMOUS
employee since 2010

The Zappos Culture is the catalyst in discovering and following your passion. Our culture is why we are able to do what we do on a daily basis.

ANONYMOUS
employee since 2010

Finally, I look forward to work each day! My favorite Core Value is #3: Create Fun and A Little Weirdness.î Who wouldn't want to be encouraged to be themselves? Thank you, Zappos, for letting me finally be myself at work, where I am free to laugh and joke and find shoes that actually fit!

ANONYMOUS
employee since 2010

The Zappos Culture, to me, means that we are all part of one great big family. We have each otherís backs and spread the love to everyone we meet.

ANONYMOUS
employee since 2010

The Zappos Culture means being yourself, living every day to the fullest, friendships and always having fun!

ANONYMOUS
employee since 2007

The Zappos Culture is fasmatasmic!

ANONYMOUS
employee since 2011

The Zappos Culture and What it Means to Me

Here is a company that truly puts the customers' concerns before its own, in a day where you see a lot of lip service to the term "giving the customer what they really need," but what they actually mean is, "We're a large corporation and regardless of what you feel, it no longer matters to us. We're still keeping your money and costing you more time."

There is now a large force pushing toward what customers are truly asking for: Respect, Consideration, An ear to hear, Compassion, Sympathy, and Empathy. There are so many other descriptive words that come to mind; however, those are a few of the larger ones that we all harness effectively in our daily jobs and in our lives. Zappos helps to put the consumer at the forefront of what drives this business. Finally, "someone" who puts their money where their mouth is, and we are a part of it. It definitely drives a satisfaction within me knowing that I contribute to the larger picture and am giving selflessly.

ANONYMOUS
employee since 2010

Our Zappos Culture is the interactions we have on a day-to-day basis that bring us together. We work hard, play hard, and get involved with each otherís lives. We care for one another just as much as we care for our customers, and it shows. The caring nature of our call center is a big contributor to our culture. We come together in times of need, whether for charity, or for a coworker as a family. What does our culture mean to me? One word: family.

ANONYMOUS

employee since 2010

The Zappos Culture meant a lot to me when I first started, and it still does. I think that we as a company should hold onto the people who TRULY cultivate and perpetuate the culture here. Core Value #5, "Pursue Growth and Learning,î is my favorite Core Value and should be encouraged and embraced in all departments.

ANONYMOUS

employee since 2010

Looooooooooove it!

ADAM Z.
employee since 2011

The Zappos Culture defines this environment, which we get to enjoy, share, and create. Because the culture is aligned with my personal values, I feel very natural and at home here. One doesn't have to look far to find a friend or someone with the same interests. Since I've been employed here, I have made many great friends!

I identify with Core Value #3 most strongly, as having fun and being a little weird is what gives life its flavor. I think that core value really motivates me to provide a positive and uplifting experience for my customers and coworkers. The actual transaction is great, but the most important part is to make a real human connection with someone ... "Here's your change." "Paper or plastic?" "Credit or debit?" "You want ketchup with that?" I don't want a straw. I want real human moments. I want to see you. I want you to see me. I don't want to give that up.

The Zappos Culture provides me the perfect platform to get those human moments because of their innovative view on business and happiness. I feel that it enables me to deliver the kind of service my customers want and to enjoy my job to the fullest.

ADRIAN M.
employee since 2009

Wow, another year has passed, and along with it, my love and appreciation for a place like Zappos has grown exponentially. Just when I think it couldn't possibly get any better, Zappos is there to prove me wrong. Whether it's good times, or rough times, the Zappos Family ALWAYS prevails and I feel privileged to be on such an amazing team.

I could literally go on for pages and pages about this place, but it comes down to ten important values ... our Core Values. They are the values by which we live our personal lives and also our work lives. When I'm faced with a tough decision, and don't immediately know what to do, I know I can rely on the core values to lead me to the promised land. They are the compass we go by, and it's truly special.

Thank you, everyone who makes Zappos a place I can call home!

Funky Cold

ADRIANNA C.
employee since 2011

I have never been in more love with a job in my brief history in the work force. In August 2011, just as you are now, Fabulous Reader, with your eyes scanning the multitude of opinions, stories, and expressions of utter love, did I with a copy of the previous yearís Culture Book. And, like you, if you have never been plunged face first into Zappos, I could not believe that such a place could be real. That they must have paid their employees for their kind words, or made them up completely. Then I joined this ... crazy, wild, caring, incredible, and absolutely amazing family of Zapponians that is the Las Vegas location. And I understood at that moment that this is something very special, and that it was an immense honor to be accepted into the extraordinary arms of this company.

The Zappos Culture, to me, is everyone involved. The people that make up the decorations, the events, and ultimately the memories are the greatest gift I could have never asked for from a job. The friends and memories that I have made are priceless; the laughs I have shared with these people, through even the toughest of times, are each a testament to how unique this place is. It truly is magical, and if you haven't seen it, it is hard to believe or understand. I have grown here, and discovered pieces of myself that had before been under-nurtured in the most extreme of ways.

To my Ziblingz, Team Hammer Time and Team R.A.C.E.C.A.R., I love and cherish you all. Thank you for growing with me, and embracing me when I venture forward. To the entire Zappos family,

thank you for living up to the over-the-moon expectations you have for new employees and guests alike. And to you, Fabulous Reader, for taking the time to read my small section in this book filled with the words of many wonderful people.

Thank you <3 ~"DorkLady"

AIMEE M.
employee since 2009

The Zappos Culture is absolutely amazing. Each employee is given an opportunity to be themselves. The connections we are able to make in this workplace are unlike anything I have ever seen in any other job.

ALANNA T.
employee since 2011

I get to be as weird as I naturally am! It's crazy to know that I can show up to work with blue hair and with as many piercings as I can fit on my face. I love the fact that the Zappos Culture lets us all be different in every way possible. We get to joke around, dress all crazy, and be friends with people we probably never would've spoken to anywhere else. Our culture is insane in the best way!

ALEXA G.
employee since 2008

The Zappos Culture means everything to me! I have been here for four years and it just keeps getting better! For us, ñcultureî is not just a word, but a way of life. We do everything here with our company culture in mind and it shows. I love my Zappos family and my job like it was the first day! Can't wait to see what the future holds for us.

ALEXIE I.
employee since 2012

Hello, my fellow Zapponians!

I just got hired with the company in May. I've been absolutely obsessed with Zappos from the day my college professor had us watch a video of Tony talking about the Zappos Culture. I couldn't be more honored/blessed/humbled to be working for such an amazing company. It is honestly a dream come true and I am so excited to see what exciting adventures my future with this company has to bring.

Love you all!

ALICE O.
employee since 2011

This is a poem but I could not put it in the format is should be in so I hope it can be read okay!!!!!!!!!!
WORKING WITH YELLOW DUCKIES -
I come from the high country far away,
Because of Zappos, in Vegas I will stay;
The Magic happens when you walk through the door, -
Something will happen to touch you to the core;
It's a joy to work with others whose core values we share,
A wonderful feeling to know they really care;
The Core Values are special, I like number three,
No one will judge me for being just me;
To be working here I am so lucky,
Just ask one of the thousands of yellow duckies;
Pink, purple or spiked-up hair,
And it doesn't really matter what you wear;
You can sing, laugh or shed a tear,
No one is on your case, there is nothing to fear;
Make a mistake? You get a hug, not a squeeze,
So give me a BIG one if you please;
Just let your imagination run wild,
Once again you can feel like a child;
Be inspired to have a dream,
Leave a footprint, be part of a team;
I feel so tiny in something so enormously grand
It makes me feel humble to be part of the plan;
Not enough room to count the ways,
I will thank Zappos the rest of my days!

ALICIA A.
employee since 2007

The Zappos Culture means family to me. I am eternally grateful to the people at Zappos. It is like having my best friends and family around at all times. I can't give back enough of what the people in this place have given me. Thank you to you all, just for being you. <3

ALICIA S.
employee since 2010

I've been with Zappos for just about two years and it keeps getting better! The people and atmosphere just make you want to be a better person. I can't wait to see what years to come bring!

ALISHA M.
employee since 2011

The Zappos Culture is unlike any other I've encountered. It truly embraces a family spirit. Everyone is genuine and accepts you for who you are as an individual. For the first time in my life, I can honestly say I love my job!

ALISON M.
employee since 2012

The Zappos Culture means I am free to be me. It means that all of us are accepted, encouraged and even recognized for being who we really are. We are always welcome to show our inner fabulousness (Is that a word? If it's not, it should be!!) To our Zappos family and, of course, to our customers! WOW is not just a word ... it's in our DNA! We WOW therefore we are!

ALLISON S.
employee since 2010

Culture is a very ambiguous word, but it is a much needed umbrella word that we use a lot here. I feel to adequately describe the culture, we would need an anthropologist to come live amongst us for a year and compose ethnography. As much as I can try, I cannot bullet point what it is. I can only say that it is unique, it is ever changing, and the majority of people here actively try to make it grow and evolve.

ALYSSA A.
employee since 2011

About a year ago, I was applying to work for Zappos. I thought I knew what the company was like, such as the culture, benefits, and work environment. On my first day of training, I realized very quickly that I was wrong. That first day, September 4th, I made over 40 new friends within my training class. I have never had a job in the past where I considered my coworkers friends! Now, almost a year later, I have experienced so many amazing opportunities. I have found who I am as a person and everyone around me accepts me for it. The Zappos Culture has allowed me to grow as a person, in my career as well as my personal life. I bring our Ten Core Values with me wherever I go. Be humble, create fun and a little weirdness, have open and honest communication in all of your relationships and most of all, be passionate and determined. I never knew a company could drive you to be the best you can be the way Zappos does. Zappos has created a whole new world for me. I am excited to see the journey that lies ahead.

AMANDA E.
employee since 2012

The Zappos Culture, to me, is like a very big family. I feel this way because my family is ALWAYS there for me. Good, bad, and everything between, yet they never judge. Their overall goal is to help me grow and be a better version of me. I feel every day at Zappos is this type of experience. I am honored to work here and look forward to walking in the door every day! I just hope that I can have an effect on ONE person or place the way that Zappos will FOREVER have an effect on me!

AMANDA J.
employee since 2012

The Zappos Culture, to me, meansîfamily.î I just started and have dreamed about working here for three years. Until fate pointed me in the right direction, I was not sure I would end up here. Even though I am new, I can already feel and notice the difference in myself and so can everyone else. I know this is my final job, because this is a new life for me and not just another job.

AMANDA V.
employee since 2011

Zappos is Amazing! I used to work in retail management, and all of my friends worked at Zappos. They told me about all the amazing and fun stories/journeys they've been on, and how much they truly loved their work family. Little did I know what I was missing. I'm almost at my one-year mark, and this has been the most adventurous journey of my life so far. It's truly a blessing coming into work, knowing that my work family and friends are all behind me. When I have had a hard day, I know I can count on any of them. Thank you, Zappos, for truly incorporating having friends/family both inside and outside of work.

AMANDA W.
employee since 2012

I have only been here for four weeks and I fall more and more in love with this place every day. In this economy, it was scary to leave my last good job for the unknown and I'm so happy I had the courage to make the leap. This job has everything I have been looking for and so much more. When you work somewhere that supports you, you become the best version of yourself and it carries over to all aspects of your life. The best part of this job is not only that I'm excited to go to work each day, but when I get home the first thing I do is ask my daughter about her day, rather than saying, "I just need five minutes of quiet to wind down." I feel so incredibly blessed to be here.

AMBER C.
employee since 2012

The Zappos Culture is refreshing. Coming from a corporate environment where I was not empowered to be myself, I was at a loss for words during my first day as a new employee. The disbelief in "Who did I trick to make it here?" I shared with a lot of new employees helped me appreciate how my job at Zappos contributes significantly to the overall positive production of the company.

AMELIA R.

employee since 2011

I am still in my first year at Zappos, but it has quickly become like my second home and family. Even when life gets crazy and work is busy, we all come together and support each other. I look forward to all the amazing opportunities that Zappos provides and can't wait to see what the next year brings!

AMY F.
employee since 2011

When I think of the Zappos Culture a song comes to mind…"WELCOME TO THE FUNNY FARM!!! Lalalala …"

This unique individual mix of personalities, styles, talent, humor, and genuine compassion for mankind makes "ZAPPOS" a family that grows together through good and bad, in our internal family roles as well as our external family and community roles.

Oh yeah, are you asking why the "Funny Farm" song?" Well, where else can you work and receive a cow/horse/ panda, all the while watching a monkey chase bananas? Where more glitter and streamers on the floor are a good thing? Where men dressed as women and are actually HOT!! Where when guests arrive, the louder we are, the better! Where PJs as work attire are supplied and promoted by your boss!!! WHAT??? YEP, YOU HEARD IT RIGHT… I LOVE MY ZAPPOS FAMILY AND THE CULTURE OF ALL OF THE LOVEABLE NUT JOBS THAT MAKE THIS MY ZEN. I STRIVE TO SHARE THIS CULTURE WITH AS MANY PEOPLE AS POSSIBLE. IT'S CONTAGIOUS! WITH NO HARMFUL RASHES OR BUMPS ;p

CHEERS!

AMY S.
employee since 2010

I love Zappos! We have such a great group of people here. Sometimes, going to work is a break from life! I feel so lucky to be a part of Zappos and everything it is growing to be! :-)

ANA G.
employee since 2010

I've been fortunate enough to be part of this family for the last two years. I've made lifelong friendships and am proud to say that I now have an even bigger extended family :) I've also gone up a size in jeans because everyone here seems to be such awesome chefs. Cheers to another year!

ANA S.
employee since 2009

Culture means a sense of family, unity and pride. It's allowing, encouraging and recognizing us to be who we are f the artist, singer, poet, comedian, scholar, dork, pink-haired kid, or the video dude with the wild afro. Yep; we are the Breakfast Club of Zappos and every year I'm here, I continue to see our culture being enriched and boy, how sweet it is!

ANA T.
employee since 2006

The Zappos Culture means trying to make someone else's day a little brighter, whether it is for customers or coworkers, family, friends, etc. Basically, it's all about choosing to be positive, rather than automatically discounting someone or something's worth and/or feelings. And about always remembering that we don't always know what that person's reality and experience is. It's about being the best neighbors we can be! =)

ANDRE N.
employee since 2008

The Zappos Culture is so exciting! I'm super-excited that Zappos has been able to share our culture with other companies through Insights, and we will now be able to share our culture with our community with our move downtown. I'm very happy and lucky to be a part of such an awesome company that is literally trying to make the world a better place!

ANDREA B.
employee since 2008

Zappos Culture probably has 2,456,578 definitions, but I define it as simply AWESOME! I am four years in, and I certainly can say that I very much enjoy working and being a part of this company because of the culture. It's what keeps us going, and keeps us going strong. Without it, we wouldn't be the company we are today. Oh, and get crazy with the Cheese Whiz! =D

ANDREA R.
employee since 2007

The culture here at Zappos is like no other company I have worked for! Come to think of it, I don't think my other jobs even had a culture. Working here I have met some amazing people, and I know we will remain friends for a lifetime. I know this has to do with the culture here at work. I am actually leaving Zappos in a few weeks, and it makes me sad. I know that I will never work for another company like this one, but I plan on taking the culture with me, so I can spread it around my new job. I am not sure where that will be, but I know that everyone can use a little Zappos Culture in their life!

ANDREAS W.
employee since 2010

I thought that I had Zappos Culture figured out, but it always surprises me. Every time I come to work, I'm blown away by the amazing people that I work with. My Zappos family really comes through for me when I need them. The Zappos Culture is the blue print by which we (Zappos Employees) live. We define the culture by living it out for each other. I love you guys.

ANDRES "BIGBOIDRE" R.
employee since 2011

Where to start ... I have been working for Zappos since the Holiday season in 2011 and from the beginning, I have been introduced to our culture. I have loved every single moment of it! Why? For many reasons that I cannot probably put in words. First of all, I love our culture because of my teammates. The friendships I've been able to build painlessly are relationships I can see myself keeping for a long time, if not forever. Our culture is the smiling and happy faces you see every day as you walk through these doors. Our culture is holding the door for people even when you are running a bit late. Our culture is the sudden feeling of happiness you get when coming in to work, whether it is your Monday or your Friday. Our culture is knowing that you have a shoulder to lean on when things are rough in your personal life. Our culture is caring. It not only takes the employees into consideration, but also considers our customers and our community. What does the Zappos Culture mean to me? It means everything!

ANDRES M.

employee since 2012

The Zappos Culture means never feeling awkward around anyone you don't know.

It's a general sense of belonging no matter who you are, where you are, where you're from, or what you love.

Zappos is acceptance for who you are. Zappos is love (in a total Platonic way of course!). Being a relatively new employee to Zappos (GO ZABOO'Z!) I experienced this culture from day one of stepping through the Zappos doors during my first interview, and I'm glad to say that it's been that way ever since. And that's what I love most about our culture.

ANDREW T.

employee since 2008

Wow!!! Can you believe it! 2012 is my fourth year with the greatest company in the world and this is my third contribution to the Zappos Culture Book!

The Zappos Culture is all about endless possibilities. It means that you are always at the crossroads and will have the opportunity to decide what path to take on your journey. The Zappos Culture is ideal, but ultimately you decide what to make of it and how it applies to you. The Zappos Culture is what contribution an individual brings to the table and how each Zappos family member will take part to enrich this culture. Each person is integral to the culture's development/growth/evolution.

Other companies may not provide the same opportunities and have only one option „ "conform." What I LOVE about the Zappos Culture is that I am part of the culture, I take from the culture and I contribute to the culture. The Zappos Culture has been a realization and reinforcement of my personal values; I will bring this experience wherever the road to success will take me.

ANDY C.

employee since 2010

Zappos is great. Live Chat.

I love, love, love the culture we have here at Zappos because it's so different from that at any other company I have ever worked for! I can come to work in my own personal style and be recognized for it in a good way. The people who work for Zappos are what make this company so awesome and we are responsible each and every day for making this company culture the way it is. I also feel we are so different from any other company because we are empowered to pursue growth and learning and to take not only our personal but also our professional goals to the next level. I have met the most down-to-earth, fun, and let's not forget special kind of people here at Zappos. I can truly say that my coworkers are my extended family! I love Zappos! Woohoo!

ANITA B.

employee since 2009

WOW - Three years at Zappos. Another great year!

ANNAMARIA C.

employee since 2011

I love working at Zappos! Here at Zappos, I am at home! I can be myself! I have always had a very bubbly personality and have always been very friendly. I have worked at places where I was told "not to be so bubbly all the time." I didn't know how to change that about myself. When I started at Zappos I saw that everyone here had an upbeat and bubbly personality! I have found my people, who love that I am bubbly!

ANNETTE R.

employee since 2011

It is an amazing place to work! Graveyard Rocks!

ANTHANY L.

employee since 2011

The Zappos Culture means be yourself. I don't have to put on a mask or hide my true identity. ItÍs ok to be weird and different because you are surrounded by a lot of other weird and different people. The culture is amazing to me because it reflects in your work, outside of work, and your personal life as well. The Zappos Culture changed my life.

ANTHONY S.

employee since 2008

First and foremost, I want to say thank you to everyone who made this year an amazing one!

This year, I wanted to try something a little different and found it put in an entry from one of Dr. Vik's emails. It's one of my favorites and I do my best to live by it.

"Day 973"
We can't put ..."What we get out of it" before we give "What we put into it."

It's the "Pay it Forward" kind of deal. Seems as though we are living in the days of immediate gratification, and many seem to focus on what they get out of something without putting anything into it. It's just not the way things work ...We need to "put into it" before we can expect anything in return ... and even then, we may not get anything back in the short term ... but in the long run, it's just the right thing to do. Yours in "Doing the Right Thing" Coach

ANTON S.

employee since 2012

Zappos ??? ?????? ??????????? ????? ???????? ? ???? ?????? ???????? ???? ???????! ??? ?? ?????? ????, ??? ? ?????-???? ??????? ??? ??? ??????!!!
Love this place.

APRIL T.

employee since 2011

Oh Zappos, how I heart thee! Let me count the ways:
1. You treasure my uniqueness <3
2. You are interested in my talents <3
3. You want to make a difference <3
4. You help me grow as a person and an employee <3
5. Most importantly, you legitimately care about me <3<3<3
To me, the Zappos Culture is something not only relevant to business, but relevant in life. It embraces the importance of friendship, caring, generosity, and doing good, just to do good! I raise my glass to Zappos!

APRILLA G.

employee since 2012

The culture at Zappos is amazing! To me it is a place where you go every day, not because you have to, but because you want to. You are with family. Everyone is friendly and courteous. Every day, there is something new to learn, either about someone you may have just met, someone you've known a long time, or even yourself. To me, Zappos is really a place to learn about yourself and grow in a lot of different directions while having a lot of fun. It is a place where every day, you get to have fun while talking to some of the most amazing people from all over the United States while sitting in your PJs and slippers.

ASHLEIGH F.

employee since 2012

In my eyes, the Zappos Culture means embracing the Ten Core Values, understanding what they really mean and making it your own. The culture here is so different from anywhere else and for me, it means I can be my fun, loving self with my fellow Zapponians and even better, with our customers. Being surrounded and embraced by this culture reminds me that I am encouraged and am able to provide best possible customer service to all Zappos customers. I am just so grateful to have the opportunity to be a part of this unique culture.

ASHLEY JJ.
employee since 2010

Since I started at Zappos, I have met the best people. Everyone always says that their favorite thing about Zappos is the people, and they would be correct. Some of my best relationships have been made here. Zappos hires good people. I also feel as if working at Zappos makes you a better person.

I was given the opportunity a few months ago to deliver a Core Value Presentation. Our Ten Core Values are very near and dear to me. I chose to present Core Value #4: Be Adventurous, Creative, and Open-Minded.î What is a Core Value Presentation? Well, I'll tell you!

Part of new-hire training is to teach the trainees what our core values are all about. Some Zapponians are asked to present a core value that they are passionate about. I chose #4 because I used to be the type of person who thought that if it was too hard, I wouldn't even attempt it. That was me, until one day I heard a quote. "You miss 100% of the shots you don't take." —Wayne Gretzky. Hearing this quote opened my mind. I thought to myself, why not? Just go for it! If it doesn't kill you, then why not? I prepared a presentation to give to the trainees to help encourage them to think the same way. To be open-minded, and not close off an idea immediately. To be adventurous, and push themselves out of their comfort zone. To be creative, let the juices flow. I teach them how the best ideas can come from anyone, and not to be afraid to express those ideas.

I love presenting this Core Value. I love getting to meet so many new people every month, and helping to inspire them.

Thanks for the read! Hopefully I can inspire you one day as well. Perhaps, I already have!!!

ASHLEY K.
employee since 2012

The culture here at Zappos is not like the culture anywhere else. You will be part of a family that gives a warm invite to be who you are as a person and to be accepted, You will always run into a smiling face or someone who can make you smile without even knowing them. One last thing: Change is a word that everyone embraces and accepts here at Zappos, because change is always happening.

ASHLEY L.
employee since 2012

I just started working at Zappos after years of hearing what a good company it is to work for. When I arrived, everyone was so happy, positive, genuine and welcoming. I thought for sure something was in the water or that they had been notified to be extra happy and nice because I was new. I waited for the bomb to drop „ but it never did. I used to go to work unhappy, sad, overworked, and depressed, praying for a miracle to get me away from my last employer. And then something happened and I went to the Zappos website and they had an opening. The rest is history. I've never been at an employer that made me feel appreciated, cared about my happiness, and wanted to build a work relationship as well as a friendship. I come to work happy, hungry to learn and talk to customers. It's hard to have a bad day. I come to work feeling like this is my second home. I appreciate everything the company has done to make me feel so lucky, happy, appreciated and part of a real team!

ASHLEY T.
employee since 2009

Zappos is a great company! Great place to work, great benefits as well! You are treated like a person, and not just an employee.

ASHLY A.
employee since 2011

Zappos is the most amazing place to be. The energy is contagious and everyone is so unique and friendly. I can't imagine being anywhere else anymore. My entire family loves Zappos; they constantly do different events so that our families can be part of the wonderful environment that Zappos has created. And of course, I now have a vast wardrobe of awesome clothes and shoes!

ASHOTTA W.
employee since 2007

Culture [kuhl-cher]: the behaviors and beliefs characteristic of a particular social, ethnic, or age group.

Zappos Culture [my version]: the total of the inherited ideas, beliefs, values, and knowledge, which constitute the shared basis of our core values.

Being more than just coworkers, we're a family that shares thoughts, visions, and ideas that become a part of a bigger picture. We are the social engineers of our time, and I'm happy to be a part of the journey. There is no better way to describe what we are a part of.

AUTUMN W.
employee since 2012

From the moment I walked through the double doors at Zappos, I felt as if I had known everyone I came in contact with for years. In the short time I have been here, I have felt so welcome and able to express myself truly, more than in any other job I have had before. It's amazing to be able to wake up every day knowing you are going to a place where everyone accepts you for who you are. We all have the ability to grow and learn from our mistakes and I really love seeing that in a company. I love the Zappos family and cannot wait to see what else lies in store!

BABE

employee since 2010

Still happy. Happy for the customers that make me smile and who appreciate the courtesies and personal attention we deliver, happy to wear pajamas at least once a week, happy for the waffle maker in the Bistro, happy for the covered parking for my scooter-badooter in the summertime, happy for Pandora playing at my desk, happy for the peeps that have been added to my pals list, happy for the treats and trinkets, happy for the benefits and peace of mind, happy for the encouragement to grow, happy for so much. Only sad thing is that my BFF isn't here anymore. But, she's happy — so I'm happy.

BARB S.
employee since 2011

Experiencing the Zappos Culture has been so uplifting for me! Each morning when I come to work, I see hundreds of beautiful reminders that we are names, not just faces; we are human, not just robots; we are friends, not just coworkers. It's amazing that something as simple as our Ten Core Values can create happy employees, happy customers and (as a bonus) a successful business. I am truly grateful to be a part of the Zappos Family!

BEN G.
employee since 2012

The meaning of the Zappos Culture, for me, is to keep an open mind, be honest, open and helpful. It means to work hard in order to play hard and have fun. Most of all, though, it means to do what you love and love what you do!

BETSU (ELIZABETH) S.
employee since 2009

The Zappos Culture has impacted in me in so many ways. I love how Zappos — as a company — shows genuine concern for employees and for the community. There are so many ways to get involved and be part of the never-ending evolution of the culture. You have employee recognition, awards, participating in charitable causes and Wishez. There is really no excuse not to get involved and be part of our wonderful culture. I am so blessed to have been part of Zappos for almost three years now. Zappos for life!

BETSY C.

employee since 2010

The Zappos Culture is AMAZING and ONE-OF-A-KIND! I love having been part of the Zappos family for the past two years!

BETTY L.
employee since 2004

Another amazing year at Zappos — but not much has changed from my last submission. One of the things that stood out for me this year is the way that we all came together as a family and got through what could have been the most difficult time here at Zappos. But because we all worked together as a family, we got through it. There are a lot of opportunities at Zappos, ways to pursue growth and learning, which you are not forced but encouraged to follow. I really appreciate this because, even though I love my Zappos family, I also have a family outside of Zappos which has prevented me from following my journey. Iím sure that with time, one day I will get to it. By the way, my kids believe that I work for the best company. They loved the picnic at Circus Circus. Looking forward to many more years at Zappos! Thanks for all the wonderful memories.

BRANDI W.

employee since 2011

I never hung out with my coworkers, outside of work, in the past. I didn't really want to (LOL). Your coworkers here at Zappos are more like the best friends you lost track of growing up. You find it pretty easy to be around them a lot more than normal. No matter what your lifestyle is or what your interests are, you will find someone here that lives it, breathes it or knows enough about it to have a full conversation with you, unexpectedly. People here talk about anything from Xena the warrior princess to belly dancing and canning jellies. Customers call us just to talk. In a large nutshell, the Zappos Culture is like a big warm hug from your loving grandma who just baked you a basket full of your favorite homemade cookies. So, from me to you, enjoy life! We are!

BRANDON D.

employee since 2010

The Zappos Culture is like an ancient civilization, filled with commonalities and things that make everyone unique, roles and standards. All in all, this culture boils down to staying true to yourself and the Zappos family as we lift each other up. But at the end of the day, you must be prepared to fight and make choices for the sake of culture, which is how it's preserved. I love my Zappos Family!

BRANDON L.

employee since 2010

Zappos has provided me with nothing less than pure happiness. The growth and development of our company and culture has left an everlasting impression on me, as well as on my family. I can always count on my Zappos family to be there for me. Thank you to my awesome Zappos fam!!!

BREANNE F.

employee since 2010

I love working at Zappos!

BRIAN L.

employee since 2012

My entire career has been spent working in jobs that I only considered a paycheck; the type of job where I dreaded waking up in the morning and even thinking about going to work. This all changed when I started working for Zappos. I have never before experienced a job where everyone around was friendly, courteous, and made me feel at home. Now, not only do I want to come to work, but in addition, the Zappos Culture has brought happiness into my everyday life.

BRIE N.

employee since 2011

Hmm ... How can I even describe the Zappos Culture? Obviously, key words and themes pop up instantly when I even hear the name Zappos: Cool, Fun, Unique, Genuine, New, Family, Friends, Growth, Innovation, Creativity, Support, and Weird. Honestly, I think our culture here at Zappos.com is definitely worth protecting. I think it's a rare, special and spontaneous thing. We have a lot of fun here. We also work really hard. You spend a lot of time with Zappos on your brain, but you make friends here that you'll have for the rest of your life. Zappos has a workplace environment unlike anywhere else. Imagine being excited to go to work! Every day! And once you're there, you stay excited! For 8 hours a day, five days a week! It's pretty cool. I feel really lucky to be here, and I hope to be here for a very long time. : D

BRIRONNI A.

employee since 2011

The culture here at Zappos is unlike anything I've seen at any other company. Being located in Las Vegas speaks volumes to how different we are. As a student, I had always viewed my job as nothing more than a tool with which to pay the bills. At other places, I never saw any real opportunities for growth, nor did I feel as if the company as a whole was out to do anything other than break the consumer's pockets in the name of "customer service." Needless to say, I dreaded going to work every morning. Zappos is a 180 degree turn from everything I had become accustomed to in the workplace. I look forward to coming here: learning, growing, making people happy and sometimes just acting like a fool. I'm surprised by the number of meaningful relationships that I've built with my coworkers — especially among my team members. The camaraderie here is refreshing. Nahmean?

BRITNEY C.

employee since 2010

I'm coming up on two years at Zappos and could not be loving it here more. I've definitely found my niche in Scheduling and have even convinced my husband to join the Zappos family! I never thought I'd be that person, but here I am. :) I find myself more engaged in the culture than ever and excited to come to work every day. I've learned so much about myself and the people around me, and truly feel that they are part of my family. Here's to another year, Zappos! Thanks for treating us like royalty every day.

BRITT A.
employee since 2011

What can I say? Where else can I wear pajamas to work while eating ice cream with my feet on my desk? In all seriousness, Zappos has been amazing, even seven months later. Our culture is unlike anything I've ever experienced anywhere, even after living in Las Vegas all my life. I get to come to work every day and see my friends, and have FUN. Knowing that my company truly cares about me and supports me is an amazing feeling. Zappos is a way of life, and that's all there is to it. I love this company!

BROOKE R.
employee since 2011

I believe that, at its core, the Zappos Culture means freedom to be an individual and express one's individuality, not just at home or in their personal lives, but also in the work environment, and to do so without the scrutiny of upper management or coworkers. I think it encourages the overall emotional health of individuals by allowing them to be themselves at all times. At the same time, with the services and classes Zappos provides, I believe the culture also promotes personal growth. This is also healthy, especially when it is promoted in a way that doesn't make the individual feel as though they are inadequate at the personal, physical, emotional, business or career level they are at right now.

BRYAN C.
employee since 2012

Zappos has been such an amazing experience so far in the month I've been here. It has helped me become a better, nicer, more patient person as well as becoming more fun and social. It has been a blast and my wife loves it. She moved from Japan to the U.S., and Japan is the king of customer service. Usually, calling customer service in the U.S. is a huge hassle and pain in the neck, but here at Zappos, itÍs so refreshing to ACTUALLY help people and hear their gratitude for it. So she loves the fact that we are the king of customer service here in the US. The culture has definitely improved my life in many ways in my short time here, and itÍs only going to get better. Domo Arigato Gozaimashita, Zappos!

CAMERON B.
employee since 2011

Do you know the difference between education and experience? Education is when you read the fine print; experience is what you get when you don't.

CAPTAIN ANOMALY.
employee since 2011

The Zappos Culture is mustering up the gamma-irradiated cells of your physiology, mutated by the freak laboratory incident of life known as optimistically-motivated-luck, and using your new-found abilities to fight the battles of the mundane Doctor Normality in the form of justice-instilling, hassle-free customer service with a strong dose of weirdness and questionable mental instability. Also, those Zappendales guys are amazing and the pure embodiment of nine of the Ten Core Values.

CARA K.
employee since 2012

Zappos has truly changed my life! I truly believe that people underestimate the impact the quality of their work life has on every other aspect of their lives. You really start to notice that when you step into a company that actually cares about you. When you wake up in the morning and look forward to coming to work, it becomes difficult to actually have a bad day from that point on. Literally. I believe it's nearly impossible to have a bad day here. We might have busy, hectic or even some crazy days, but the second you walk through those doors, you feel a sense of family and happiness. YES, happiness *f* at work, crazy, I know! From my very first day, I finally enjoyed working and stopped wishing I could have just stayed in bed each morning. It's amazing the things you can accomplish when you have a whole company backing you up, encouraging you and watching out for your well-being. Zappos makes life better!

CARLA ANN.
employee since 2010

"People rarely succeed unless they have fun in what they are doing."
-Dale Carnegie

We have fun here every single day, and for that we are lucky.

CAROL T.
employee since 2008

The Zappos Culture is our fun and unique work environment. It is the appreciation of everyone's talents and the ability to use them to make our company a great place to work and to do business with!

CATHERINE C.
employee since 2011

The Zappos Culture is a state of mind. It is all about love, family, kindness, hard work, community, energy, and happiness. It's like a recipe; mix all of the above listed ingredients, stir, sprinkle a little weirdness and out comes ... the Zappos Culture!

CATHERINE M.
employee since 2009

My favorite Core Values are "Build a Positive Team and Family Spirit" and "Create Fun and a Little Weirdness." What better place to do those things than at an Amusement Park! So when I think of Zappos, I think of being at an amusement park with the best games, food and rides. I enjoy working here and hope to be here for a while more. Thanks, Zappos!

CC.
employee since 2007

Another amazing year and I am STILL flabbergasted every day when I look forward to coming to work! I'm never bored. Never uninspired. Never tapped out. I'm challenged, supported, encouraged, and empowered. I love it here.

CHANE S.
employee since 2011

I've been working here at Zappos for about eight months now. All I can say is that, as an employee, Zappos is the MOST unique place for anyone to work! I've forged some close relationships here and for the first time, I can actually have some fun while doing my job — imagine that! It is because of Zappos that I have faith that a company can "do it right" when it comes to taking care of its employees.

CHARONNE A.
employee since 2011

The Zappos Culture, to me, is a lifestyle. And not just a lifestyle, but one that is positive and rewarding. Working at Zappos has allowed me to be myself and to embrace my own ethnic culture. It's like a melting pot of various cultures and ideas all rolled into one. It also means driving change and becoming a better person. The culture allows me to appreciate each person for who they are.

CHE F.
employee since 2011

I feel that the Zappos Culture is a social environment where you can work while enjoying the things that make you happy. It's a family type of atmosphere because you build connections, and friendships with your coworkers and they grow to the point where it doesn't even seem like you're at work. You're "WOW"ing our customers with your service, but feel more like you're enjoying time with friends.

CHELSEA P.
employee since 2010

Shout out to all my Gila Monsters! Thank you, Zappos, for always allowing me to pursue what I'm truly passionate about. I don't know where I would be without you!

CHEREE H.
employee since 2004

The Zappos Culture means that you have the ability to share your thoughts/ideas, bring enthusiasm, display your creativity, build open and honest relationships with your coworkers and most importantly, have the freedom to be yourself. ZAPPOS = FAMILY!

CHERYL R.
employee since 2009

Whenever I walk through the doors at Zappos, it is always a WOW moment! Happiness is definitely expressed throughout the building. You can't help but catch yourself smiling, even when no one is around. Working here has definitely brought out the HAPPINESS IN ME!!! Yeah, Buddy!!!

CHEZ V.
employee since 2009

Once you experience the Zappos Culture, you will be forever changed. It is such a unique and inspiring culture. The positive energy that it creates is contagious. Once you have been immersed in the culture and learned its core values, they become embedded in your lifestyle. Eventually, the culture is spread to everyone you come across. The Zappos Culture is "happiness in a box" that we can deliver to everyone!

CHRISTIAN M.
employee since 2012

WOW!!! It really is the only way to describe Zappos, not only for most of our customers, but for the employees. Everywhere you go in our buildings, people are smiling! And honestly, since I've started working here, I've become so spoiled! I find myself in disbelief when I'm outside of work and someone doesn't do something as simple as hold the door open for me, just because I've become so used to having that done for me at work ... and I´m used to so many other nice gestures as well. When my friends and family complain about their jobs, I can't say one bad thing about mine to chime in ... and I LOVE IT! This is definitely the last job I will ever have. Zappos = LOVE. <3

CHRISTIANE T.
employee since 2010

The Zappos Culture means "family." It is amazing how everyone on your team becomes your extended family. As we move on to new teams and meet new people, our family continues to grow. We become invested in each otherÍs lives and care so much about them. I find myself proud of everyone I know as they progress in their Zappos journey and I know that they feel the same about me.

CHRISTINA L.
employee since 2008

Every year I write about what the Zappos Culture means to me, and every year it changes for the better. I've come to realize that the Zappos Culture is purely the generous and selfless interactions that we have with one another. It's all about the love, baby!

This year has been full of unexpected surprises, struggles, and beautiful moments. It's our culture that allows us to come together in times of heartache, and celebrate the joyous occasions. Most importantly, our culture allows us to have fun and be ourselves...

Knock Knock!
Who's there?
Yoda!
Yoda who?
Yoda leh ee-hoooo!

CHRISTINE B.
employee since 2008

I'm so excited to move downtown! I can't wait to have our employees get even more involved in the downtown community. I would have never thought I'd move downtown, but we're already searching for a new apartment!

CHRISTINE M.
employee since 2011

Wow! My husband was watching T.V. one day and Tony was on. My husband called to me and said, "You should put an app in at Zappos, you're just like the people he's describing." So, in January of 2011, I submitted an application to Zappos, and here I am.

It took from January of 2011 to September of 2011. It was hard work and a lot of waiting but I knew the end of the trail would be well worth it. And it was and still is. It's nice to work around positive and happy people, and since I've worked here, coming to work has been a pleasure. Feeling intimidated, being scared of losing my job, feeling people are talking behind my back — these were things I feared when I first started but, that came from prior jobs. Now, I don't even think about them and if those thoughts enter my mind well, they leave as fast as they arrive. We are all human and in reality, I would have to think that kind of behavior does go on, but I feel so strong within myself since I´ve been working here that those fears have no place within me anymore. I guess that's always been something that has bothered me. Being an employee here has given me the freedom and the strength to NOT be afraid anymore, here at Zappos or in my personal life. Thank you, Tony for being so consistent at making Zappos successful and, thank you, Zappos, for the culture.

CHRISTOPHER H.

employee since 2010

The best way I can describe working for Zappos ƒ It is like they thought of everything that a normal company would never do, did it, and put it on steroids!!

CHRISTOPHER L.

employee since 2010

The most important thing about the Zappos Culture, to me, is that you are allowed to be yourself. Your quirky personality is not only accepted, but embraced. It's not every company that will allow you to form a "Sexy Man" band, and go around the office crooning poorly performed melodies to coworkers. Not only were we able to do that with no musical talent whatsoever, but we were even able to perform on stage in front of the entire company! I think everyone has that rock star dream, and though we are all well aware that we have no talent and are by no means rock stars, we each got to live that dream for five minutes that day.

It's unique experiences like these that make Zappos special. You are able to fulfill dreams that you never thought possible. Mix that with the fact that I love coming into work every day just to talk to my coworkers, and I can't imagine being anywhere else right now.

CHRISTOPHER P.

employee since 2011

What can I say about working here that hasn't already been said by some of the other entries in this book? Here are some things that immediately came to mind:

1) My desk is covered in toys
2) My friends list on Facebook has increased by about 200 people in a few short months
3) I've attended so many Zappos parties that I've lost count of them

It really is an amazing place to be. I am incredibly honored to come in to work every day and be able to hang out with all my friends in such a rewarding job. Even on the busiest or most hectic days, I leave happy and satisfied. Oh, and the free Lucky Charms in the Bistro help too.

CHRISTOPHER R.

employee since 2010

I am on my second year here at Zappos, and I couldn't be happier. There is such a family feeling here, and everyone is genuine and kind. I look forward to coming into work every morning, and working with all these wonderful people. I want to say "Thank you" to Zappos for letting me be myself here. I feel very comfortable in my skin, and there are not many places where you can do that!

CHRISTY C.

employee since 2010

I love my job. I know that if you have made it to my entry, you've already heard this from more people than you can count. The only thing that I may be able to add is that I feel this way because we are a family. Not just in a "We are all friends" or "We hang out all the time" way. It's a little bit more. Just like a real family, we are not perfect and have our ups and downs. What sets Zappos apart from anywhere else is how we handle it. If we make mistakes, we forgive. If there is tragedy, we grieve together. If someone succeeds, we celebrate with them. As a family would do, we help each other grow and become better than the day before. We are just people, but at the end of the day we are here for something more. We have common ground, and we build it up together. Also, the free coffee is great.

CINDY M.

employee since 2010

After being here over a year now, the Zappos Culture has, to me, been a fun, wild, creative, learning experience. Not only for the brain-building knowledge, but for the fantastic relationships that I have built and will take with me for the rest of my days. Also, the ones that I have not made yet, but are still to come!

CLARENCE R.

employee since 2008

To me, the Zappos Culture is what binds all the employees together. It helps us keep up morale during tough times. It's also an excuse to go drinking at any random time. :)

CLARISSA R.

employee since 2008

I have been a Zappos employee for the past four and a quarter years. I have enjoyed it immensely. I have worked with other companies and there is no comparison. I look forward to coming to work each day and feel bad if I can't make it in. There is always something new and different going on. Zappos is a company that allows me to be myself, provides the resources for me to give the best service possible to my customers. I look at it as my own little store. What can I do to help this customer and make a difference? Although older than many of the employees, I am young at heart and I am not made to feel any different because of my age. We help each other and cheer each other on in all walks of life. I wish all companies could treat their employees at least half as well as we are treated here. Although casually dressed, we are very professional and creative and give our suggestions regarding 95% of all projects going on within the company. We are involved in the community. Zappos is my family. Funny, I went to have a medical test and when asked who to contact, I wrote "Zappos.com."

I love my growth as a person. I have learned patience, and learned not to say that I cannot do something. Instead, I say "Show me." Anything is possible and I know I have great support in all aspects of my life, at work or personally. I have friends that have been made along the way. I hope to be here for a long time to come.

CODY B.

employee since 2007

The Zappos Culture means being able to be myself. It means knowing that even though others might think I'm "weird" or "different," that it's those quirks that make me a good fit here. When people are comfortable being themselves, they excel. That is what our culture does. It allows you to take all of your strengths, even the quirky ones, and turn them into something great.

COLE M.

employee since 2012

The Zappos Culture, to me, means being happy, making others happy, and treating each other the way you'd want someone to treat you, or better yet, your parents. I look a little weird compared to most "social" norms and Zappos encourages me to be myself, to have crazy hair, to have my piercings, to not keep my tattoos hidden, and while doing this, to continue to grow and build myself and also my career here. I've just started, less than a month ago, and I already know this is a place where I belong. Small acts of kindness are everywhere, and I feel that we actually take the time to attempt to make each other smile. The other day, I was out shopping with my best friend and I kept smiling at people and saying "Hi" to them as they walked by me. She looked at me kind of crazy and said, "Why do you keep doing that? You don't work here." I don't care, smiling and saying "Hi" created the same response from them. So far, in just these few weeks, the Zappos Culture, to me, means being happy and spreading it however possible!

CORINA C.

employee since 2008

I love my job. I love the people I work with. I love the family that the people I work with have become. Carpe Diem. It's worth it.

COURTNEY S.

employee since 2010

Nowhere else can I go to a place where I get paid to deliver WOW to customers and socialize with my friends! I have never laughed so much and truly felt like I belonged anywhere else as much as I do here at Zappos. Because I'm so happy, it's only natural that I want to deliver the best customer service I can, which in turn produces happy customers. It's such a simple idea, treating employees right, and Zappos knows what it's doing! I <3 you, Zappos!

COURTNEY W.

employee since 2011

It can be quite difficult to even begin to describe how "at home" Zappos truly makes you feel. Even though I have been here since October of last year, I still find myself excited every single day to see what's next in store for me and all of my Zappos family. Also, I could have never imagined being as close to my colleagues as I am at this point. The culture here is bright and beautiful, with a ton of new friendly faces popping up and keeping things fresh. There are so many opportunities to grow towards something bigger than just you, and I am nothing less than completely enthralled with what is to come with Zappos and our tight-knit breed of happiness ninjas. I think the greatest thing that everyone keeps in mind here is that the culture does not come from a book, a guideline, or even our willingness to come here every day. It comes from all the pieces of the puzzle every employee brings to the table, and how empowered we stay and grow towards a better and brighter future.

CRISTAL O.

employee since 2010

I enjoy coming to work every day, even if it's at 5 a.m. I feel lucky to be a part of the Zappos Family and the experience. Working here, I see how I've grown and I'm anxious to see what more I will become.

CRYSTAL H.

employee since 2010

This is now my second year working here at Zappos and it's been another year of awesomeness! Our culture is not only reflected in the diversity and fun-loving nature of our employees, but also in the joy and gratitude we hear from our awesome customers! Delivering WOW service and going above and beyond while at the same time building a family spirit with both coworkers and customers is what our Zappos Culture is all about! I'll always be grateful to have Zappos in my life!

CRYSTAL M.

employee since 2005

The Zappos Culture means you can be different. You can be yourself. You can be expressive. Our culture is a mixture of people with new ideas to help our company soar to higher heights.

D (DYAN).

employee since 2008

I love my job! I have been here four and a half years and I can't think of a better way to spend it than with my friends and family here at Zappos!

DAIL T.

employee since 2007

I think one of the greatest things about working at Zappos is that you are given entitlement to "do your own thing" for every customer you come in contact with. Doing whatever you feel you need to do to WOW the customer is encouraged. It gives us a great feeling of satisfaction and really sets us apart from all other on-line retailers.

DANIKA J.

employee since 2008

It's been four and half years, and I still feel privileged to work for a company that has what I consider to be a superhero culture. We stick together, through the good times and rough times. Seeing everyone pull together during the WMS project, the holiday rush and the security breach blew me away, and reminded me how strongly we believe in our core values and our mission to succeed in WOWing our customers, and the world. At the All Hands meetings, everyone gets "powered up" (get it? LOL) about the change and opportunity that is available and soon to come. As He-Man would say "we have the POWERRRRRRR!"

DARLENE K.

employee since 2008

What does the Zappos Culture mean to me ... Hmm ƒ 24/7 Outstanding Customer Service with the best Customer Service Reps in the world, being able to toot my own horn as well with my last statement :), having fun with all of my Zappos family members on a daily basis, Team Building events (a shout out to the French Toast Mafia, you know who you are), meeting great new people all the time, being able to mentor new and upcoming employees and seeing the look on their faces when that call ends with a happy customer, and also, for the first time, allowing me to partake in the Bald and Blue event this year! I actually got my head shaved to help raise the funds that the company donated to the Nevada Children's Cancer Foundation. I can't wait until next year to do it all again! Zappos rocks and I'm blessed every day when I walk through the doors to find out what's in store for me in the future.

DAVID B.

employee since 2011

The Zappos Culture is a mixture of fun, work, and a dash of organic nature.

DAWN E.

employee since 2009

I've been at Zappos for almost three years and I must admit that this is the GREATEST JOB EVER! I've never worked at a place where I LOVE coming to work in the morning. Zappos treats its employees with the utmost respect. It's such a great, family-oriented company. I never thought jobs like this existed. I go home in the evening with a smile on my face every day. Zappos has changed my whole outlook on life and my family will tell you the same.

DEBORAH H.
employee since 2006

evolve (Verb) Develop gradually, esp. from a simple to a more complex form.

We are evolving — and evolution affects every aspect of our company. I must adapt and evolve.

DEREK C.
employee since 2007

The Zappos Culture is inspired and driven by all the amazing individuals who make up our family. By always following our passions and striving to reach the next level, our culture will continue to grow as we grow as a company. No matter what challenges we face moving forward, our culture will hold strong as long as we empower ourselves and others to always drive the ideas we have to fruition.

DEREK N.
employee since 2010

It's been a tough year at Zappos, but I think our culture helped keep us together during challenges that would have upended other companies. Whether we were all in the trenches during a difficult warehouse systems changeover, working our fingers to the bone during a hectic holiday season or uniting as a company to address the security breach, we really demonstrated that our culture is not just words on paper but actions that hold true. While it wasn't easy, I'm prouder than ever to say I work for this company and to work with the people I do.

DIANA A.
employee since 2007

When I first started at Zappos, I was amazed with everything the company had to offer and its culture, etc. That was back in 2007. Fast forward to now, 2012. As the years progressed, I've gotten to see the company blossom like a beautiful flower. I am blessed to have been given the opportunity to work for such a wonderful company that values its employees. I mean, how many jobs have company picnics, holiday parties, vendor parties, happy hours, spirit days and team buildings? Also, how many jobs let you go into work in pajamas? Working at Zappos changed my life outside of work; I now have lifelong friends that I know will still keep in contact regardless of whatever path life takes us on. Let's do this, Zappos!

DIANA M.
employee since 2010

There is a lot of support and guidance here that I haven't experienced elsewhere. To me, the Zappos Culture means "Unity."

DIANA O.
employee since 2005

The Zappos Culture is one of a kind! It's unique, it's fun and it truly allows us to be our individual selves. It's what separates us from other companies. The culture is what has brought us close as a family and allowed us to grow with one another. Our culture is super-special and it's because of all of us that have made it as special and unique as it is. It has allowed me to be myself and have a ball at work. :) There is no Zappos without our culture. We would have no identity without it.

DIANA S.
employee since 2012

The Zappos Culture is a new beginning for me. I started a new chapter in my life and starting at Zappos played a huge role in that. At a time when I really needed comfort, support and encouragement, I was offered a position with the company. From the very first e-mail to New Hire graduation, I have felt welcomed and encouraged to be who I am and to grow in my personal life and professional life. I can't wait to see where things go from here and am excited to be growing with a company that values it employees and encourages a family-type setting!

DIANE M.
employee since 2004

I've been here for eight years now and am loving it! I feel blessed to be a part of this family where fun is prevalent and wowing is our thing! :)P I can't wait for many more years of happiness. Zappos truly delivers happiness!!

DINA D.
employee since 2010

Z-any A-ss P-eople P-roviding O-utstanding S-ervice! That's us in a nutshell. Wear your PJs, grab a double espresso from the Z Cafe, participate in a Nerf» gun battle, wave at a passing parade, shave your head for charity and help out our customers! That was on Thursday. What's in store for tomorrow? Who knows? Whatever it is, it's going to be fun! It doesn't get any better than this!

DONNA G.
employee since 2004

Zappos is the most amazing company I have ever worked for. Our Customer Loyalty Team is empowered to make the kinds of decisions our management can. It is a very positive culture and employees are given many opportunities to grow, both personally and within the company.

DONNA H.
employee since 2005

Definition of Life: The condition that distinguishes organisms from inorganic objects and dead organisms, being manifested by growth through metabolism, reproduction, and the power of adaptation to environment through changes originating internally. Definition of Zappos Culture: See above.

DONNA M.
employee since 2012

I am a new employee here at Zappos and I absolutely love it!!!

DONTRE W.
employee since 2012

This is only my fifth week here and if I could describe my experience here at Zappos in one word, it would be "WOW!" It's literally THE BEST JOB I HAVE EVER HAD!!!

Before I even heard of Zappos, I heard many great things about its culture and how work doesn't even feel like work. I thought to myself "No way, there isn't any place like that." So I signed up for a tour to see exactly what the culture is like and man, was I wrong! I mean, everyone that works here is so freaking nice! There are decked-out cubicles, nap rooms, and even the restrooms are cool!

I loved it so much that I took a second tour and that's where I felt that it was definitely time to apply. One of the best decisions I ever made! It feels good to be a part of the family. I'm not going anywhere, anytime soon =)

DUKE C.
employee since 2005

Imagine a wall, say, a white wall, a very large wall, in fact. Kinda boring, right? Now say someone splashes some blue paint on it. Then another person splashes some green paint. Then someone with red paint, then orange, then magenta, and then cobalt blue ... not too boring anymore right? In fact it's kind of cool, catchy, maybe even inspiring. Well that's pretty much what our culture is. No, not paint! It's the multiple layers of individuality, creativity, ingenuity, and passion to create a place where we can enjoy ourselves and find happiness!

Rock on, Zappos!

DYLAN M.
employee since 2007

Our Zappos Culture smoothes out all the rough edges. When there is discussion that could have turned into an argument or a day that you start off wanting to throw away, the culture smoothes it out. It's what makes it possible for us to deliver happiness.

EBONY M.
employee since 2007

Guess what? I am still here! I just had my five-year anniversary! Need I say more? The one thing that I have wished for is now coming true. I will no longer have to travel a total of 38.55 miles to and from work five days a week. I cannot wait for the Big Move to Downtown Las Vegas. Woot Woot!

EDWARD B.
employee since 2011

It has been quite an adventure this year. We have all been through quite a bit as a family. I think the one big takeaway for me this year would be that people are everything. Zappos is about real genuine human beings and better yet, about friends. Without friends, I don't think it would have been possible for me to make it through all that has happened personally and professionally. I'm looking forward to a great year.

EFRAIN F.
employee since 2010

After two years of working at Zappos, I am still blown away by everyone's energy and commitment to the culture. It's truly infectious! Not too many jobs come along that can be described as "fun!" Zappos rocks!

ELISA D.

employee since 2012

The Zappos Culture means a lot to me! I love the fact that no matter where I came from, how weird I am, or how society may portray me, Zappos as a whole is very accepting and has come to me with open arms. I appreciate the welcoming vibes I get from every single person I have encountered since I've been a part of our family. Our culture that we strive to have is so important to us and I love that! I am so proud to be a part of something more. I feel as if being a part of this wild, wacky, and weird culture has made me more open and honest with who I am as a person. The Zappos Culture brings out the right "me," which makes me all warm and fuzzy inside. The culture means the world to me!

ELISSA S.

employee since 2007

I feel that the Zappos Culture is different from all the other company cultures out there because of the employees — who drive the culture to be diverse by having the freedom to be themselves. It takes a special group of people to cultivate this type of environment, and without these unique individuals, our colorful company culture would not be possible.

ELSIE F.

employee since 2005

Working at Zappos is absolutely the best work experience I've ever had. Not only can I be myself, but also I'm empowered to WOW my customers both inside and outside the company. At Zappos, we are like a big family; we all care for each other and also have fun together. Our core values at work help me not only in my work area but also in my personal life - helping me to be a better mom, a better friend, a better person in general. I'm so blessed to be here and be part of the Zappos Culture. I love my job!

ERIC S.

employee since 2007

The Zappos Culture is contagious! Pick up the phone and talk to someone in CLT or come out to Las Vegas and take a tour of our offices and you'll find out why. Some of the symptoms include being adventurous, creative, and open-minded, along with creating fun and a little weirdness. You're definitely not the same person after you've had a Zappos experience. This infectious, yet good feeling has a trickle-down effect with those you have contact with. Zappos is spreading and delivering happiness to all.

ERIC Z.

employee since 2008

It has been a pleasure to work at Zappos. Everyone I know here is dope and Zappos has taken very good care of me. Looking forward to working at Zappos for years to come!

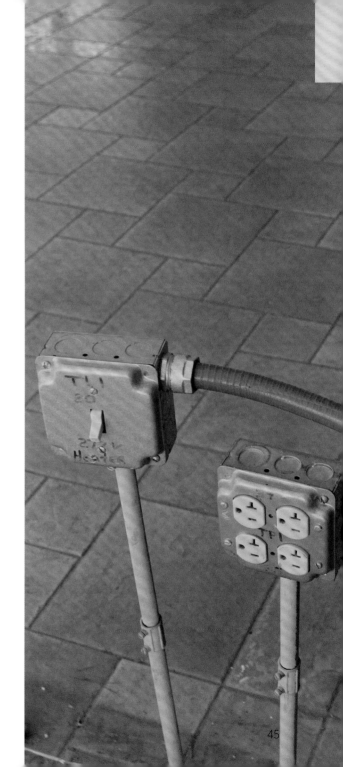

ERICA D.

employee since 2009

The Zappos Culture is definitely unique. This is the only company I know where people are encouraged to have fun and be weird. I love that we have events where we can all get together and mingle with other departments.

ERIK L.

employee since 2007

The Zappos Culture means opportunity to me. I haven't worked in a place where I felt my opportunities are as open as I feel them here. Beyond that, the culture is the people I work with every day, the relationships I have built with others, and the feeling when I leave that I've put in a good, full day. I wouldn't trade the experiences I've had here for anything; I think they've made me a better person.

ERIKA P.

employee since 2007

The Zappos Culture is about inspiring others to push beyond mediocrity and be the best.

EVELYN L.

employee since 2011

I absolutely love the culture we have here at Zappos. I have worked for companies in the past that had great-sounding core values tacked onto a wall, but that's as far as they went. It's great to work for a company that really lives and breathes its values. It really makes this feel like a worthwhile company to be a part of. It's not some dead-end job; it's a place that seems to be full of opportunities.

FIDEL W.

employee since 2011

First off, WOW! Zappos is amazing. I've been here eight months and I still get goose bumps walking through the door. I love being here and I love chatting with our customers. Every day is always different but always filled with smiles. Coworkers have become family and their families have become my family. The best feeling about coming to "work" is knowing that my job is to put a smile on our customers' and coworkers' faces. If you haven't taken a tour yet, please do! Look for me; I'll be the one with the biggest smile :)

Thank you, Zappos.
Thank you, customers, for always being awesome.
Thank you, partners, for always being there.
Happily Humbled

FRANCES M.

employee since 2010

I don't know what I'd do without Zappos. Probably get my dinner from a garbage can. A black and orange cat sittin' on a fence. A Stray Cat - if you will.

In all seriousness, I feel safe here. I trust the people around me and I know I can confide in them. People here care about me, and I care about them. They are what make Zappos so great. Everyone works together. We're a team, and even more, we're a family. I <3 my Zappos Family.

FRANKAVEN L.

employee since 2011

Kindhearted individuals.
Accomplished beyond measure,
Cool under pressure.
Hugs all around,
Optimistic bound.
When you are empowered, KACHOW!

GABRIEL R.

employee since 2012

I have been working for Zappos for only two and a half months and I already understand why the Zappos Culture is so unique. It makes the work environment very welcoming. I can always count on anyone to offer assistance or advice to me, even if I don't know them! We are allowed numerous opportunities to get to know one another through events, meetings, work functions, etc. These opportunities allow us to bond together, creating a family-like atmosphere. Everyone who works here has a piece of our Ten Core Values inside them; they share them with all the new people like me, which makes this an awesome company to work for.

GARRETT M.

employee since 2011

Do you remember the first time you trained your first unicorn? Well, that's kind of what it is like working here at Zappos. It's work, but it's the most fulfilling and fun career I can think of. The only other job I would want to have would be a Teenage Mutant Ninja Turtle, but let's face it, I'm not a ninja. It feels great to know someone can change your day in a single phone call. I try to live our core values throughout my life, especially Core Value # 3. Come on down to Zappos HQ

GEORGE R.
employee since 2009

Hey, Zappos! Thanks for making work actually FUN ... there's never a dull moment here and I appreciate every bit of it. I look forward to many more fantastic years :)

GERALD M.

employee since 2008

I'm constantly amazed, amused and blessed with Zappos. As we move forward to the incredible vision that we will and have become, the frequency of the amazement, amusement and blessings have only increased. As always, Zappos gives us motivation and support to help deal with the pace of change. They do this by providing us with some of the most sought-after speakers in the world and by developing company support on almost any subject you can think of. Zappos is a company that always tries to maintain a solid heart for its customers, employees and community. Anyone knows it's a difficult balance to please everyone all the time. However, I can say with confidence that Zappos maintains this balance better than any company I've ever worked for and strives to protect that balance. I am proud to be a part of it.

GIGGLEZ.
employee since 2011

Becoming a part of the Zappos family has been truly unbelievable. Moving from Los Angeles, California, I have found a home away from home. When you walk through the doors here, there is an energy that cannot be described. I'm honored to be a part of this amazing company.

GINA E.
employee since 2011

What can I say about Zappos? - hmmmmm ... wow, wow, wow, wow, wow, wow, wow, wow, wow! Oh yeah, and of course, WOW!

GINA W.
employee since 2007

The Zappos Culture is unmatched. You really have to be here to feel it. It's intangible, for the most part! =)

GIOVANNA W.

employee since 2007

Zappos has helped give me a feeling of self-empowerment that spills right over into my life and my daily decision-making process.

As an employee at Zappos, I have benefited in my life as an musician/actress from the fantastic experiences I've had being here, from being featured in a Zappos commercial as a "Zappet" to having my band, "Justus," in which I am lead vocalist and bassist, perform at the City of Las Vegas Corporate Challenge in 2012.

The positive, "anything is possible" spirit of Zappos has given me the ability to laugh and have a great time with the thousands of customers I've personally had the pleasure of speaking with - because I have tools available at my fingertips to do all I can to help "make people happy"! The feeling of being encouraged to have an "I Can, We Can" attitude with each and every customer I help, and not one of limitations, makes me understand that providing a completely positive, one-of-a-kind customer service experience is possible, over and over again!

Zappos helps grow big dreams from tiny seeds, and they have found the way to incorporate the right people who will rally together to help continue to build a beautiful reality!

GRACE A.
employee since 2010

After coming to Zappos, my family has grown by a few hundred people. Working here is more than just a business relationship. Everyone genuinely loves and cares about one another. No one is a number or a means to an end, which is what makes coming to work every day a pleasure.

GREGORY R.
employee since 2008

The Zappos Culture is extremely unique, to say the least. It is not about decorations. It is about building people through building family relationships. Yes, we do have fun, but we also work hard. I truly hope that everyone continues to work super-hard at building close relationships.

HANK M.
employee since 2011

To me, the culture here at Zappos means being allowed to be myself at work, letting my personality shine through, having fun and making friends. Also, it's all about hot dog day.

HANNAHLIA T.
employee since 2011

The Zappos culture — it's what I feel was missing in my life in regards to work satisfaction. Not only has it erased the line that separated my work life from my personal life, it's what brought them together. Happiness is contagious, please spread it to everyone you know! Every day is a new day to learn and embrace each core value. They are what separate ZAPPOS from other companies, but they should stand as an example of what a company should be. I am proud to call myself a ZAPPONIAN CULTURE NINJA!

HARMONI S.
employee since 2010

One word: Thankful.
Okay, another word: Happy.
Maybe one more word: Inspired.

HEATHER A.
employee since 2010

Zappos is the best thing that has happened to me. I've learned and grown so much since I started here. The lessons I have learned have helped me to be a better mom, daughter, wife and friend. I will be forever thankful for the lifelong friends I have made. I look forward to my future as a Zapponian.

HEATHER H.
employee since 2012

This picture says it all! æThis is how 'Humble' (Core Value #10) our whole company is ... Kaitlyn and I were only working at Zappos for two days and Tony, our CEO, was willing to 'Create Fun & A Little Weirdness' (Core Value #3) by allowing us to take this super-cool picture for our "New Hire Photo Challenge!" I KNOW we are going to love it here!

HEATHER H.
employee since 2012

Being new at Zappos, it's a little hard for me to really sum up exactly how I feel about the culture here, but I definitely feel that our Core Value #6, "Building Open and Honest Relationships," is a huge part of what makes this place so special. This value makes it possible for people to maintain their personhood within the structure of this large company. This policy allows me to be honest, not only with others, but also with myself. With this honesty, I get to be who I am every day, and this makes my days bright.

I love coming to work every day because I know that the people I see every day are here because they want to be and that they are the person they were meant to be because they are empowered. That said, have a fantastic day!

HECTOR G.
employee since 2006

I am glad that I found this company where you can have so much fun working. That sounds weird but it's true. I have been with the company for almost six years and am still enjoying it the way I was on the first day.

HELENE T.
employee since 2008

It's been an awesome year! Looking forward to the big move downtown in 2013. As always, Zappos is still the one!!

HOLLY F.
employee since 2006

I am so grateful to Zappos for all the opportunities that I have been given to grow and learn, both personally and professionally. I have made lifelong friendships from working here, and my coworkers always help to keep me laughing and positive. Zappos really is unlike any other place I have ever worked at, and it means the world to me.

HOLLY K.
employee since 2007

To me, our culture doesn't really have a defined shape ... much like an amoeba. :) The culture you'll find within ZCLT won't be the same culture that you'll find in Merchandising. Even the teams within those departments will have their own culture. But that is what is so amazing about it! It is something that we grow and shape through our daily interactions with everyone we come in contact with. Our culture is the invisible force that keeps propelling Zappos forward and keeps me driving home from work with a smile on my face.

HYATT R.
employee since 2012

I've only been at Zappos for a short amount of time, but I can tell you that the culture here is amazing. I'm encouraged to have fun, help others, deliver some smiles, and be myself while doing it. The time I've spent here so far with this zany group of like-minded individuals has made me a better, happier person, both in my job and personal life. I enjoy coming to work, I enjoy putting a smile on a customer's face, and I enjoy the family spirit that we have here at Zappos. The people here aren't my coworkers; they're my friends. And that's what it is all about.

IRENE V.
employee since 2007

The Zappos Culture can be defined in many ways, but to me it means "family." I look forward to coming in to see my coworkers/friends every day. I have been fortunate enough to meet some wonderful people here and for that, and many other reasons, I am thankful to be working for such an amazing company.

IVAN S.
employee since 2011

Zappos is, honestly, the best company I have ever worked for and I have been around the block! Amazing people that truly care about one's feelings. I have been WOWED!

IZZY P.
employee since 2010

Our culture is what makes us unique. I feel Core Value #7, "Build a Positive Team and Family Spirit," sums up the Zappos Culture this past year. With the warehouse update and security breach, Zappos has been faced with a lot of challenges that really tested our company. I feel we came together as a family, held our standards high, and got through tough times. This is mainly due to our company culture. I love my job at Zappos and am proud to work for a company with an amazing culture.

JACQUELINE Y.
employee since 2008

Our culture here is unique, amazing and untouchable. Can't wait for the upcoming years — it's been fun!

JAIME S.
employee since 2007

Culture in some civilizations is now a thing of the past. Their culture is only preserved in books and publications, photographs and rare findings. Their cultures have evolved with time, making history. I think that our Zappos Culture is defined by our history and the unique experiences that shape our company. Since we're a young company, everything we do to shape our culture now is more important than ever! We need to define ourselves right now. The Zappos Culture means defining ourselves and shaping the things to come, much like a sculptor shapes his masterpiece.

JAMES H.
employee since 2009

The Zappos Culture allows you to be yourself and encourages you to think outside the box! This is what makes Zappos the best place to work!

JAMES L.
employee since 2007

The Zappos Culture takes individuals and makes them part of a large family with many goals - everything from helping each other whenever possible to the bigger picture of helping out the community whenever possible. Plus, doing all this with a "can do" attitude and knowing the joy received when you know you're doing whatever you can to make the world a little better place through your actions.

JASMINE K.
employee since 2006

To me, culture is the equal embodiment of greatness and humility. Culture is Zappos.

JASON C.
employee since 2011

The Zappos Culture means that I can make a direct and positive impact on the team I work with (Team R.A.C.E.C.A.R., where you at?!) and on the company as a whole. Any idea that I wanted to pursue or contribute to was considered and often times embraced. Through this process I am inspired by others on a daily basis, and for that I am thankful. Godspeed, Zappos!

JASON M.
employee since 2012

To me, the Zappos Culture is all about being yourself and having fun while getting the job done efficiently. I've only been here a month and I've already learned a lot, and have a ways to go, but, I've made a lot of new friends too. This is the best job I've ever had.

JAVIER C.
employee since 2012

My experience at Zappos since I have joined has been nothing but amazing. The All Hands meeting, the culture, the opportunities, training, and attitude here can't compare to those anywhere else. I am basically a Las Vegas local, and growing up here and hearing about Zappos ... it was a dream to get a job here. I cannot wait to continue in my journey with this company and grow with it. I know I have found the company I want to spend the rest of my life with. I thank Tony and the company in general for the opportunity to join the Zappos Family, and I hope I can play my part and grown and learn with everyone here.

JAY W.
employee since 2012

I had been here for nearly three months at the time of the request to do this entry for the Culture Book, so my experience is limited. On the other hand, I have a fresh and new look of Zappos, and each day teaches me something new and exciting. I have had experience in many different work atmospheres. I have had the regimented, uncaring employer to something new, Zappos, which is care-free but productive. The structure exists, but it is masked by a friendly, empowering sense of freedom. The core values that the company uses as their guidance seemed strange at first, but with time, I found that they do help make it easier to assist the customers in the best manner possible. I also have to say that since my coworkers are a pleasure to be around, the positive feeling from everyone carries over to the customers too. I have never before been so fortunate as to have customers calling in with a problem in their order and not be screaming at me. It is truly surprising and refreshing. The customers have even called in and asked if they could combine returns to help the company save some money in shipping. I never thought I would ever hear of a customer trying to help a company save money in that fashion. If every employer used a similar business plan, perhaps more employees would be happier at work and there would be less sick time used in this country. Nothing is perfect, but Zappos has done such a good job, you can overlook the imperfections that arise from time to time.

JEAN D.
employee since 2006

I love our culture! I have never before worked anywhere where I looked forward to going to work each and every day! We have many opportunities presented to us in job growth, seeing our ideas come to fruition and providing the best customer service in the industry! We have amazing benefits here and not a week goes by that I have not stated how lucky I am to work here and be a part of something I would have never thought existed! Thank you for letting me be a part of the Zappos experience for the past six years and I hope for many more to come!

JEANINE L.
employee since 2007

The Zappos Culture is quite unique and different from anything I have ever experienced before. Where else can you come into work and be completely yourself? The diversity of the people here is something you would never find somewhere else. It's a fun place to work and very comforting knowing they like you for you and welcome your quirkiness. Parades, games, potlucks, shenanigans ... what more could you want. Definitely a sight to see.

JEANNE M.
employee since 2012

Zappos has been a once in a lifetime experience. I have never met so many truly caring people as I have at Zappos. It is all and more than I ever expected it to be. In the short time I've been here, I am more positive, determined and willing to help all that I know and don't know. I love Zappos!

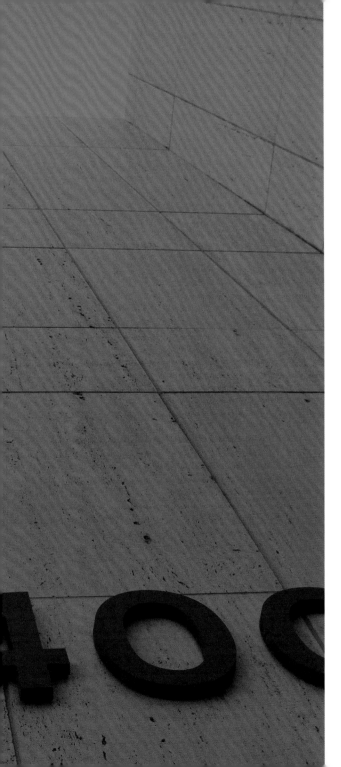

JEFFREY L.

employee since 2006

Free lunches are great.
So are our great benefits.
Can't wait for next year. Zappos Haiku!

JEFFREY T.

employee since 2010

The Zappos Culture is making friends into family and working to make the environment a better place. I have made lifelong friends while working here and look forward to spending time with them each day. We take care of each other and make sure that we have a good time while getting the job done! It is different here each day and I really enjoy speaking with great customers! There are tough days, but working with people you like in a relaxed environment makes the job totally worth it.

JEFFREY W.

employee since 2011

Hello everyone, I want to start by saying that I am lucky to work for such a wonderful company. Are we perfect? No, but we do a lot of the right things very right. Do we work hard? Yes. I think the biggest misconception about Zappos is that we are all fun and no work. We work extremely hard and have many of the pressures that outside companies have. In conclusion, I love coming to work every day and seeing the same wacky smiling faces. I apologize if I used the word "we" way too many times. I am writing this at 3:39 AM and my tooth hurts!

JEFFREY Y.

employee since 2010

The culture is what makes Zappos such an awesome company! Not only does it make work fun but it also creates a sense of camaraderie within the office. It's really nice to WANT to go to work every day.

JENN B.

employee since 2010

First of all, I would like to say "HEY" and thank you to everyone I've met and built a relationship with while working here. This is so much better than a yearbook!! Pictures bring back great memories, but reading about the experience speaks volumes. The Zappos Culture is unparalleled and, in my opinion, cannot be mimicked. Mahatma Gandhi said it best, "No culture can live if it attempts to be exclusive." The great thing about Zappos is that we strive to embrace our culture and it seems to spread to other people and their workplaces. I look forward to seeing how the Zappos Culture develops.

JENN D.

employee since 2009

The Zappos Culture means the world to me. It means that I don't have to dread coming to work. It means that I know I have an extended family outside of my blood relatives. There are so many people I can count on when needed and I wouldn't trade that for anything!

JENNA E.

employee since 2011

The Zappos Culture, to me, is coming together as a whole and being a family.

JENNI M.

employee since 2007

Zappos = Fun
Work = play
What the Zappos Culture means to me is that I look forward to coming to work, and spreading that joy to everyone that comes in contact with me. I <3 CLT! I am looking forward to many years of work and play with Zappos!

JENNIFER G.
employee since 2010

At first, the Zappos Culture was very different from my other jobs in corporate America. I was unsure why people were so nice and friendly. The first few weeks, people were holding doors open for me, smiling and always so helpful. I was very skeptical, but I gave into the culture and made friendships in my training class. right out of the gate.

I was very excited to start my journey at Zappos. com, but I had no idea that this company would change my life. I love the fact that most of my close friends are actually now my coworkers. We really do hang out more outside of the office then I could ever imagine.

I would like to give a Special Thank You to Tony for thinking outside the box and creating such a "Fun and Unique" Company and business model.

I am so grateful. This company has been so good to me and my family. My five-year-old son Ryan actually asked me, "Mommy why do you have to go to Zappos and party without me? "I advised him that although we do party and have fun, we also WORK really hard. I am excited to see our company culture get even better when we move downtown.

JENNIFER G.
employee since 2010

Culture means a way of life. Culture is different to many people around the world. It can be how and where you live, the clothes you wear, what you eat, the music you listen to and much more. It can be a particular society with different art and manners. Culture can be behavior and characteristics of a social group or organization. That is what is so great at Zappos. Everything is rolled into one.

JENNIFER T.
employee since 2011

Wow, this last year has flown by! Again, I feel so blessed to be here at Zappos. I know God brought me here for a purpose, and I'm having more fun than I care to admit finding out what that is! I have made so many new friends and LOVE MY JOB (if you can even call it a job!). I am the happiest now that I've ever been in my entire life!

JENNIFER W.
employee since 2007

I love Zappos ... because we all go together like bacon and eggs ...

JENNY K.
employee since 2010

WOW, did I just complete a day of work, or was it a day of fun?!

How about both?!

That's how I feel, just about every day. Even when it's stressful, I'm continuously reminded of just how lucky I am to be surrounded by all these amazing people.

Zappos cultivates an environment that has allowed me to grow personally and professionally, all the while blessing me with life-long friends. I'd write more, but I'm late for a parade! Until next time ...

JEREMY E.
employee since 2012

The Zappos Culture is unlike any other. It's an awakening of sorts. It makes me feel alive and ready to help others and spread my passion for life! It's refreshing to have open communication from everyone here. I feel free to be my weird self and express my opinions freely and openly.

JESSI F.
employee since 2007

The Zappos Culture is a unique work environment that all employers should strive to have. Almost every employee is ready to offer a smile, a kind word, and open doors. We are not only allowed to be a little crazy and strange while at our job, it's encouraged! The Zappos Culture helps bring the employees together to create a more family-like atmosphere, and encourages people to learn and grow for the better.

JESSI K.
employee since 2009

Let me tell you what the Zappos Culture means to me ... It means a place that you go to work that is COMPLETELY stress-free. A place where you can be yourself (and show off your tattoos proudly)! Zappos is a family for sure!! I have met a lot of friends here that have turned into really close friends... I've been lucky to be here for over three years. I'm sure I will be here for many years to come.

JESSIA C.

employee since 2010

It's hard to really put a definition on the culture around here because it means something different to everyone and it changes all the time, depending who you are around. For me, I guess it's best defined by examples. For me, the Zappos Culture is:
• wearing stripes so much that it becomes your trademark
• taking your afternoon break with your best friend and giggling all the way outside
• daily multiple high fives with your lamp
• having shenanigans on the Rdesk with Blewis, VR, and Mookie
• randomly yelling "Dey took ur derbs" and the whole team responding back
• the whole team laying on the floor doing "fab ab February"
• telling John K he looks healthy
• having like 50 different nicknames
• fist pumping and singing 'call me maybe' with your team
• having your awesome adopt-a-team adopt YOU :]
• having everyone on your adopt-a-team nicknaming each other "Steve" and using "Steve" to replace half the words in your zuddle crash
• building relationships with high fives
• hugs with your BFF that result in incident reports
• dressing like your lead on his birthday
• visits down the row from Stephen — I mean Dylan
• putting pictures of gila monsters all over Chelsea's desk
• jokes about Stelio Kontos
• being a total creeper (or being totally creeped on)
• i'm like, "No, girlfriend! There's not no tornado in Las Vegas!"

JESSICA B.

employee since 2006

Our team efforts create individual attachments to a larger cause. What is this larger cause? That's for everyone to define for themselves. For me, it's being the best me I can be — at work and outside of work — friendly, courteous, driven, creative, and fun. If we're all the best we can be and inspire others to do so too, well that's a pretty darn good start :)

JESSICA D.

employee since 2007

Each year I am with Zappos, these entries become harder and harder to write, as I love our unique culture more and more with each passing year! So ... I am going to try and keep this one short and sweet. ;)

 For me, the first word that comes to mind when I think of the Zappos Culture is ... acceptance. I know of few businesses in the world that promote the idea of 'being yourself' the way Zappos does. Every day, I am encouraged to provide my opinions on matters, to show my silly side, and to be open with my ideas. I have been given/earned a number of outstanding opportunities along my journey at Zappos, and I have also made my share of mistakes along the way. However, the acceptance of my mistakes and the willingness of my leaders to help me grow is what really sets the Zappos Culture apart from all others, and is what makes it so incredibly special to me! Thank you for another opportunity to share my love for this one-of-a-kind company!

JESSICA M L.

employee since 2011

I am almost at my one-year mark here at Zappos and it has been the best experience thus far for me. The culture here makes this place what it is today. Everyone makes you feel at home - we are just one large family that has each other's back. We are united by each other's strengths, helping each other on whatever path we wish to follow. I have never been at a job that is here for its employees just as much as it is for its customers. It simply amazes me! The best part of it all is, we can be at work and have fun!

JESSICA O.

employee since 2012

Zappos has been WOWing me from the very beginning, ever since I met a couple of Zappos employees while at my last job. I noticed a difference in their overall character — a genuine happiness and friendliness that certainly wasn't common at my current job or really at any of my past jobs. I was interested in finding out more about the company.

I did my research, and ultimately was very excited when I found out they were taking applications for CLT. From my first day of training, I noticed how well organized it was, yet also very fun and a little weird. This company is not only run well, but is also fun to work at. I have never experienced anything like this in my life. I truly appreciate the opportunities that are available at Zappos; I'm definitely looking forward to what the future brings.

JESSICA O.

employee since 2005

In my many years here at Zappos and on Earth, I've learned that change is constant. My own personal culture has transformed over the years, along with the Zappos Culture. It changes for the better as we are growing in knowledge about ourselves and what we want. The culture keeps us grounded and focused on who we are and how we want to be perceived as we continue striving forward towards our goals.

JESSICA P.

employee since 2012

Zappos - WOW is all I have to say! I've worked for a lot of companies, many that claim to be a family, to help you grow and give support, but this is the only one that actually does all that. I didn't know anything about the company until my best friend said I NEEDED to apply and there was a job bite coming up. So I hurried up and pulled my resume together and prayed. Two weeks later, I received an email that said they had gotten my resume and I needed to take some tests. An interview was finally offered to me two weeks later. When I walked into the building, I knew this was my future home away from home. It took me two months till I was able to start and I have loved every minute of it. I've only worked here for five weeks and have met so many awesome, friendly, people. It doesn't matter what department you are in or what you do, we are all the same, we are all here to do one thing, to WOW!!!!!

JESSICA P.

employee since 2009

Oh Zappos, I still have a crush on you after three years! In those three years, I have been lucky enough to become a phones team lead (the Angry Birds and the Cave) and most recently the lead of the Resource Desk. What fun it is leading a bunch of pirates! I love the freedom to decorate our areas and take on a fun persona at work. The team buildings are glorious, I've had the opportunity to go paintballing, BBQing, midnight bowling, to the wax museum, and the neon boneyard. Happy hours, All Hands meetings, and lead raves ... we know how to party. But what really makes the Zappos Culture? The crazy, zany people, of course! It really is a family and we make each other stronger!

JESSICA R.

employee since 2012

I've wanted to work at Zappos since I was 16. I worked at Port of Subs, and a lady from Zappos always came in and always told me how great a place it was. I went home that night and looked up Zappos blogs, and was immediately in love. The work environment was unlike anything I'd ever seen, and I couldn't believe a place like that existed. Seven years later, I'm finally working here, and it is everything I imagined. There is so much fun, passion, and excitement to be at work every day. I used to dread waking up and going to work, but every day I look forward to driving here and wondering what I'll experience. The culture is just a mixture of everyone loving their job, because they are encouraged and given all the empowerment to really WOW the customers. The Zappos Culture is a mixture of crazy shenanigans, driven employees, and the awesome customers who give us a reason to show up each and every day!

JESSIE H.

employee since 2012

The Zappos Culture is all about being who you are as an individual. I have never been in any environment that promotes being the best (and weirdest!) possible version of yourself as much as this company does. I can honestly say that I am a better, more well-rounded person because of the wonderful people that I interact with on a daily basis. I've noticed that I have replaced "Zappos" with "we" in my vocabulary when talking to friends and family about the company. I love my job!

JEWEL R.

employee since 2007

Zany!
Amazing!
Positive!
Productive!
Open-Minded!
Sensational!

JILLIAN M.

employee since 2011

The Zappos Culture is something near and dear to my heart. When I think of Zappos the first word that comes to mind is "family." Since day one, every person that I've met has been there for me with open arms, from my days in training and my time on the floor. These wonderful Zapponians have been there to help guide me and mold me on my journey through Zappos. I am internally grateful for everyone involved in this company.

JIM C.

employee since 2006

2006 - What a year! The Wii was born, iTunes' billionth song was downloaded, ("Speed of Sound" by Coldplay) Facebook was opened up to anyone over the age of 13, Dick Cheney accidentally shot his friend (maybe ex-friend now) in the face during a hunting trip and I got hired at the greatest company on the planet! A lot of other cool and interesting things have happened since I started my amazing journey with Zappos and I count my blessings every day for them.

When I started with CLT, my job was to deliver WOW through service by answering calls. Earlier this year, I had the honor of speaking at a conference, representing Zappos in front of business leaders from all over the world. As I reflected back on my journey, I couldn't help but think that this wouldn't have been possible without all of the incredible opportunities Zappos has given me, as well as the support and genuine feeling of family I have felt in the six years I have enjoyed here. My gratitude cannot be adequately expressed here, so I will simply say, "Thank you."

One more thing. I will attempt to leave you with a small bit of encouragement. The greatest mistake anyone can make is to do nothing because you believe you can't make a difference. You can make a difference.

JIM G.

employee since 2005

You'd think that after writing six Culture Book submissions over the course of six years that I would have run out of things to say. However, all within a year's time between submissions, a lot of things have changed. Luckily for us, they have changed for the better!

The Zappos Culture is ever evolving, as it should be. This year's go-around deals mostly with the involvement of our culture in the downtown Las Vegas scene. With the big news released that we are moving downtown soon, I think it's awesome to see that we've been making concerted efforts in trying to bring our culture to the growing downtown scene.

As everyone hopefully knows, our culture is loving, accepting and all-around awesome and honestly, the downtown area could use all of the above! I hope that by the time I get to write next year's Culture Book submission, our culture will have spread further and even deeper into the downtown area.

Go, Zappos, Go!

JINA B.

employee since 2011

They always get me when I'm hung over or look like sh*t.

JO L.

employee since 2007

Community
Unity
Love
Team
Utopia
Relationships
Everyone
:D

JO'D D.

employee since 2011

The Zappos Culture really is like nothing else. Where else are you encouraged to be yourself, and even a little weird, build a family environment, have managers who genuinely want to see you succeed at everything you do all while getting to talk to people all over the country and do anything in your power to WOW them and make their day? Every employee here is a firm believer in our culture and that's what makes us so special and different from every other company out there. Here, you don't just apply our core values for a small amount of time while you're in the office; you really begin to live them in your life.

Shout out to my Kachow family!

JOE K.
employee since 2008

Being a part of the Zappos family is amazing for a number of reasons. All of them individually keep me here, but all of them together create a feeling and atmosphere most won't find through work. Zappos has helped me make personal goals a reality as well as career goals. I've been here for four years and plan on many more! I can't thank Zappos enough! Be sure to tour our facilities and see our amazing culture when you can!!

JOEY N.
employee since 2011

Since day one of being here, I've experienced nothing but amazingness. Our culture is one of the greatest things in the world to me. Why is it so important to me, you ask? Well, fun and little weirdness is who I am, and what I stand for! I get to come to work and see all my friends, have as much coffee as my body can stand, and I get to make people smile, laugh and be happy! What's not to like about that? Also, there is always something new to learn. You never know what you are going to take away once your day is over. Plus, all the managers and supervisors have been nothing but amazing as well. It's unlike anything one could ever imagine in a job, they actually want you to succeed! How crazy is that?! Mix happiness, friendship, family, knowledge, FREE coffee, personal style and music together. It's an explosion of culture! It's hard to find these days; Zappos got me feeling cultural! It's really cool!

JOHN D.
employee since 2005

Zappos - what a great place. I've grown in many ways while working here, and I've met some pretty nice people. I still love BBQ!

JOHN K.
employee since 2009

Working at Zappos has changed my life. I can confidently say that I'm a better person than I was when I started over two years ago. Every lead, supervisor, and manager I've had has been invested in my growth, not just professionally, but personally as well. It makes your life so much less stressful when you know that the people you work with care for you like a family member. I feel like my journey here is just starting, and I'm excited to see where Zappos takes me.

JOHNNY G.
employee since 2010

On the first day of training, I realized that this was not going to be like any job I had before. The first month of training was a blast and I got really excited about the culture here at Zappos. I am a few months shy of two years now and my thought from the first day is still true — I will never have a job like this again in my life.

JON R.
employee since 2011

Coming together from all walks of life, meeting and interacting with total strangers for the first time and feeling as if you are talking with a friend that you've known for years - that is what the Zappos Culture means to me. The culture here, coming from any other workplace where I've been, has been pretty much a culture shock. What company would give you the power and the knowledge to improve yourself and grow? Not any that I know of so far. The people here are the most random bunch I have ever encountered, but I wouldn't trade it for anything. The definition of culture should have Zappos in parentheses, because without these people, this company would just be a jazz without soul.

JONATHAN P.
employee since 2011

Who loves Zappos? I love Zappos. Is it true? Mmm-hmmmm. I do, I do, I do — oooo!

JONETTE C.
employee since 2012

At Zappos, we ALL deliver WOW and happiness to our customers through our amazing service each and every day. We also learn to embrace and drive change in our everyday lives.

At Zappos, we always manage to make time for the important things like creating fun and a little weirdness in our workplace! We are always encouraged to be adventurous, creative and open-minded. As Zappos employees, we always have the chance to pursue growth within the company and we are always learning something new. I find that it's easy to build open and honest relationships with coworkers by simply using many forms of communication.

At Zappos, it's effortless to build a positive team and family spirit with the amazing and unique people we work with. Zappos shows us how simple it is to do more with less. It's easy to be passionate and determined to make this company the best when you work here. I am truly humbled to be a part of the Zappos Family! For the first time in my life I can actually say I LOVE MY JOB!

JORDAN R.
employee since 2007

I'm very happy to still be here at Zappos. I have grown as a person and made many friends in the time that I have been here. I can't wait to see what happens once we make the move downtown.

JOSEPH M.
employee since 2006

The best part of working at Zappos is the sense of satisfaction of everybody pulling at the same end of the oar ... from non-customer-service employees jumping in to help on the phones during the busy holiday rush, to employees across all divisions supporting bake sales and BBQs to help local charities, to volunteering time and talent in such endeavors as back-to-school backpack filling or the Las Vegas Marathon, there is a sense and feeling of family and unified purpose that is almost impossible to find anywhere else ...

JOSEPH P.
employee since 2011

The Zappos Culture means that no one here is a stranger; we're a company of over two thousand friends in a city where most people don't even know their own neighbors (but we're working on that). Not only that, but we keep close ties with an extended family out of state. We're privileged to work with engaging, exciting people in a place that nourishes ideas and values individuals. Our culture could be the spark that starts a corporate revolution in how both employees and customers are treated.

JOSHUA P.
employee since 2008

To me, culture means knowledge, beliefs, habits, and laws that are specific to one group of people or one society. I believe that being different is very important within a culture. If we were like everyone else, we wouldn't stand out the way we do. Zappos is full of this kind of culture and you can tell by just walking through the offices of 2280, 2290, and of course the best building, 2300!

JOY M.
employee since 2010

I AM so fortunate to have been a part of the Zappos family and to have shared time and space with an AMAZING group of people! Because of Zappos, I was able to fulfill many lifelong dreams, like going to New York during my favorite time of the year (Christmas), attending the charity: water ball, meeting one of my heroes (Tyler Perry), visiting the gravesite of my favorite singer (Aaliyah), among other wonderful experiences that I'll cherish for the rest of my life! Thank you so much, Zappos & Tony Hsieh! Love & Light, Pua <3

JOYCE E.
employee since 2006

OK _ now it's year five for me and things are still improving, the culture is stronger, and I am even more blissfully happy. We had an unfortunate incident earlier this year, and I could not have been any prouder of the way we came together as a company (as a family). Leadership was great, but CLT — pop yo collar — because we came together and showed "them" what we are made of (sorry to end this sentence with a preposition). Our next large project is the big move downtown. I know things will come together as planned because that's just how we roll.

What does the Zappos Culture mean to me, you ask? It means never having a bad day because of work.

JULEZ Z.
employee since 2010

The only way I could love Zappos more is if it were made of jelly beans.

JULIE G.
employee since 2011

The Zappos Culture is everything I was hoping it would be! I've been here 10 months and it keeps getting better and better!

Before I ever thought about working at Zappos, I read Tony's book, "Delivering Happiness," and it just clicked with me: this is where I belong!

The focus on amazing customer service and the unique friends and family atmosphere was something that I really identified with.

I feel as if I'm able to be myself and really grow and progress here. I'm not only encouraged to express new ideas and drive change, but I'm also supported to do so - as opposed to being threatened or intimidated into meeting high standards (as many companies seem to do). Zappos does an amazing job of coaxing great ideas out of people and encouraging us to be ourselves. I never feel as if an idea of mine will be judged or scoffed at. I always feel as if I have a voice and my opinion matters.

I love it here - I'm so grateful to work for such an amazing company and with such awesome people!

JUSTIN F.
employee since 2009

Our Zappos Culture has delivered on so many levels over the past year, including being involved in charity events and community. The latest All Hands meeting was the best I've experienced since I began in 2009. I feel this company is something special that invests a lot into its employees - and that pays off in the long run. Being a part of the Zappos Insights Events, Goals Workshop, various Pipeline classes and now in the leadership team allowed me to grow personally and professionally. We have the ability to cross-train in a variety of ways. This gives the employees the confidence to pursue growth and learning and it's highly encouraged. Looking forward to the rest of 2012 and beyond.

KAITY B.

employee since 2011

The Zappos Culture is like a big party, hanging with your friends, feeling welcome, loved, and always having a shoulder to lean on. At Zappos, you can be your complete crazy, fun, silly, weird, loud self and not have to worry about being judged for being YOU! It's the best feeling to walk into work every day knowing that you can wear what you want and be who you are and be welcomed with open arms. The Zappos Culture has helped shape who I am today, at work and outside of work.

KARA H.
employee since 2008

The Zappos Culture, to me, means community. If something needs to get done, everyone pitches in to help out and make sure it gets done. It doesn't matter if it is someone in Dev or Marketing or ZCLT, we all come together as a team and a community and make sure that Zappos is the best company we can make it.

KARA L.
employee since 2012

Since I am new to the company, my outlook on the culture may be a little different than some. When I first came for my interview, it was crazy, people walking around, having a parade, everyone looking like they actually liked being at work ... NO WAY!!! What I actually saw was people being themselves, and a company that actually let them do it. Our Ten Core Values mean different things to different people, but to me it means just be yourself and you'll be accepted and loved for it.

KAREN H.
employee since 2011

I am happy to be part of the Zappos Family and Culture. It is exciting to see all of the friends that I have met learn and grow within the company. I am looking forward to continuing my journey and watching as things change with our move to downtown Las Vegas.

KARLA C. AKA MCCALLISTER

employee since 2010

Zappos is my second home. It's where my (Zappos) family is, where my support structure and support is, and where I have fun. If Zappos were not my workplace, I would call it my hobby! Because of the great culture we have built here and the great customer service experience, even if I come into work in a bad mood, it only takes 30 minutes of friends and a wonderful Zappos customer to turn my day around. I have never experienced office politics or backstabbing because of promotions. When someone is promoted, everyone else supports, encourages and praises his or her accomplishments.

I think one of things I love most about The Zappos Culture is that we are encouraged to take chances, and if we fall short, we are given feedback to help us learn and grow from the experience. Zappos is how a workplace is supposed to be: loving, supportive, imaginative, different, fun.

KARLI F.

employee since 2012

My favorite thing about the Zappos Culture is that I get to be super-creative at work and every call I take is a chance to meet a new friend.

KATHERINE F.

employee since 2009

One of my favorite things about working at Zappos is that I feel like I work at the DisneyWorld of call centers. As a customer service rep, I am empowered to treat every customer the way I would want to be treated. It's a rare commodity to get great customer service these days for internet purchases. Our customers constantly tell us how awesome we are and often end chats or phone calls with ïl love you guys.' I'm willing to bet that DisneyWorld does not get as many "I love yous" at the end of a visit as we do!

KATHERYN G.

employee since 2007

I have been here for almost five years. And while change is constant and part of our core values, this still is the best company I have worked for. I especially love the functions and culture events and also seeing fresh new faces that have just gone through training. It is like welcoming a whole new generation to our big family. Awesomeness!

KATIE V.

employee since 2011

To me, the Zappos Culture is amazing. This is the only place I have worked where, when I come in, it's like coming to hang out with my friends and family — not like coming to my job. Every morning I'm welcomed by my smiling teammates and throughout the day I find myself laughing non-stop. I believe that if it wasn't for the Zappos Culture, this place would be like every other call center. The culture is also apparent in the way that we assist our customers. The Zappos family members have so much love and pride in this company that they will do whatever it takes to help build the Zappos name and WOW our customers.

KAYLA P.

employee since 2012

Zappos, to me, means so much more than a job. It means a way of life - and a way for me to change my life. It means opportunities that I never would have seen or experienced without Zappos. I love my job. I love coming to work every day. I love my coworkers, and the way everyone acts toward each other. The culture here is unlike anything I've ever seen before, and I sincerely wish other companies would take after it. We may not be enough to change the world, but a little at a time sounds like a good rate to me.

KAYLA Q.

employee since 2011

The Zappos Culture means being able to be yourself. By being yourself at your job, you are happier. Not only does being happier help you, it creates a great team and work family and it also pleases our customers! It is so rewarding to read the "WOWs" and "OMGs" from our customers via email each and every day. Working together as a team and embracing our awesome culture really does make our workplace somewhere special and unique.

KEIR F.

employee since 2008

The Zappos Culture means various types of people intermingling and coming together for the common good.

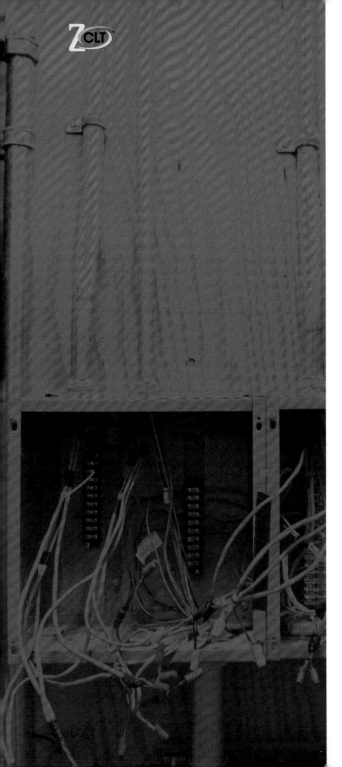

KELLI A.

employee since 2010

The culture here is unlike any other, and I'm so excited that I've had the opportunity to experience it! We're encouraged to live our Ten Core Values, and I really do eat, sleep, and breathe them every day. I love working here because when we're presented with a challenge, we really work together and get things done, but we also know how to relax and enjoy ourselves when the time is right. Zappos just wouldn't be Zappos for me without a nap room and genuinely happy people everywhere you look. I heart your face, Zappos!

KELLY M.

employee since 2012

I believe that what makes a company great is how it handles itself when it makes a mistake. Every company is great while things are going right, but what happens when mistakes happen? Here at Zappos, all of us are given the tools as well as the trust to actually make any type of issue right. We understand that we are not perfect and that mistakes are bound to happen. But we also understand how important is for us to take responsibility for our mistakes and to be honest with our customers, whether good or bad.

KELLY S.

employee since 2011

From the moment I first researched Zappos as a potential company to work for, I fell in love. After being here less than a year, I have to say that Zappos still WOWS me every day. Not only is it a fun work environment, but the people I work with have such positive energy, are super-supportive, and are genuinely nice people. I have built so many friendships while working here and never have a day where I dread going to work. In fact, I almost get bummed out when the weekend rolls around. Zappos truly has been such a blessing and I'm very thankful to be part of a company whose main goal is to deliver happiness!

KELLY S.

employee since 2011

When I think about our Zappos Culture, I immediately think FAMILY. While I may have just begun my journey here at Zappos, I have to say this was one of the quickest (and biggest) families that I have ever gained. I am thankful every day for the blessing that this job has been. Having graduated from college — where I was immersed in a very close-knit community of friends — just over a year ago, I know they were the hardest thing to leave behind when I moved home. Transition and change is never easy. I have always been told, "Grow where you're planted." I used to take that quote for granted, thinking it was cheesy, until it finally came to fruition this year.

My coworkers have been a huge support system. They continue give me the confidence to stand by that quote. I've worked for companies where you only see people during your work hours and nothing more. However, our Zappos Culture truly cultivates a unique family environment. You learn to work hard together, spend time with one another outside of work as friends, and to love each other in spite of each other's antics — like family. Some would call us a cult. I would agree, and make the argument that you can't have the word culture without the word "cult". Because we spend such a great deal of time together — not just working hard, but having fun together — it really transforms the work environment. Instead of Monday morning being something to dread, I look forward to kicking off my work week. And I'll admit — there are even times when I feel anxious on days off because I miss my team.

Our culture is what makes our company truly unique. The fact that we continually embrace it is what continues to keep us close together —and I LOVE IT!

KELLY W.
employee since 2010

The culture at Zappos is definitely unlike any other! It's amazing to see an entire company that is vested in every employee! You can feel how special it is every day. I am grateful to work with such amazing people who care about each other so much!

KELLYE T.

employee since 2010

I can't thank Zappos enough for all of the amazing blessings I have received over the years! Zappos has been a safe haven, crazy party, learning experience, and the home where all my Las Vegas family resides. The amount of physical things and experiences I have been able to enjoy is beyond measure, but the most important of all is the impression left upon me. Starting at Zappos at 18, I have grown into the person I am today due to the huge impact this amazing place and the people who work here have left on me. So, from the bottom of my heart, thank you for everything from the delicious soup in the Bistro to the best 21st birthday a gal could ask for! :)

KELSEY W.
employee since 2010

Every day something happens that reminds how lucky I am to work for such an amazing company and how fortunate I am to be surrounded by so many terrific people. To say it simply, I love Zappos!

KENNETH B.
employee since 2012

The Zappos Culture endorses success on an interpersonal, mental, and professional level. Plain and simple. Initially, in nurturing your interpersonal abilities to work well with others, voice ideas/concerns, and be surrounded by constructive mentors and leaders. Secondarily, as an aspiring professional, the culture allows you to use your talents in departments and capacities that you might not consider. It challenges you to not just talk about it, but be about it.

Lastly, each person at Zappos has the potential to have joy in their lives because of what they receive from this culture. Never mind anything monetary in a struggling global economy. The struggle against our own perspectives is waged daily and because of the culture at Zappos, joy has the upper hand. Creating a little fun and weirdness, remaining humble, and pursuing growth and learning are elements of a job that, if implemented properly, can improve every person's mental health (whether they think they need it or not).

The culture makes this a great and wonderful place!!! The people who take it with them into the rest of their lives make the WORLD a better place! GO, ZAPPOS, GO!!!!

KEVIN K.

employee since 2010

There is so much to say about Zappos. First and foremost, it is a truly incredible company, not only to work for, but to be a part of. There is usually a clear line between business and play; however, Zappos effectively blurs that line without sacrificing productivity. Being here doesn't feel like work. It feels like a second home. We are all working, but we're working for more than just a paycheck. We're working for the betterment of this company; we're working for each other. We're all working to be a part of something greater. It's an amazing experience. As with all things in life, we aren't perfect. But that isn't a bad thing at all. We're still growing strong and improvements are made on a daily basis. Our future has never looked brighter and I'm very much looking forward to what we will accomplish.

KENNIA G.
employee since 2010

The Zappos Culture is like coming to work and feeling like you just walked into your second bigger, louder, brighter, crowded, and more eccentrically decorated home ... and clocked in.

KERRY M.
employee since 2012

I just started working at Zappos in February and I can't imagine a better place to work. I moved from Michigan to work here, and even though it wasn't the easiest thing to do, I don't regret doing it for one second. Everyone that I've met here is so nice to talk to and be around. The relationships I have been able to build with my training class have been amazing. I certainly see myself working here for many years to come!! =]

KEVIN L.
employee since 2011

Zappos is a great company to work for. It has helped me grow and change in many aspects of my life. I look forward to growing and changing with this company. The Zappos Culture, to me, means being with friends and having a good time while fulfilling customer needs.

KEVIN M.
employee since 2012

"I HATE MY JOB!!!" How many times have you heard someone say that???

I can honestly say that I have NEVER heard that phrase uttered at Zappos! And why is that? Well ... what's NOT to love here? Everyone you meet is always open, honest and equally helpful, no matter what the situation. Everyone is more than willing to help anyone with anything. Need help moving something? Everyone will help you! Need someone to hold the door for you? Everyone will help you! Need someone to give you advice or help? Anyone can and WILL help!!! The people here are simply AMAZING!

Zappos is easily the best place I have ever worked and even more importantly, it's the best place I could ever hope to work!!! And it's all because of the wonderful, amazing, talented, cheerful people!!! And that helps explains why I LOVE my job!!!!!

KEVIN T.
employee since 2008

The Zappos Culture means a lot to me. It is what really separates us from the other companies out there. It takes the stressful jobs that we all do here and makes them fun and less stressful. "These few dollars you lose here today are going to buy you stories to tell your children and great-grandchildren. This could be one of the big moments in your life; don't make it your last!" —John Dillinger

KIANA L.

employee since 2007

The Zappos Culture means so much to me! It has definitely changed me in so many different ways. It's not something that I only live by in the office, but it has become a way of life for me and is something that I will forever be grateful for.

KIMBERLY B.
employee since 2010

To me, the Zappos Culture means that we are courteous to each other and back each other up. It's also nice to know that when bad times occur (in your personal life) there is someone who will care. We truly are a family here!

KIMBERLY N.
employee since 2008

The Zappos Culture, to me, means family. I feel like coming here is my second home. I have people here who support and care for me, and who are always there for me. I do not see myself being a part of any other company besides Zappos.

KIMBERLY R.
employee since 2011

This is my first year here at Zappos and my first entry for the Culture Book. I have to say that for the first time in my life, I am so thrilled and thankful to be a part of something so special. I love coming to work and being with such a great group of people who, in a short time, have become my family.

KIRA K.

employee since 2010

Zappos is zapparific! We have fun at work every day. It is great to jump out of bed every day and look forward to going to work. I enjoy the friends and family I have met here at work. This is a company that does follow its core values. My favorite is #5, "Pursue Growth and Learning." I love all the opportunities I have here to pursue growth and learning.

KRISTEN F.
employee since 2010

I love Zappos. I love culture. I love the Zappos Culture — hey, hey, hey! It's true, I've been here for almost two years now and I'm still in puppy love. From the day I started, I knew that I was in my element and in a place where the possibilities were endless and no door was ever closed ... unless there's a meeting in progress. Our culture allows us to be who we want to be and find out what we're passionate about, as well as giving us the outlet and core values to manifest our ideas. I feel very blessed to have the opportunity to work not only for a great company, but alongside such amazing, passionate and talented people. Not everyone in the world can say that they've participated in a water-balloon fight on the walk into work, answered e-mails while wearing football pads, thrown a pie in the face of a supervisor for charity, or been to battle with a Nerf gun, but I have, all thanks to Zappos. What's not to love? So, here's a big thanks to Zappos for allowing me to be fun and a little weird and for the chance to put a smile on strangers' faces.

KRISTEN W.
employee since 2011

This much I know. I did not know what it meant to have best friends until I started to work here. For that, I am truly grateful and will always hold them dear to my heart <3. That much I am sure of.

KRISTINA S.

employee since 2011

So far my journey here at Zappos has been amazing. I love the culture! My favorite Core Value, by far, is #3 "Create Fun and A Little Weirdness!!!" I enjoy being goofy and making people laugh :) I can't wait to experience all the new adventures in the future here at Zappos ... Cheers to all my Zapponians!

KRISTINA T.
employee since 2011

The Zappos Culture is about community. At work, we are blessed enough to be able to laugh together, rejoice when someone receives a promotion and support each other through tough times. Zappos strives to create leaders as well as innovation in the workplace. They encourage us to be ourselves and use our skills to help this company advance. I am truly thankful that I am able to experience the beauty of this culture, because it is unlike that of any other company.

LACIE J.
employee since 2010

Zappos always seems to amuse me. It is always one step ahead and ready to take on any challenges that may come. It's been a great year and doesn't feel like I've been working here for two years. Time flies by when you are having fun! I was just promoted to the Racecar Email team and am having a blast! Thank you for the chance to purse my growth and learning! "Keep Calm and Close More Threads!" That is all for now, until next year! =D

LAILONNIE H.
employee since 2008

The Zappos Culture means "family" which is important in my book. We play together, we look out for each other and we inspire each other. No one ever forgets your birthday or anniversary and everyone is a priority. Our culture is the foundation for all of the happiness that's provided by each and everyone in this company. There is never-ending love, loyalty and respect from my extended Zappos family.

LAKESH M.
employee since 2007

To me the Zappos Culture means we are a passionate, determined, adventurous family that is fun and a little weird. :-)

LAURA C.
employee since 2007

I'd like to think of Zappos as my home away from home. I've invested much time, out of pure enjoyment, building lifelong relationships with my teammates and have created very dear friends. I take much pride in saying that I work for Zappos, because this is more than just a job. I also value the bonds between myself and the people I work with, because they are more than just coworkers. Since my employment here began, there's been so much growth and amazing goals concord. The future holds great changes, and for us, the sky's the limit. There's nowhere else I'd rather be than here, because we set records, exceed goals and expectations, dream big, make changes, party hard, deliver the WOW in and out of the office, and we never give up. It's amazing and honorable, to be a part of our company and its exceptional growth.

LAURA F.
employee since 2011

The Zappos Culture is a hard thing to put into words because it encompasses so many things. It's friends and family. It's a positive learning environment. It's not being afraid to show who you are but most importantly, it's about finding out who you can be. I absolutely adore all my fellow Zapponians and am truly grateful for being able to be part of this amazing journey. Shout out to my Kachow family!

LAURA M.
employee since 2005

The Zappos Culture to me means random things. Coffee shop, connections, fun and reaching for goals.

LAURA S.
employee since 2010

I have been with Zappos since November of 2010 and what a difference there has been in my life has been since joining the Zappos family! I have made great, true friends and have grown both in my person and work life. The experiences I have had at Zappos have helped me make my personal life better as well. I love our customers; they make coming to Zappos every day a joy, not a job! The environment is very open and friendly and we are encouraged to be our own person. What an AWESOME place to have for a second home!

LAUREN C.
employee since 2006

I really believe this year was one of personal growth. I have learned so much and have been able to develop my leadership skills over the past five or six years. However, this past year has been one of huge personal changes; all the things I have learned about how to be a great leader have come in real handy in my personal life and I truly feel that I have grown and matured. To me, this is the embodiment of our culture. There is always a balance of work and life, and when I can start putting the things I have learned at work into other parts of my life and take myself to newer and higher levels, I truly feel fulfilled; I believe that I am living and serving the higher purpose our company has set out to accomplish. I feel very grateful to work with amazing people who keep pushing me forward to greater and greater things!

LAUREN E.
employee since 2010

I have been here for two years tomorrow and I still love my job! There aren't days where I don't want to come in and I genuinely look forward to coming into work. Sometimes, I miss my team on weekends! There are not many people who can say that. I certainly count myself lucky to be part of this amaZing company. Our culture is so very important and integral to our success. As Aristotle said; "Pleasure in the job puts perfection in the work." We work hard because we love our customers. Here's to many more years, Zappos!

LAURIE B.
employee since 2012

About four years ago, I took a tour at Zappos. It was the best 90 minute tour ... ever! All I could think about was, "How do I get to work there? ... these are my kind of people!!!" So, I pursued my dream job and now I'm an official Zapponian. As I write this entry, I have been with Zappos for 24 days and in that time, I've had a blast! Zappos is a place that accepts you for who you are, what you wear and however you wish to look. It is a joy to come to work every day. I have the opportunity to meet new people every day who will welcome my craziness and wackiness. It's so refreshing to be able to come in to work each day with a smile and pass along my happiness to others outside of the workplace. Thank you, Zappos for accepting me into your world. I can't wait to see what the future holds!

LEANN T.
employee since 2012

I started a little over three months ago. I have worked in call centers for a good portion of my career, and let me tell you, Zappos is not like any of them. This place is amazing! In the short time I have been here I have formed my opinion of what the Zappos Culture is. I believe that Zappos has created an environment that is very motivational; there is a sense of respect, no matter who you are. I am able to be myself without any judgment whatsoever, which is awesome! I have also created some really great friends in a matter of months, which is unheard of. I really enjoy working here and I think if everyone could experience the culture here, the world would be a better place. :)

LEANNE T.
employee since 2012

Wow. I mean ... WOW. It's the beginning of my fifth week here at Zappos and I cannot believe how at home I feel. I have had friends that have worked here for years and they always talked about how much they loved it. They also all told me to apply. I hesitated at first because I didn't think working in a call center would be that great. Boy, was I wrong! Zappos has changed everything I ever thought a call center would be. I actually look forward to coming in to work, sitting at my desk and jumping into the calls! It's so much fun talking to people in all parts of the United States and helping them shop and pick out just the right shoe color or dress style. It's also good to work in a place where everyone is happy and friendly every day. It has made me more happy and friendly, more patient and more willing to help in any way I can. This has been a life-changing experience.

LESLEY L (TMOTD).

employee since 2011

The Zappos Culture is an amalgam (love that word!) of hard work and hard play. Lots of work, always done with the customer uppermost in our hearts and minds, and lots of hard play, a little less customer-centric. It's a way to wake up each day and not regret going to work, but instead knowing that I'm going to be with friends and coworkers with a common goal. The Zappos Culture is thoughtful, considerate, funny, quirky, socially aware, compassionate and energetic. It's a way to be part of a larger community, while still maintaining our individual identity. It's awesome!!

LETHA M.

employee since 2007

I have now been here four and a half years and damn if I don't still love this place! What a gift it is to be able to say that you love your work.

LINDA T.

employee since 2006

The Zappos Culture is, by our definition, to be different and to set the tone for all other organizations and companies. The Zappos family's goal is to aim to be honest, humble and family-oriented. All of these are great qualities that any parent would want from their children. I'm in love with the fact that this is the focus from Tony Hsieh. It's important to me that he still plays a close and intimate role in keeping our core values a vital part of what makes our culture so coveted. If there is any secret to be had about why our environment is thriving, it would be how strongly we try to uphold our core values.

I have to mention that I am closer to the person I want to be every day because of the benefits of being a part of this family. The attention so meticulously given to our health insurance, our lunch options, the consideration given for arriving maybe five minutes late to work — all are characteristics that make my work life enjoyable. I'm utterly grateful for what I have and don't have in life. The major events that recently took place in my life are all thanks to Zappos. This is my story and this is my example of how our culture affects me. Thank you for listening!! :)

LINDSAY F.

employee since 2012

Everything is Culture. It's your accomplishments and the accomplishments of others. Culture is how you live your life every single day. It makes you ... well, YOU.

LINDSEY G.

employee since 2011

I've met some pretty amazing people since starting at Zappos. When I was making the decision to accept a job with the company and uproot my life in California, I was more concerned about what the company had to offer me, instead of what my coworkers could add to my life. My greatest part of personal growth that I have achieved since that time was discovering that I had my priorities backwards. My coworkers aren't really my coworkers — they have become my extended family. When I come into work every morning, I look forward to laughing with them. We commonly turn to each other for advice. We know each other's significant others, families and pets! We "get" each other's sense of humor. Most importantly, we have truly supported each other through thick and thin. When my wife and I were trying, unsuccessfully, to have a baby, it was my "extended family members" that gave me a hug each disappointing month and reminded me that "the best things that are meant to be, come with time." So, all this is true of finding my Zappos family.

I've worked for other companies in the past where they didn't want us to talk or "fraternize" because they thought it slowed production. I'll say this to the disbelievers — look at how we pull through during the holidays or how we came together during an unfortunate situation like the security breach. That type of dedication, passion and hard work comes from having this family-like atmosphere.

LISETTE M.

employee since 2010

I have been blessed to be part of the BEST company for the past two years! I am so proud to represent such an awesome company! Zappos has taught me the true meaning of friendship and what family spirit is all about. I look forward to being part of the Zappos family for many years to come.

LIZA H.

employee since 2012

I have finally found My Dream Job!!! I love working for a company that is Making a Difference in this world!

LIZZY G.

employee since 2012

Zappos is LOVE. That is the only possible way I can describe it. The culture here means everything to me, and it is more than I could ever have asked for.

I have never felt so at home in any other place in the world, or met as many lovely people as I have here. Each person I have encountered in my short time working here has been both unique and incredibly loving, and I can't get enough of it.

Zappos encourages each of us to be different, and I think that plays a huge role in the family-like environment that flourishes here. It encourages us to be strange and wonderful, and that makes all of us happier. When we're happy, it makes it very easy for us to love everyone. And I certainly do.

I love you all, and you're amazing.

LORI K.

employee since 2005

Zappos is more than a job, it is an experience, and after seven years here the experience continues. I believe the Zappos Culture is the foundation that keeps us bonded and moving forward. I bond with my coworkers and they are my extended family. Also, Zappos creates an atmosphere of trust and creativity. All ideas are welcomed and I have seen many of them implemented around the office. I appreciate the fact that as a customer loyalty rep, I can actually provide my customers with service. I have the freedom to do what needs to be done. I wish I could find Zappos service everywhere, but I know I can take my Zappos Culture with me everywhere I go and that is worth a lot.

LORNE S.

employee since 2006

The Zappos Culture, for me, is about the fun I have at work and outside of work. When we had our Christmas Party in the Aria, I went by myself. I had so much fun with different coworkers, laughing, drinking, and enjoying the moment. Zappos employees know how to have fun.

We also have Happy Hour at work; we toast each other, then get back on the phones. ONLY at Zappos!

I love to have fun with other coworkers and create memories. For example, one of my coworkers had a birthday. In fun, I sent her an email to congratulate her on her 21st birthday (she was not 21). I also stated that she can now DRINK and gamble with the adults. I gave her a birthday gift of wine, poker chips, a deck of cards and "The Dummy's Guide to Gambling." She loved it.

We are a company that creates fun and it's a little weird. My coworkers will be my friends for life.

MADISON F.

employee since 2012

"Our minds are as different as our faces: we are all traveling to one destination; -Happiness; but few are going by the same road."—C.C.C.

MARA K.

employee since 2005

To me, the first things that comes to mind after being here for seven years is that culture is and has always been number 1 to us at Zappos. We all believe in our culture, we are One Big Happy Family, equality for all. We all come from different backgrounds so first and foremost, treat each other with full respect, deliver WoW through service, do more with less, be creative - we all are creative here. Fun - always fun. Parades. Zappos is the best!!!

MARANDA N.

employee since 2010

What does the Zappos Culture mean to me? It means many things to me ... building relationships, meeting new people, making connections, learning new perspectives, keeping an open mind at all times, humbling myself and not being proud, trying new things, and thinking outside the box. This culture has taught me to enjoy my life, because you never know what the day will bring, so live it like it was your last!!

MARC T.

employee since 2011

I appreciate all the culture that Zappos brings into my life, from hanging out at the cafe to MAN BAND practice up in 2300. It just amazes me how much they influence you to do whatever makes you happy. I think it's what makes coming to Zappos every day different and amazing.

MARGRET H.

employee since 2008

As I write my entry into this year's Culture Book, I reflect back on almost four years of employment here at Zappos. It has been four wonderful years of both personal and professional growth. Zappos has allowed me to change emotionally, spiritually, even physically. I am a much calmer and more well-rounded person. That is because I love my job and enjoy coming to work every day. Zappos has provided me with a place to exercise and exercise classes that I have taken advantage of, and they are improving my health every day. Zappos has given me a huge extended family that I love dearly. They have become my second family. We have a free-flowing, open-door policy here at Zappos. Our leaders are always available and accessible. Growth is encouraged and promoted here. I was just moved up to our Live Chat team. Had it not been for the encouragement from my Lead and Supervisor, I might not have tried out for the team because I am a bit timid about these things. We have a great support system in place here. This is how Zappos is run. You are encouraged to grow. You are encouraged to spread your wings and fly. Zappos loves to see growth from within the company and I am proof of that. I love my new team here at Zappos. I look forward to writing in next year's book; who knows what team I will be on then, but I do know that I will have the support of Zappos behind me all the way!

MARINA M.

employee since 2007

The Zappos Culture, to me, is a way to live life in and out of work. It is funny, because you find yourself holding open doors for people at the store or bank, since it is something that becomes second nature here at Zappos. You also find yourself smiling outside of work. You hear about the culture, then once you are exposed to it, it all becomes clear and I love that it has stayed so strong through the years. I know I said this already, but it is second nature to live it, breathe it and let it consume you.

MARION B.

employee since 2011

Our Zappos Culture is what I live by, day to day. I believe in our culture and core values! The culture is what sets us apart from so many companies and I feel that's why we are so loved. The core values have reshaped my life as a whole and they are what I look up to. Thank you, Zappos, and I love you!!

MARISSA G.

employee since 2007

Zappos has definitely changed my life in more ways than I can imagine. I love being myself and being a part of such a warm environment. Everyone is so loving that I feel like I am in the presence of family, not coworkers. The culture alone is what has me hooked on Zappos. The benefits are out of this world and the care that everyone shows to one another is beyond what you would expect at a place of employment. I am grateful to have been able to experience Zappos and I definitely see myself retiring with Zappos.

MARK C.

employee since 2008

The Zappos Culture ... to me it means waking up and going straight to work in whatever I have on ... it just means me being me 24/7! It's nice to just really relax at work and feel so comfortable. Even the people here are so great! It's been the best job I've ever had and I'm very thankful for it. I must say it's an honor to be a part of the Zappos Culture and I love every second of it!

MARLENE K.

employee since 2005

People, passion, perseverance! It's been a year of growth in so many ways, and those three things are what keep our culture alive and strong.

MARQUES S.

employee since 2012

Hello,

I just started at Zappos and I'm loving every minute. I've been with the company for just five weeks so everything is new. I must say everyone is so sweet, patient, and willing to make you feel right at home. I love the fact that Zappos wants you to progress within the company. Most of the companies I've worked for didn't want you to grow and would keep you from growing. Most other companies I've worked for wanted to throw you under the bus in order to advance, whereas Zappos is the total opposite — it wants you to grow not just professionally but personally. I'm very excited for the opportunity that was given to me and excited to grow my career with the company.

MARTHA P.

employee since 2005

The Zappos Culture, to me, is being accountable for your actions and words while being accepted for who you are. Our culture is about providing the greatest service to our customers and finding a way to continue to WOW them with our creative solutions. Basically, make it as easy for the customer as possible and be the best version of you every day!

MARY T.

employee since 2007

I could go on and on about what the Zappos Culture means to me ... the culture here is still unlike anywhere else. I have been here for five years and still, to this day, consider myself VERY BLESSED. I still very much enjoy coming to work every day because I know that I get to come to the Disneyland of the business world. =)

MATT D.

employee since 2011

The Zappos Culture is the ability to have a marriage between the individual and their role at work. Most positions at other places ask you to become the person that a particular role/position requires. However, at Zappos, we're encouraged to make the job reflect who we are. It's a balance between work and life, which is very necessary to success, not only as an individual, but as a company as well. I love it!

MATTHEW F.

employee since 2010

The Zappos Culture symbolizes individuality, passion, honesty, and integrity. This is a company in which each one of us truly feels a part of one big, crazy, fun, and slightly dysfunctional (in a good way) family!

MATTY M.

employee since 2011

My journey started here with a PEC card from a Zappos employee when my mother made an order. I put in an application, flew 2600 miles just to tour, and then flew back to Las Vegas two months later just to interview. After my interview, I received notification I was hired. What an experience it's been. From the highest of highs to the unfortunate lows that we've experienced, it's been an incredible ride. I truly found the meaning of family when I joined Zappos. The people in this company are incredible.

Being part of the Corporate Challenge solidified those views. I've never made so many friends and new family members as fast as I did with Corporate Challenge. It was a gratifying experience to be a part of something so special to Zappos and the family experience it brought to me.

This year will bring bigger and better things for Zappos. We will be one step closer to our new home. A vision will be reached; ideas and dreams will come true. Rather than a scribbled idea on a sticky note, you will be able to walk through the doors of that idea.

I can't thank the company enough for what it has done and where it has brought me to today and I can't thank that person who took 15 minutes out of their day to make my mom that PEC card enough. It's truly special what a Zappos experience can do for you. Thank you, Zappos!

MAURA S.

employee since 2003

The Zappos Culture: It's not about the parties, it's not about the happy hours, or the fantastic company All Hands meetings. It's not about parades, dress up days, or BBQs out in the parking lot. It's about being there for each other, about being a good teammate and being supportive. It's about working hard while enjoying what you're doing. It's about trust. That's what the Zappos Culture means to me :)

MEL C.

employee since 2009

The Zappos Culture is about being there for one another and this past year has been the perfect example of just how true this is. I lost my best friend, Amber, one of our Zappos employees. It was overwhelming to see the outpouring of love and support from my coworkers, some of whom had never met her, but were still affected by the loss in our family. Because of everyone, we were able to raise money to help her family cover the cost of her funeral, but more importantly we were all able to celebrate Amber's life and grieve with people that truly cared about her. I will never forget all the people who were able to help me get through such a difficult time. Thank you, Zappos, for being so much more than a job and for being there for me through the good and the bad. I can't think of a single place I'd rather get up and go to every day.

MELISSA D.

employee since 2012

Eight weeks ago, I experienced a life-changing event. I began my CLT training. Nothing could have prepared me for the total immersion into the ZAPPOS CULTURE, which began immediately. The trainers are wonderful and a little weird. On the second day of training, Megan and Kristi broke out their dance routine, in their tutus (of course they were wearing tutus, it was Tutu Tuesday), dancing to "I'M SEXY AND I KNOW IT." At the beginning of training, we were told that as long as we worked at ZAPPOS, we would probably remain friends with our classmates. At that time, I didn't even know anyone's name but now, I feel as though I could call on any person in my training class, Zaboomafooz, to help me if I needed them. Why? Because we were encouraged to build open and honest relationships with each other. We shared things about ourselves while playing "Two Truths and a Lie." We went on scavenger hunts with our teams, and learned to depend and rely on each other. In the beginning, all of the fun stuff seemed like time fillers but they weren't. The people at Zappos know that in order to get to really know someone, you need to see them differently than working beside them. You need to see how someone plays a game like "Catch Phrase" in a team-building exercise, or how they complete a task with an impossible time frame. That is when quirks and personality cracks and attributes come out. There is always a method to the madness here at Zappos. Fingers crossed, it's the last job I will ever have.

MELISSA M.

employee since 2006

Zappos has helped me to walk in love, laugh with spirit, and learn with passion.

MELISSA Z.

employee since 2011

You do not realize how much your job or career can affect your daily happiness until you love what you do and have a natural comfort level with your coworkers (teammates). It's about nurturing your talent, no matter how different your talent is. Your growth depends on the risks you take, and risks are encouraged. It's not a competition, it's a ladder. Each experience here truly molds your character; you learn discipline and how to make to most of the negative. You learn that it is acceptable to make a mistake, as long as you learn and that if you eat 200 cupcakes every week, you will gain 20 pounds and you will learn to "Just say no." And oh, how hard it is, cakes, candies, bacon pot lucks (yes, only at Zappos) ... I could go on and on. It's about having a work ethic, learning, embracing, observing and most of all, chancing and risking the things you never thought you would!

MERENAITE S.

employee since 2008

With the Zappos Culture, I feel a sense of pride and I am very proud to be a part of it.

MICHAEL A.

employee since 2008

I've been at Zappos nearly four years and I am happy to be part of the Zappos family. As we know, it's a unique culture. Zappos remains a unique place to work in the world of business and I like being part of it. This past year has been challenging for everyone, for all of us who worked during WMS and then the security breach. It's been challenging to customers as well, but I'm happy to see they are back in force. There are still things that need to be fixed, and I am sure that will happen as time goes on. We've had to use almost all of the Ten Core Values this year and I'm grateful that they are available to give us something to use.

MICHAEL B.

employee since 2010

It seems that it just never gets old! Here I am, one year later and still, I'm loving every minute of my job, the people around me, and the overall work environment. The Zappos Culture is truly outstanding in every way possible. I have the luxury of working with such a great team that makes my job special and makes me happy to come to work each and every day. I could go on and on about how great it is to be a part of this, but it's just the family environment that put this over the top for me.

MICHAEL S.

employee since 2010

It is an amazing feeling to be excited about coming to work every single day. The people here are always so positive and welcoming. It blows me away to see such a large group of people working hard as well as having fun. The Zappos Culture allows me to be the same person I am at home as I am at work, and that is a feeling that cannot be matched.

Zappos is bliss.

MICHAEL S.

employee since 2009

This culture has become my life! Zappos has become my life! Everything that I have learned since 2009 has helped me realize my own potential and has inspired TONS of different goals and dreams. It has had a positive effect on how I interact with my family. And it has given me some the best friends I have ever had. From my first day at Zappos, I knew that here is where many doors will open and lasting relationships will grow. Above all, it has given me the opportunity to spread love, encouragement and happiness in a way that I could never do anywhere else. Regardless of what happens going forward, the Zappos Culture will ALWAYS be with me, wherever I go. This is my little light, and I'm gonna let it shine. Let it shine. Let it shine. LET IT SHINE!

MICHELLE C.

employee since 2010

The Zappos Culture is one of the many reasons I love to come to work every day. It's the culture that allows me, as an employee, to grow and be myself. I feel as if I am a part of something bigger than myself and that inspires me to find ways of making our company better.

MICHELLE M.

employee since 2006

What does the Zappos Culture mean to me? It means happiness, family, strength, craziness and most importantly, it means love. We incorporate our culture into everything we do — our work, our relationships and our play. The culture is US and it's our responsibility to nurture and protect it!

MICHELLE U.

employee since 2012

Well, all I have to say is before I came to work at Zappos one month ago (yes, I'm a newbie and I'm from England) I would say I was quite a bit more reserved. Now, it's all about "outside the box" for me. I have participated in Nerf» gun battles and lots of fun activities and dancing. I have bonded with my coworkers, big time! I must say I have never had so many people smile at me and say hello and the most important one for me is that everyone holds the doors open for one another (we do that a lot in England, you know). I feel that I worked very hard to get this job and I feel lucky to be a part of the Zappos team.

MIGUEL H.

employee since 2011

Yo, this amazing place has allowed me to be myself. The culture is a fantastic interpretation of what a work environment should be: fun, energetic, genuinely inviting, free-spirited and weird at times. We all work really hard, and we play hard too. Thanks to Zappos, I have time for my artwork, Marley, Woody, Allison, family and friends. I will not forget to live. Thanks, Zappos. Peace out, yo.

MIKAL G.

employee since 2007

Five-plus years at Zappos and I am still being WOW'd. A lot of movement has happened over the past five years and I don't see us slowing down or tethering off in the near future. I have had a lot of growth this past year too! It is awesome working in an environment that can still surprise you after five years. I love our ability to just be ourselves and this has never changed since I joined the company. I am very fortunate and thankful to be working for Zappos. Rock on!

MIKE D.

employee since 2010

There is something here for everyone. I am participating in a bike relay race, a running relay race, a 38-mile hike, a marathon, and the Tough Mudder this year. That is just a small part of the activities offered here but there is always something to look forward to. We are free to pursue our passions and initiate new things all the time.

MIKE S.

employee since 2005

The Zappos Culture is not a preset way of acting or being. It's people.

MONABEL S.

employee since 2011

I love the great family atmosphere here at Zappos. It's been a great experience so far. I look forward to many more experiences!

MONICA G.

employee since 2011

To me, the Zappos Culture means to live the core values and to seek to bring them out in others.

NA'MA B.

employee since 2010

Look, Mom! I'm a published writer!
É <-- That's a picture I drew for you of Steven Tyler singing.

May the Force be with you.

NAOMI S.

employee since 2010

I moved to Las Vegas two years ago from Denver to start my job here at Zappos. I left behind all of my family and my friends and moved with what would fit in my car, ready to start my new life — my new adventures. I didn't realize how hard it would be to be away from everyone. Little did I realize how much I would grow to love my new Zappos family! Everyone really helped me feel wanted and appreciated. It was hard working on holidays, especially Christmas, away from my family. But with the help and support of everyone here at Zappos, I truly felt a part of a huge family. Since then, I've worked every weekend just so I can spend my holidays with my adopted family! Zappos has done so much for me since I've been here. I've been totally WOW'd by everyone here. All the little things that most people don't think of, I truly appreciate and can't thank everyone enough for. I never thought that I would get the opportunity to be a part of such an amazing company, one where my thoughts and opinions matter. One where my own personal thoughts and experiences (and weirdness) would be appreciated and taken into consideration, on an everyday basis. I love my job here and I don't plan on leaving anytime soon!

NATASHA G.
employee since 2005

I still can't believe that I've been with Zappos for almost seven years!! WOW! I've watched this company grow from merely 150 people in our department to close to 400! It's been an amazing journey and I wouldn't change any of it for the world. What you read on the blogs and see in the media is true — Zappos truly takes care of not only its customers but also its employees. I've learned so much from every single individual that I've come into contact with. Being part of this amazing company has truly changed my life.

NEAL G.

employee since 2005

The Zappos Culture means coming to work each day and being able to just be yourself. It is amazing to see so many diverse people all working together in one place. It is truly a "special" place.

NICHOLE D.
employee since 2012

The Zappos Culture is something that is uniquely created by each customer and employee alike. I have only been here a few months and am already striving to make my experience here amazing. I don't want to just have an impact customers, or coworkers, but on myself and people I am close to outside of work as well. Working here means that much to me. We live in a town that is pretty much centered on customer service, but I think that we excel compared to most others (with that humble attitude, of course)! I have always had jobs where customer service was needed and working for Zappos encourages a better attitude and pushes you to walk out the doors and keep that attitude. Our culture is one in a million and we're only looking to expand that and I'm proud to work for a company with so much growth ... now and in the future!

NICHOLE N.
employee since 2012

The Zappos Culture is finding a place to work that you never wanna leave. You're surrounded by people who all have a little bit of weirdness in them, just like you. Trust me; I've had some jobs from hell. The first day I came to work for Zappos, it was like a curtain had been lifted, and there was this amazing place to work, plus bacon. You come in each day and people are smiling and opening doors for one another, it is impossible not to feel great. Zappos allows me to be the person I have always been, a ball of fun.

NICK A.
employee since 2012

The Zappos Culture has been very eye-opening. It is the first place I've worked where I'm constantly reminded how important learning and growing as an individual can change the company for the better. Even more amazing has been the idea that each one of us has a voice and our voice will be heard.

NICOLE C.
employee since 2011

Well, I'm sure many of you can relate to this, but before I started to work at Zappos, I HATED going to work. I would wake up in the morning, try to think of something fun and exciting to get me through the day and pray for the best. Now I really do enjoy coming to work every day. I love hang out with my team during our team buildings. I never thought it was possible to enjoy going to work.

PAMELA A.
employee since 2009

I feel lucky to still be a part of the Zappos family today, almost three years since my hire date! This place has taught me that once you find your passion, the hard work will be worth the future outcome. I love this place and hope to be able to continue to be a part of it as long as I live in Vegas!

PAMELA C.
employee since 2010

This year at Zappos had many challenges, as we all know. We pulled together as a team and overcame these various challenges. I feel it has made me stronger as a person and made our culture even stronger. Every day, I'm thankful for having been given this opportunity to work for such a great company. I'm proud to be a Zapponian.

PATRICE C.
employee since 2007

Wow! Another year has gone by! I can't believe it has been over five years since I joined the Zappos Family. It's such a pleasure to spend my day at Zappos. I'm always learning, growing and having fun. I enjoy the positive, friendly and a little quirky work environment. You can't help but enhance your personal life with that fun and positive Zappos spirit. It is amazing being here, and I am proud to be part of the Zappos Family.

PATRICIA N.
employee since 2006

I have been here for five years and the time as gone by so quickly. Time truly flies when you are having fun. Zappos has really become my family and has truly been there for me when times were hard. I cannot think of a better company to work for and be happy to represent. I never stop telling people about Zappos and how proud I am to be part of this family.

PORSHA P.
employee since 2008

Going on my fifth year, and I'm still here! I've said as long as they will keep me I'm not going anywhere. As always, I am thankful for the freedom that they have given me; to be able share my artistic side is a blessing. I am always ready for their call, so I can paint the town!

PRECIOUS B.
employee since 2011

The Zappos Culture means the world to me. Zappos became more than just a job almost immediately. I learned just how much Zappos becomes your family when my mom passed away during my new hire training. The people at Zappos made one of the most difficult times in my life a little bit lighter. I will be forever grateful to the kindness I was shown, and am still shown to this day. I feel very blessed to be part of the Zappos Family and am excited to grow with it.

PREMILA N.
employee since 2011

The Zappos Culture is its own brand of weirdness, happiness, openness, honesty and the best part of it all, the unity amongst ourselves as a Company to rally around our CEO, trust him enough to let him rule, take this Company towards higher grounds involving the PEOPLE, whether it is the employees themselves or our customers.

PRISCILLA G.
employee since 2007

The Zappos Culture is the epitome of amazing.

QUINTAYE P.
employee since 2006

I can't believe it's been six years already! Definitely looking forward to many more!!!! Thanks, Zappos!

RACHEL S.
employee since 2012

The Zappos Culture is a fun and unique experience!! Friendly faces are everywhere and I have conversations with people I have never met before. They have a way of making you feel part of the team right away.

RACHELL H.
employee since 2010

I LOVE my Zappos family! It's great to be excited to come to work and spent some time with my extended family. I love getting the time and opportunity to communicate with coworkers and learn more about them. It's great to have open communication with fellow employees, in turn, making it easy to communicate with customers.

REANDRA D.
employee since 2008

I am so amazed and pleased to be writing my fourth culture book entry! This has been a long journey with many more miles ahead of me! Being in ZCLT has taught me a lot!! I love making new friends, inspiring the new hires and seeing old faces that never get old! Zappos has allowed me to make life-long friends and some of the best friends ever! I love how inspiring everyone around me is. I appreciate the encouragement from other leads and even people from other departments. I look forward to continuing my journey with Zappos, and exploring more that Zappos has to offer. I plan to be a part of the growth and can't wait to continue making an impact on those I come in contact with! I <3 my Zappos Family!!

REBEKAH N.
employee since 2006

The Zappos Culture, to me, is having lifetime friends who are more like family.

REGAN H.
employee since 2011

The Zappos Culture is simply amazing. I feel it is really similar to what we call the "Aloha Spirit" back in Hawaii. This "Aloha Spirit" is a feeling of genuine love and kindness for the people but also for the place. Here, the people are my coworkers (or friends as I like to call them) and the place is Zappos. Zappos feels like an island community. A place where people are a part of something bigger than just themselves. A place where people come together with a common goal and work towards achieving it. So what are we trying to achieve? I believe we are trying to set an example or a standard, if you will, for how a company should treat people. Not just how it treats its customers but also its employees. We prove to the world that it is possible to be successful and treat your people really well, whether they are internal or external. We demonstrate that happiness can go hand in hand with productivity and a sense of purpose. Simply put, we prove that kindness with a focus towards happiness in business can be profitable if harnessed and directed properly. I love my job and I love the company I work for. I love Zappos. Most importantly, I love the people I meet and work with every day. Perhaps that is exactly what The Zappos Culture is — Love.

REGINA N.
employee since 2011

The Zappos Culture, to me, means accepting everyone as an individual, and knowing that we determine what it takes to uphold the culture that we work so hard to build and maintain. Compared to other company cultures, The Zappos Culture allows us to be accepted for who we are, determine our own destiny, and work hard all while having fun!

RIAN C.
employee since 2009

It has been a whirlwind year for my Zappos career. This company has provided more opportunities to me than I had during my years in college. I have met some of the most amazing people and I am happy to call them my family. Zappos has taught me so much and I am so very lucky to have been a part of something so great in my lifetime. "Thank you" pales in comparison to the gratitude that I want to express towards this great company and the people who have embraced me as a Zappos Family member.

RICHARD E.
employee since 2008

The Zappos Culture is about creating a friendly environment and striving to perform at your best. We work together as a team to accomplish our goals, and we help each other out to find solutions. The Zappos Culture means, work hard, play hard, and be respectful to yourself and each other. The Zappos Culture also extends to our community, with activities such as charity events and outreach programs. We have held summer and spring camps for our kids where we share with them the values of Zappos. One last thing, may I suggest that you participate in the Goals Workshop. It can help you reach your goals in your career, life, or whatever goals, large or small, you may wish to achieve. I enjoyed my time in the workshop and I apply the techniques I learned each day.

RICHARD P.
employee since 2011

The Zappos Culture is amazing. It's what truly makes this an incredible place to work. The positive energy and support we all share with each other is inspiring. Zappos rocks!

RICKI M.
employee since 2004

My eighth anniversary is coming up quickly, and as we grow bigger and bigger, we focus more and more on the Zappos culture. In 2004, every employee knew every other employee — their birth dates, their home addresses, their families and friends, their hobbies, and even what they had for breakfast. That is no longer possible. It is a comfort to know that great efforts are made, every minute of every day, to protect and preserve the spirit of cooperation, as well as the warm, fuzzy, feelings we all have for the company, and our fellow employees. As we grow larger, and larger, herculean efforts will be necessary from all of us, to protect the greatest asset we have — our culture.

RITA S.
employee since 2006

Every year we get busier and busier. We have grown so much and so fast that it is difficult to get to know the new family members and also to keep in touch with the people we have known and loved along our journey that is this crazy Zappos family. We are doing the best we can to be true to our Zappos Culture. I am excited for the move downtown where we will hopefully have more of our family interactions since we will be all in one space.

ROBBIE M.
employee since 2006

What does the Zappos Culture mean to me? The first thing that comes to my mind is "family." The relationships that I have built in the five years I have been here have been awesome, and I appreciate how open we all are to each other and how accepting we are. I can't wait to build more relationships as the years go by.

ROBIN G.
employee since 2006

I never hit the lottery, I never hit jackpots, and I never find money on the ground. But I work at Zappos, so I am very lucky. I do not have enough time or space to enumerate all the reasons why this is lucky. I have worked here for six years and the people I have worked with and the situations enrich my life daily. I hope I work here forever!

ROBYNN J.
employee since 2010

Well, here we are! I cannot believe that I am close to my second year here at Zappos! Time really does fly when you are having fun. My transitions have been absolutely amazing with the company. I could not dream of a better workplace. Aside from the perks, the people are truly genuine, and that gives me something to look forward to each day.

ROCHELLE W.
employee since 2011

The Zappos Culture, to me, is having a family unit away from home. It's us being able to express ourselves and the ability to grow from within as well as throughout the company.

ROCKNE H.
employee since 2009

Let's see ... third year at Zappos and third submission to our wonderful Culture Book. The amount of gratitude I have for this company is still as strong today as it was since day one. I think that the pursuit of growth and learning comes to mind when reflecting on the journey I've taken this past year. I was able to progress mentally and physically, paying much due to Zappos. I don't quite know where the future will lead me, but I'm thankful that this company continues to make individuals realize their full potential as well as fostering any endeavors they may have. It certainly has caused me to believe that and my journey is therefore real-life proof. Third year down and as always, thank you Zappos, for bringing out the best in me!

RONISUE R.
employee since 2010

Zappos is a wonderful company. The job is something you can find with several different companies, but the environment makes Zappos the best place to be. They feed you, clothe you (I have a Zappos T-shirt drawer), keep you entertained (GO ZAPPENDALES!!), and provide you with many other essential and not-so-essential needs. There is no better place to come to work five days a week.

RUBEN R.
employee since 2009

To me, the Zappos Culture means family! There is definitely a sense of family here. We're not just business here. We have fun with each other by incorporating our core values into our days and making a family-oriented atmosphere.

RUBY A.
employee since 2008

Never knew about culture until I came to Zappos. I truly think that having a culture at your workplace is great.

SAM O.
employee since 2011

What's up, Zeeps (Peeps)?
I thought I'd like to say a few words about the happiest place on earth. I've been here at Zappos for a little over a year and I can't believe it! I can honestly say that Zappos has changed my life altogether. I've been through some hard times these past few years and being here at Zappos has helped me get through these tough times. I look back a year ago when I started here and I've changed all around for the better. My life has done a full turnaround and I wouldn't be where I'm at if it wasn't for this awesome company. This is a place like no other and I appreciate this opportunity to the fullest. I've really Embraced and Driven Change this year and I can't wait to see where my Zappos brick road takes me next. I could go on and on about Zappos, but my fingers would be too tired to finish! Until next time, folks!

SANJA S.
employee since 2009

Contagious ... that is the best way I can describe the Zappos Culture (just ask my friends and family). The personal and professional growth I have experienced since 2009 is nothing less that. Amazing! I am forever grateful and forever changed for the better, just by being here.

SARAH K.
employee since 2011

To me, the Zappos Culture is going to an amusement park or river rafting, it's walking into your parent's house smelling your favorite meal, it's hiking to the top of Mount Everest, and it's being at the mall with your best buddies. So obviously the Zappos Culture isn't really ALL of those things, but the feelings are mutual. Our culture is fun, comforting, challenging, and makes it so much more enjoyable having your best buds that you've met along the way by your side.

SAUNDRA J.
employee since 2009

Zappos is so much fun! It has great people with very different personalities, which I think is what makes up a big chunk of the culture here.

SAVANNA H.
employee since 2011

It's hard to put into words what the Zappos Culture means to me. The Zappos Culture is being able to come to work in your pj's and no one says a word. The Zappos Culture is being around a group of people and when you break into song, they just follow up with the rest of the lyrics. It's about finding family in the people that you work with.

SCOTTIE K.
employee since 2004

Only Climax Blues Band's song, "I Love You," can describe what the Zappos Culture means to me! :)
"When I was younger man
I hadn't a care.
Foolin' around
Hitting the town
Growing my hair.
You came along
And stole my heart
When you entered my life.
Ooh, babe, you got what it takes
So I made you my wife.
Since then I never looked back
It's almost like living a dream
And, oooh, I love you.
You came along
From far away
And found me here.
I was playin' around
Feeling down
Hittin' the beer.
You picked me up
From off the floor
And gave me a smile.
You said, you're much too young
Your life ain't begun
let's walk for awhile.
And as my head was spinnin' 'round
I gazed into your eye
And thought, oooh, I want you.
Thank you, babe, for being a friend
And shinin' your light in my life
'Cause, oooh, I need you.
As my head was comin' round
 I gazed into your eyes
And thought, oooh, I want you.
Thanks again for being my friend
And straightenin' out my life
'Cause, oooh, I need you.
Since then I never looked back
It's almost like livin' a dream
Oooh, I got you.
If ever a man had it all
It would have to be me, And, oooh, I love you."

SEAN H.
employee since 2009

The Zappos Culture is what keeps me wanting to come to work every day. The energy and feeling of family spirit comes naturally. It is something that I am very thankful has not changed since the day I started, over two and a half years ago.

SEAN M.
employee since 2006

The culture here is unlike any other I've ever been around. There is a sincere depth of caring for each other that goes beyond being an employee or coworker, and a support system for both your personal and career goals. With this kind of nurturing environment surrounding us, it is no wonder we are able to be the incredible company that we are!

SEANPAUL E.
employee since 2008

Through my personal and professional life, Zappos has been a huge part of it. It has been four years and as we move on to the future, Zappos will still have that huge impact in my personal and professional life.

SHAEA L.
employee since 2012

I like to think of Zappos with, like, big eagle's wings, singin' lead vocals for Lynyrd Skynyrd with, like, an angel band, and I'm in the front row, and I'm hammered drunk.

I like to picture Zappos in a tuxedo T-shirt. 'Cause it says like, I wanna be formal but I'm here to party too. I like to party, so I like my Zappos to party. I like to think of Zappos like a muscular trapeze artist.

I like to think of Zappos like a dirty old bum. He's comin' up to me, and I'm 'bout to sock him one, cause, you know, he's a dirty old bum, but then I say, "Wait a minute, there's something ... I don't know - special about this guy."

I like to think of Zappos like a shapeshifter, or a changeling, like that guy — You ever hear of that TV show, "Manimal"?

SHANAE G.
employee since 2011

For me, the Zappos Culture means growth ... you learn to fully embrace who you are and learn to love the uniqueness of others. I can personally say that I have come out of my shell so much and I have learned to be comfortable being myself.

SHANE B.
employee since 2012

I only just recently started working with Zappos but I've already grown to love it. I've worked in the Customer Service industry for roughly 12 years now. This is the first job I've worked where Customer Service is the actual goal. Too many companies focus more on the profit aspect of their business models while foregoing the level of customer service that people crave. It's refreshing to able to work for such a company

SHANNON C.
employee since 2008

I still remember the day that I started working at Zappos. We had training throughout the week, and then the weekend came. Most people wake up on their day off, and embrace the time to decompress. But I wanted to be back at work. That's how in love I was with the company from the beginning. True story!

Well, that was four years ago. Four incredible years! It has been an adventure and I am overjoyed to be on this wonderful ride. Each day brings something new and exciting. Perhaps a parade, or a team potluck. Never a dull moment! I can't imagine ever working anywhere else. Zappos is a dream and I am thankful every single day to be part of it!

SHANNON M.

employee since 2007

What does the Zappos Culture mean to me? After being with Zappos almost five years, it has changed my way of thinking when it comes to customer service, and treating the person on the other end like they're the only one that truly matters at that moment. Zappos taught me to think outside of the box and understand that it's not about me; it's about getting the job done and having fun while doing it. I'm enjoying the PEC (personal emotional connection) the most. After all these years, I love bringing a smile to that person that calls and wants to talk or truly NEEDED something and couldn't find it and I did it without rushing them. Allowing people to talk to me like we are friends and shop for hours finding that perfect item for that special event - that's the Zappos Culture to me!

SHANNON P.

employee since 2010

"Every individual matters. Every individual has a role to play. Every individual makes a difference." _ Jane Goodall

It's really hard to sum up the Zappos Culture in so many words, but I feel this quote does a pretty good job. Zappos is more than a fun place to work and even more than a friendly place for customers to call for assistance. It's a lifestyle and mindset. It's getting up every day, feeling good about what your place is in the world, and working with amazing individuals towards a common ultimate goal. I feel so blessed to have been a part of Zappos and its culture for the last two-and-a-half years. Thank you!

SHANNYN M.

employee since 2012

Before I was hired, Zappos was described to me as "Disneyland without lines" and "adult daycare." After working here for the last month, I'm stoked to say that it's both. It's rare to find a place to work where you feel like you're not just part of a team, but a family, and where you're encouraged to be a little off the wall. The energy here is unbelievable, and everybody here is awesome. I feel like I'm bragging when I talk about my job, but I can't help it ... every aspect of it is nothing less than amazing, and I feel super lucky to be a part of this!

SHARON R.

employee since 2007

The Zappos Culture, to me, means loving my job! Our culture and Ten Core Values allow me to be creative and adventurous. Also, to:
Be a little weird; have a lot of fun at work with both our customers and coworkers;
Be free to be open and honest in the work relationships;
Be offered constant learning and development on the job in areas that I choose to pursue;
Be ready to embrace change, which helps us grow both personally and as a company, which also keeps things fresh, new and different ... while making them even better;
Be able to fully assist our customers and WOW them in the ways that I feel I would like to do;
Now ... how many places other than Zappos can you do that without getting into trouble? None that I've ever seen or worked at before ... and I'm VERY old and have worked at MANY places through the years! WOW! I've found my home away from home at Zappos, and I'm lovin' it! :)

SHAUN S.

employee since 2010

The Zappos Culture still continues to amaze me. Even with all of the issues we went through in the last year or so, everyone stays banded together, believes in each other, and pushes through any challenge that we may face. It's awesome to see the drive and determination with this company, and I still say "ZAPPOS FOR LIFE!

SHEA K.

employee since 2012

What does the Zappos Culture mean to me? Family, Friends and empowerment.

SHEENA B.

employee since 2010

The Zappos Culture, for me, is a way of life.

I have been here for three years now and everyday seems as though it is my first. You cannot sum up the Zappos Culture into one sentence or even a paragraph. To be honest, our culture is so diverse and unique, there is no proper definition for it.

Every day, we strive to better ourselves and to better our culture as a whole. To me, the most important thing that makes up our Zappos Culture is the unity we have. Our relationships with each other are the foundation of our culture. We learn, we teach, and we grow together. Every individual is a big part of this family, whether you are helping in facilities or assisting customers on the phone or making sure we have the inventory for our site. Without each helping hand, we would not be able to stay afloat in some way.

I look forward to coming to work each and every day because I know I am a part of a bigger picture, whether it's helping a customer shop for that perfect pair of shoes for their wedding day or helping my fellow team member reach their goal to succeed further in the company. I love knowing that my fellow workers are really just an extension of my immediate family.

And I wouldn't have it any other way.

SHEENA G (BEENA).

employee since 2008

Another year has gone, and I'm still ever so smitten with my Zappos Family.

I was once told that an ancient Chinese curse reads, "May you live in interesting times." This year has been a challenging one for all of us, yet I am continuously amazed by the power of a strong team whose members genuinely care about each other. This year has been the most "interesting" one I've experienced in my four years as a part of Zappos, and yet it's the one that I'm most proud of.

Our folks in ZCLT handled WMS like champs, embracing and driving change every day while WOWing their customers. The whole company banded together during the breach, and I was in tears at the sight of all of the other departments dropping what they were doing to go all hands on deck when we needed their help. We truly are a team, and while the opportunities we get to show it aren't always under desirable circumstances, I'm grateful to have had the chance to be a part of it and make even the tiniest difference in someone's day.

This year has also given me the chance to develop and nurture some of the most amazing people I have ever met _ leaders who have blossomed and come into their own, and who have taught me as much as I have tried to teach them. I am so proud of you all!

On a personal level, this year has been difficult as well. Once again, my Zappos Family stood with me, cried with me and hugged me until I couldn't breathe to get me through it. When I needed to be distracted, they went out with me and kept me company _ no questions asked. When I needed a moment to be selfish and complain, they listened and assured me that it would be okay. When I needed to be given a reality check, they did so kindly but firmly. Most of all, they loved me for my faults and made it bearable to make a decision that wasn't easy, but was right. You know who you are, but thank you so much to all of you. I couldn't have gotten through this without you. Cheers to mustache tattoos, sushi, beers, tutus, Wacky Wiener Wednesday, superheroes, beer pong, the FC, and Insert Coins. I can't wait to see what the next year has in store for us!

SHERRI-LEI S.

employee since 2010

Aloha, Universe!! I can't believe that another year has gone by and it's time to write something new. There have been so many challenges and changes. Embracing drive and change has been the focal point of my year.

I continue growing spiritually, mentally, and socially. I have so much to be thankful for that it's hard to keep my thoughts on track.

I feel blessed for the opportunities and experiences presented at Zappos. I have grown more with the books provided for self-education, pipeline classes to expand professionally and the guest speakers that come in and get me excited to help create change within my community.

I continue to share my journey with anyone who wants to know about Zappos. We play hard but work harder.

SMILIN' ROB.
employee since 2004

When you find something great, you'll fight for it. Over the years, there have been lots of ups and downs, but we've always come out ahead. The past year has been an interesting one, but I know that we're in the process of making a much stronger team and family. I've seen this before, and I'm optimistic for the future. You can't have the good until you've shared the bad, and our culture is about turning challenging situations into positive results. For me, I want to share past stories with others so they understand that a tough day/month/quarter is only part of the process of making us stronger. We bond when the team is challenged, and we learn how to be better the next time we have to put on those working boots.

This is a special place filled with some great characters. We're fun, quirky, intelligent, and inspirational. Each day brings an opportunity to learn, teach, and have a hearty laugh. I'm a better person because of Zappos and that's something that will always be with me. Thank you, Zappos family.

SOFIA K.
employee since 2009

Two and a half years in. Still loving it! Looking forward to the endless possibilities that the Zappos future holds.

SONYA J.
employee since 2012

What does the Zappos Culture mean to me? It's the difference between liking my job, and LOVING my job! I started just a few months ago (March '12) and I can honestly say that the culture we have here, as a company, is absolutely amazing!! It's something as simple as being able to be yourself. Individuality may be frowned upon at other companies, but it is absolutely embraced and encouraged here. :) On my first day of training, I was told that the people I met that day would become my second family. Having come from my previous jobs where "you're not supposed to be friends with the people you work with," I was ever the skeptic. But sure enough, as days and weeks passed, I found myself caring about these people as if they were my brothers and sisters!! I found myself wanting to be around these people OUTSIDE OF WORK??! WHAT??! That's just crazy, right? Not at all ... not even a little bit. I just attribute it to the people that Zappos hires, and the freedom we have to LOVE our jobs. I LOVE, LOVE, LOVE it! And I LOVE this company for what it has done to change my outlook on the future!!

Oh and one more thing ... Trip OnederZ FOR LIFE!!! Class 111! :)

STEFFANY B.
employee since 2012

The Zappos Culture is all about balance. It is basically a place that allows you to be yourself. It has managed to successfully strike a balance between autonomy and structure. Allowing the company employees to be themselves, in return, gets them to perform great work. Zappos has managed to create a strong foundation and belief in its core values. By accomplishing this, by allowing people to freely fall in love with the company as a whole, the end result is a bunch of people who care about each other and the company.

Zappos is generally is a company that stands for honesty, reality, forward thinking and hard work. Most companies manage their employees with fear and dictatorship. They don't allow opinions and ideas in the workplace. Zappos allows growth in the company and in the end, that allows the people of Zappos to grow as well. By allowing the employees to freely share their ideas and opinions, and offering advancements through the company, Zappos steers away from having employees become complacent and bored. Everyone wants to work for a company that allows them to be themselves and to share what goes on in their heads.

The Zappos Culture is the best because at the end of the day, it is forward-thinking about what is going to be the best for the company and the customers. It is real; it allows us to speak to the customers with no script. It offers a friendly environment, where we can all be ourselves and make new relationships. At the end of the day, Zappos is the best because it has managed to not only find how to balance out the company but how to also maintain that balance with eloquence.

STEPHANIE H.
employee since 2012

When asked what the Zappos Culture means to me, the first thing to instantly come to mind is that it is the most incredible working/family experience ever! Zappos isn't a job ... it's an exciting experience that is never dull or boring! It's not the same daily routine, clock-punching, paper-pushing-type job either! ... It a party with a paycheck, as my dad has put it to me!

When I came to Zappos I had no idea what to expect. I hadn't even heard of it before, honestly. I came in at one of the hardest times of my life and now I can't be any happier and more thankful that I accepted the most amazing opportunity EVER!!! Becoming a part of Zappos has paved an awesome path for me! I am extremely honored and excited to be here!

STEPHANIE H.
employee since 2010

The culture at Zappos has changed so much over the years as we grow and expand. One thing that will never change is the people. I have met my best friends here and they will always be my family. I am grateful for everything Zappos has given me!

STEPHANIE H.
employee since 2007

The Zappos Culture is like no other! I love coming to a place where I can be myself and not worry about being judged. I love wearing whatever I want ... especially my yoga pants during the busy holiday season! ;] I have made lifelong friends at Zappos and am blessed to be part of an amazing company!

STEPHANIE L.
employee since 2012

For the first time in my life, I can say that I am 100% happy. When I first arrived at Zappos, I assumed that as a new person I would feel awkward and that I would be hazed by my coworkers. I was surprised when Zappos employees welcomed me with open arms and it actually seemed as though they were glad that I had been hired. I am so thankful every day for my new family :)

STEPHANIE T.
employee since 2006

I can't say that I know where to begin. Another year has gone by again. It seems like yesterday that I walked in the doors of Zappos, and I'm sure I've said it many times before, it might have been the best, most life-changing day of my life. I'm sure that makes no sense. It's a place where I can be myself, even after six years, and growing up with a place that I not only can call a "job," but also a family. A place where anyone who knows me, REALLY knows me. They have been through my ups, my downs, what I look like in my pajamas and even worse, what I look like hung over. I can't say that I'd know what I would be doing without Zappos and my Zappos family in my life but it wouldn't be the same, nor would I. Even my daughter knows how to say "Zappos," or she often just says "mommy work!" She's like part of the family there too! I get to keep meeting new people, expanding my family and horizons, and I love every minute of it! I can't wait for another year, more family, more friends, and great times! Bring it!! :)

STEPHANIE W.
employee since 2004

The Zappos Culture is about being happy in the workplace - about feeling appreciated, valued, treasured! Zappos takes such good care of us that we are truly spoiled. This is a place where our opinions count - where our feedback is welcome and taken into consideration. It's a place where I can be me! I've been here for eight years and I still feel very blessed to be on board!

STEPHEN A.
employee since 2011

The Zappos Culture simply means bringing a positive attitude to work every day _and really, can you even call it "work?" I'm doing things here, but it's not laborious, it's fun because the culture here is all about fun, positivity, encouragement and having a good time. If that's "work," I'll work forever!

STEVEN A.
employee since 2011

I'm less than a week away from my one-year anniversary of working at Zappos. I've read the three things you need for job satisfaction are autonomy (you have some say in what you do or how you do it), complexity (you encounter new or unique situations often) and connection between effort and reward (you can see the fruits of your efforts manifest in a tangible way). I would agree that sums up a good place to work.

But add to that a sense that you're not so much "working," as just hanging out with a lot of interesting, funny and staggeringly diverse people, who happen to be getting lots of work done, and you've got Zappos _ delivering happiness and organizing hilarity since 1999. Bring on year two.

SUSAN A.
employee since 2012

The Zappos Culture, to me, means the ability to be whoever you are both externally and internally. You do not have to pretend to be anyone else but who you are. You can actually be comfortable in your own skin. The culture breeds being kind to all and being humble. The Zappos family is a very special group of people. I am very honored to be a part of the Zappos Family.

A new family member, 2012.

TAMA C.
employee since 2007

I believe that our Zappos Culture is the backbone of the company, and the glue that binds us all together. Without the fantastic culture, we wouldn't be the same joyful, happy, insane workplace that delivers the message of happiness we strive to send throughout the community.

TAMARA H.
employee since 2010

Zappos is full of fun, wonderful people. It is fun to work here and make long-lasting friendships. Providing great customer service and WOWing customers makes each day a great experience!

TAMI L.
employee since 2007

The Zappos Culture is what you make it. Through the years I have been a part of the Zappos family, I have seen changes to the culture. Those changes are a direct reflection of what each and every individual contributes as well as what they take away from it. Our culture is unique, it is special, it should be treasured. I am proud to be a part of the Zappos Family and will always do everything in my power to keep our culture alive, fresh, and positive, and protect it in my day-to-day interactions, both inside and outside of the office.

TAMMY R.
employee since 2009

The Zappos Culture ... that brings about the word "WOW" for sure. It is a unique environment, to say the least. Since day one, I have been astounded at the different people and personalities here. However, even with those differences, there is a level of respect, understanding and acceptance, since we are all one "family." In the beginning, it was hard for me to believe that these people — some of whom seemed so different from me — would really become my family. I am happy to say that they definitely have. Each new shift brings about mixed emotions, knowing you will be leaving the team you have grown to know and bonded with, but excited by the thought of getting to know more of your other family members better. Our Zappos Culture and our bond is what make us the company and "family" we are.

TAMRA J.
employee since 2008

The Zappos Culture means "freedom" to me. It means being able to be myself, joke around, have a great time, and rely on others, while not having to worry about stupid corporate things. We are free to show our creativity in our work and get the job done however we need to. It's nice to feel free and have the freedom to show our personalities at work.

TANAI M.
employee since 2008

The Zappos Culture means a lot to me because it has taught about the importance of friendship. Working here, I have been able to meet my best friends and find people I can really count on.

TANYA S.
employee since 2010

My journey at Zappos has been amazing. I am going on two years here in July. I wouldn't give it up for the world. No matter what might get thrown at us, as a company we always seem to pull together and get things done. This is something I never got to experience prior to working here. Our Ten Core Values make it so easy to talk with everyone. I love that I don't only think of them while I am at work, I think of them outside of work. Being a part of the Zappos family has made me realize that it's nice to know that my work is very much appreciated while I am working. That is also something you don't find very often. The relationships I have made here with the people I work with will follow me for the rest of my life. I just want to say, "Thank You very much, Zappos for making me a part of this amazing family!"

TARA M.

employee since 2008

Zappos, you never cease to amaze me. Every year, I write about growth and change and how much of it there has been for me over the course of the year. This year has been no different. Zappos, you always provide me with new opportunities to grow, not only at work but also in my personal life. This year was a tough one for me. I had struggles to overcome, struggles that seemed daunting and unrelenting at times, but with the strength that Zappos has helped me foster and the family ties I have made within this company have kept me in positive spirits. I know that no matter what I have to face, I have an entire Zappos Family Army behind me to support and help me reach all my goals. I love all my Zappos Family a whole bunch!!!

TEE I.

employee since 2010

Working at Zappos is like sitting cross-legged ... on top of the world.

TERI M.

employee since 2012

When I first started the interview process, I was given a previous year's Culture Book. At first I thought, "All of these people can't possibly be that happy and love their jobs." But then I got hired. And it all started making sense. This is the most fun I have ever had working and I'm loving it. I've only been here a couple of months, but from the very first day I knew this place was special. The people make it special. Everyone is so friendly. You can't help but have a great day the minute you step on campus. It's so much fun we should pay Zappos to work here!! And when you're this happy at work, you can't help it from spilling over into your life. From the Nerf» wars that break out, to the team building events, to the All Hands meeting, every single day is something new, different and fun! I love this place!!! I hope to be a Zapponian for the rest of my life!!

TERRELL T.

employee since 2011

The Zappos Culture, to me, is about being who you are 24/7. As simple as it sounds, it's actually a hard thing to accomplish. At my previous jobs, I had to put on a mask and an attitude different from my own, or even jeopardize my connection with customers because of company expectations. It seemed as if the companies wanted to build rapport, loyalty, and customer interaction but didn't want to you spend to long with one person — which just felt contradictory. I'm so glad to be part of something that lets me connect with customers my way, and to the best of my abilities. Thanks, Zappos!

TERRY D.

employee since 2011

A friend presented me with a Culture Book to read before applying for a job at Zappos. I started to cry reading how people were happy and how the happiness seemed to bleed over into the employees' personal lives. I wanted a piece of this action. The Zappos Culture is an important part of my work life, but I notice it has also impacted my personal life in a way I didn't think would happen.

I have become a more patient and calmer person. I have always been one to help someone in need and always thought I was a caring person, but applying our culture to my personal life has brought me inner peace. My soul seems to have been rejuvenated and the culture has brought me into contact with so many new people that I now consider a part of my family. The values and culture at Zappos have helped me to grow as an individual. Being in a place where I can express my feelings and where I can just be me has constantly made me smile and be thankful that I could be part of this great company.

THOMAS C.

employee since 2009

People used to laugh at my 97-hit e-presence. I was ashamed to Google my name and find out that I had less likes than yesterday's viral video. Nobody would return my friend requests and I couldn't tell the difference between a tweet and a telegram. THEN I discovered the patented Zappos E-Presence System. In only a few short weeks, I was on the top of the trending topics, and I'm getting more retweets than I had ever dreamed possible. The Zappos method made me such a complete specimen of e-manhood that I hold the title, "The Internet President of the World." Thanks, Zappos!

THOMAS S.
employee since 2007

The Zappos Culture is about being one big family, where you can be yourself and not have to act differently. It's different from other companies in that one of our Ten Core Values is "Create Fun and a Little Weirdness." I'm unaware of any other company that would promote that as a value. I've been here four and a half years and have seen the culture really being cultivated over time. The company really cares about the employees' wellbeing and is constantly coming up with ways to make things better, when they are pretty darn good now.

I can't wait to see how the culture flourishes once we move to our new campus, where everyone will be all together in one building.

TIFFANY C.
employee since 2012

The Zappos Culture is the feeling you get knowing you are happy to go to "work" and that people are happy you are there. It is wanting to experience everything that Zappos has to offer, rather than needing, or feeling obligated to do so. It's noticing that from the first person you see as you walk in the doors right through to the last person you see leaving through them, everyone is going to be smiling at you. Zappos has taken me, and made me not only part of a team, but also part of a family. Wherever I end up, I will forever be grateful, and honored to be part of Zappos.

TIFFANY C.
employee since 2011

One of my favorite things about the Zappos Culture is Core Value #6, "Build Open and Honest Relationships with Communication." I think Zappos allows you to express yourself and also makes you willing to be open to feedback from the leads and to us as ZCLT. I have had great opportunities to learn and grow from some of the others, including Leads and Management. I look forward to many more positive growing years with "open and honest relationships with communication."

TIFFANY L.
employee since 2005

Zappos! Oh how I love you, let me count the ways! As usual, you continue to amaze me with everything that you have afforded me in my personal/professional life! Thank you for providing us with amazing benefits like a free gym, a cafeteria/bistro, a coffee shop, paid benefits, team buildings, amazing parties, just to name a few. Though these benefits are amazing in and of themselves, what is even better is the opportunity to touch other people's lives and be a part of their journey. To work for a company that allows you to build a connection with each other and truly cares about making a difference in the lives of others in such a positive way is one of the most rewarding experiences one can ask for. I am truly blessed and thankful for each and every day that I come to work and get to have new interactions and experiences.

Every day is different, it just keeps getting better! I love you, Zappos!

TOM S.
employee since 2008

Our Zappos Culture and our Ten Core Values are our guiding beacons as we grow Zappos as a company. I believe in our Culture and our Core Values. As I speak with many of our customers, they believe in them, too. This creates a strong bond between our customers, our visitors, our friends, and our employees!

TONY AKA ESKO.
employee since 2011

I have never worked in such a friendly place in my life. From the first time I came to interview right up until today, everyone greets you with a smile, says good morning, and just feels happy to be there. What an amazing place to work, a place that even when you aren't having the greatest day, everyone around you picks you up, and makes sure you leave with a smile.

TONY F.
employee since 2009

I've worked at Zappos.com since September of 2009. I feel so fortunate for having been accepted for this job after being a victim of the severe economic downturn that ravaged the Las Vegas area. Since starting here, I am very impressed with the way the company treats its employees, and the generosity shown towards us. It's also impressive to me how approachable the management is at every level and how willing they are to listen and help whenever possible.

TREE
employee since 2007

Wow, this is my fifth year at Zappos and I love it as much as I did five years ago! We have made more changes than I can count in the past five years, some good, some bad. But through it all, it is still about our customers. They are the reason we are here. At the end of the day, I can honestly say that I have done everything in my power to help our customers. I look forward to another five-plus years!!!

TREVOR H.
employee since 2011

What the Zappos Culture means to me ... that's a tough one to put into a few sentences. The culture is what makes me excited to come into work in the morning, I work way earlier then my body feels I'm meant for, and yet every morning when I come in, I have no choice but to smile because I cant get five feet inside without being greeted with a smiling face and a polite, "Good Morning." The culture here is such a happy family environment that it just makes you end up being a part of it without even trying. Something as simple as holding a door will get three "thank yous" from anyone who walked through that door. We're a big happy family here ... and crazy as this place may seem, I love it.

TYD1.
employee since 2010

The culture here has taught me many things. It has taught me to look beneath the surface and find the deeper meaning in everyday interactions. It has taught me that no matter what I want to do, I can. And the best thing it has taught me is, your blood relatives are not your only family. Sometimes you can find family where you least expect it. Thank you for everything, Zappos!

TYSON W.
employee since 2009

Most, if not all of us, enjoy our Zappos Culture. And many of us strive to protect this culture. As the last year passes and it is time to contribute again, I think of the great American cultural anthropologist, Margaret Mead. When asked how America could find a richer, more diverse culture, she said:

"If we are to achieve a richer culture, rich in contrasting values, we must recognize the whole gamut of human potentialities, and so weave a less arbitrary social fabric, one in which each diverse gift will find a fitting place."

We do not claim to have found a national model for cultural perfection, yet I believe that in our attempts to create a more effective and appreciative workplace, we have (rather inadvertently) stumbled upon a model of company culture that directly connects and compliments our current national business environment. One that I truly believe Miss Mead would support.

VERONICA J.
employee since 2005

Stay thirsty, my friends.

VERONICA M.
employee since 2010

It is my second year here at Zappos and I feel so incredibly blessed. My friendships have grown stronger and my love for Zappos is endless. I am so happy to be a part of the Zappos family!

VICTORIA P.
employee since 2010

Ahh ... Zappos! My home away from home _ and yes, I mean that positively. Where else can you and your spouse work for the same company and still be treated well and as individuals? I have had many opportunities to grow, learn and develop over the last couple of years. I have also met some really amazing people who have helped me along this journey and who have become family. All I can say is I am very lucky and I am truly grateful.

VINCENT Q.
employee since 2010

Hi ho, hi ho, it's off to work I go ... Hold up, wait a minute! You call conversing with our nice customers, having fun with your coworkers "work?" I don't think so! After being here for two years, I've found out how lucky I've been to have this "job." Zappos has enabled me to re discover my interest in being a DJ, which I had shelved for over 10 years. They allowed me to share my interest by letting me entertain others. The leadership year has looked after my career and shown me the potential that I didn't see in myself. I've never had the opportunities available to me that I have here. I'm eternally grateful to be here every day that I step inside these doors.

VINCENT V.
employee since 2008

Coming in strong / For real, we roll deep / Getting attacked, we react / Came together with no slack / Ask me? / That's what you call having each others' back / Now tell me please, what we really know about that?

Didn't die / Back and ready to fly / To deliver happiness if you're sittin' there wondering why / With no limits we can touch and even pass the sky / Strong values in our core, so don't even try.

Making sure you get this / Can I get a witness? / WoWin' till we breathless / Too many skills to kill / Z be keeping it real / Game face when we hit the field / If y'all feel the same, then let me know how you feel!!!

One Team, One Dream.

VIOLA H.
employee since 2007

The Zappos Culture means stepping out of my comfort zone and doing things that I would never have believed I would do. For instance, after working here over five years, I became a mentor and an ambassador (all on the same day). The craziest thing I did was to shave my head for charity.

When I wear a Zappos shirt, I have many people walk up to me and ask, "What is it really like to work there?" I am more than happy to share my everyday experiences with them. When I am finished talking with them, many want to come and work with me.

I am pleased and honored to be a part of the Zappos Culture.

WANDA H.
employee since 2005

I have been with Zappos for six and a half years and I am still amazed at how wonderful it is to work here. I have the most amazing coworkers. For a company with this many employees, we are still like a family. I am surrounded by people who are honest, kind and who truly care about each other. I wish everyone could be so blessed.

WAYNE R.
employee since 2011

Zappos is such an amazing company to work for! It's refreshing having a job that allows me to do what I am passionate about. I have been at Zappos for almost one year now, and can't believe the amount of opportunities that I have had to progress, both personally and professionally. I have made so many close friends in my time here that now, coming to work is not really like work at all. I can't imagine ever working anywhere else.

WENDY ZEE.
employee since 2010

As I approach my two-year anniversary with Zappos, I look back and realize that the past year has been fraught with challenges coming from many different areas. To have been able to work alongside this group of people during these challenges has given me an even greater respect and love for each of them. Zappos knows how to come together in times of crisis and in times of celebration. This cohesion, I believe, is what sets us apart from other companies and is what makes us successful on so many different levels.

WESLEY D.
employee since 2012

What does the Zappos Culture mean to me? Well, to put it simply, it means being myself all day, every day! I have never had a job where I get to come to work and I literally don't have to change anything about who I am. I get to come to work every day being myself, having fun, meeting new people and spreading my own personal brand of fun and weirdness to everyone I meet! Being able to do that makes every day a wonderful and fun new experience that I would not give up for anything. Thank you, my Zappos family, for making my job not just wonderful but one of the best parts of my day.

WHITLEE M.
employee since 2012

"Create Fun and a Little Weirdness" is exactly what attracted me to this amazing company. While I was working for my last employer, all my coworkers constantly told me that I was 'weird', and I always said 'thank you' in response. Being weird is a compliment to me because it means you are different, you color outside of the lines, and you don't fall into the status quo. I have not been with Zappos for long, but in that short time, it has been verified for me that, yes, Zappos is different. Where else can I have Tutu Tuesdays, Wacky Wednesdays, and Thumb Wrestling Thursdays? I feel like I can be myself here because everyone shows his or her true colors. I am so happy to be a part of this family and want to share the Zappos experience with the world. So you see, being a little weird is who I am and I get to come into work every day and express that! In turn, by loving what I do, I deliver happiness to our beautiful customers!

WILLIAM L.
employee since 2011

The Zappos Culture means a whole lot to me! It's a perfect blend that consists of working hard and playing hard. When these two things come together, the results are amazing! Working hard allows the company to grow a lot and become very successful. It shows that we are very dedicated and committed to helping our customers and are here for them 100%.

Playing hard can be looked at in many different ways. Sometimes we do it as a "reward" for all of the hard work that we do. Also, we play hard because it's a good chance for us to all come together as one and get to know one another better. It brings a lot of cultures and diversity together to create a nice blend. This will create tremendous results overall which will lead to a lot of success. A lot of companies can learn from this technique. Also, a lot of companies should apply our formula and culture! It'll benefit them all! ZAPPOS 4 LIFE!!!

YARDLEY M.
employee since 2011

To me, the Zappos Culture is what makes this company, the employees and the environment here so unique and unlike anything else I've ever seen! True story.

ZACH W.
employee since 2010

The Zappos Culture, to me, is ... Customer Service. Whether you are selling world-famous coffee or flipping brand-name burgers, operating a car wash or working as a valet -. whether you are protecting valuables during overhaul after knocking down a fire, cutting open a car to rescue a child, or performing CPR, all the way to performing open heart surgery ... or whether you are working at Zappos, you are in the "People" business. You are providing customer service. You automatically have the responsibility to fulfill the needs of each person you come in contact with directly, as well as indirectly ... and as with any of these jobs, you need to be very good at what you do. You need to be raising the bar, and be exemplary. Zappos does this very well.

MAUREEN S.
employee since 2010

The Zappos Culture means different things to me, depending on the week. Sometimes it's more about creating fun and a little weirdness, other times it's about doing more with less, or open and honest communications. The thing I love the most about our culture is the fact that it reflects so many of my beliefs.

BRER BEER RABBIT NIGHTTIME MODEL

2012 VENDOR PARTY

WORLD MARKET CENTER

STICKER
ADDICT
IN THE WILD

ZAPPOS COOKBOOK
COVER (DUH)

ZAPPOS COOKBOOK

ZAP CAN COOK

**THE WSUP
AAAAHHHH**
SUNGLASSES
CONFIGURATION

2011 RANDOM FUN

ZAPPOS SHIRT DAY

PURPLE ALERT!
SET OF THREE

RED ALERT!
SURPRISED MODE

2011 VENDOR PARTY

THE COSMOPOLITAN

D

AN E

DOES NOT
COMPUTE
ERROR 3241

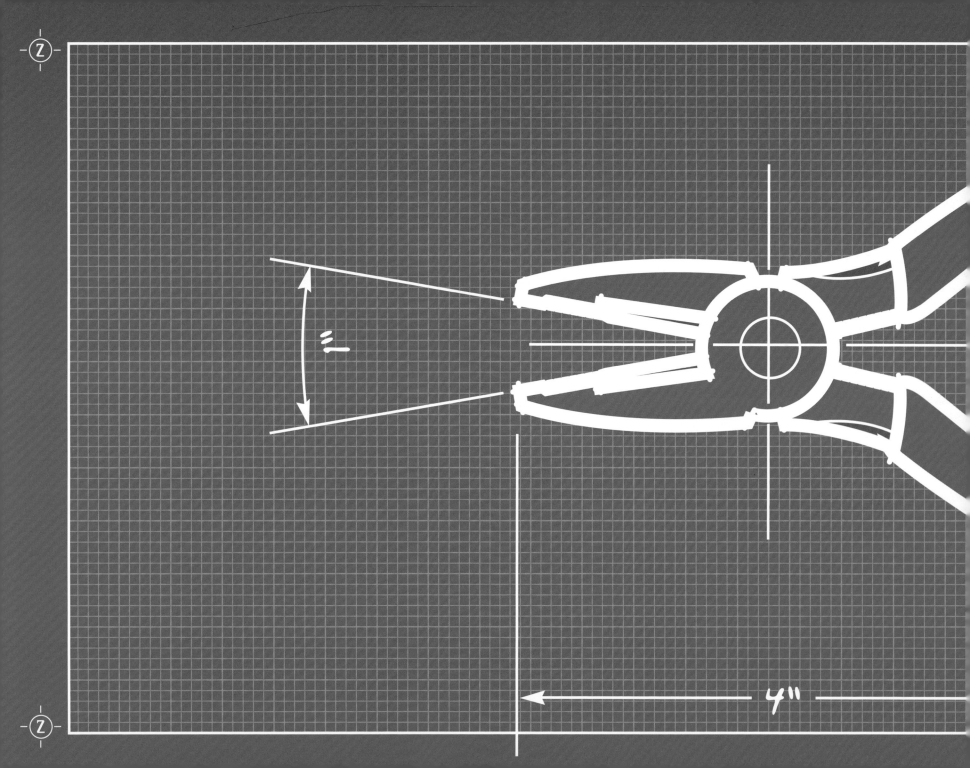

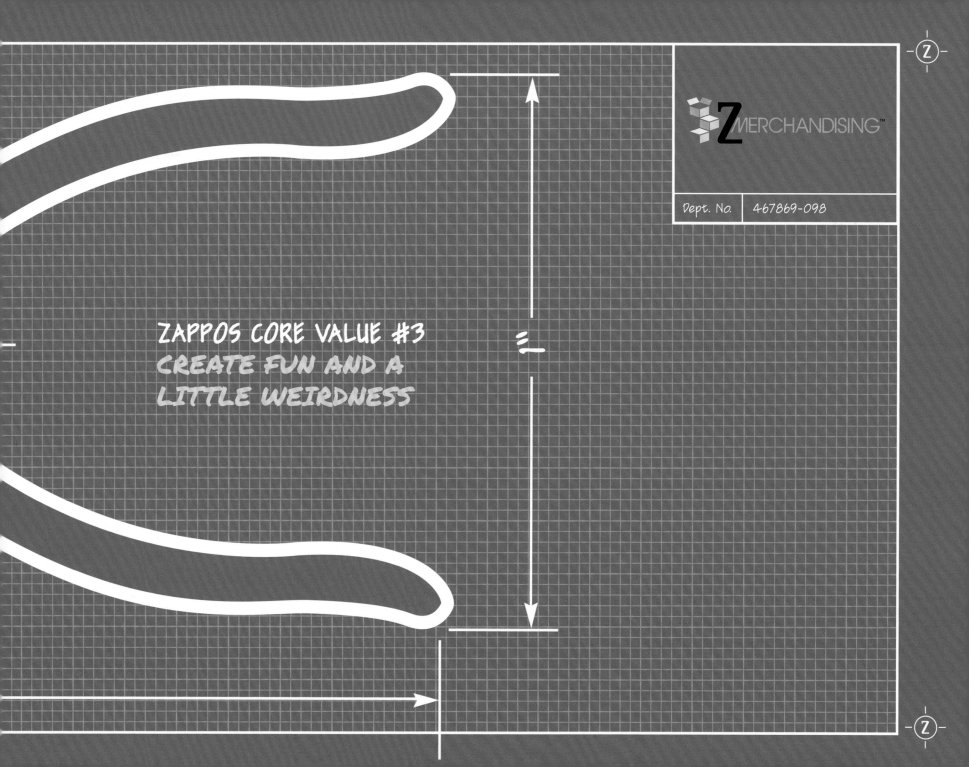

ZAPPOS CORE VALUE #3
CREATE FUN AND A
LITTLE WEIRDNESS

MERCHANDISING™

Dept. No. 467869-098

ANONYMOUS
employee since 2009

Even after being here for three years, every day is unexpected! I cannot imagine myself doing anything else for the rest of my life. The people you work with and the memories you share are truly priceless.

In my books, Zappos is unique and successful because they invest in their employees. If you are truly passionate about something in this company, you will get it! How many people can say that?

ANONYMOUS
employee since 2005

Collectively, the employees are the creators and drivers of the company's culture. Ultimately, the Zappos Culture continues to evolve as the company grows. Luckily, being part of this culture has made an impact in my life. Traditionally, stories are told and new ones are formed, enhancing the culture. Unexpectedly, the Zappos Culture has become my work and my work, my culture. Respectfully, the employees live and breathe the culture. Eternally, the Zappos Culture will always be its employees.

ANONYMOUS
employee since 2011

So like, right now, for example. The Haitians need to come to America. But some people are all, "What about the strain on our resources?" Well, it's like when I had this garden party for my father's birthday. I put R.S.V.P. 'cause it was a sit-down dinner. But some people came that did not R.S.V.P. I was, like, totally buggin'. I had to haul ass to the kitchen, redistribute the food, and squish in extra place settings. But by the end of the day it was, like, the more the merrier. And so if the government could just get to the kitchen, rearrange some things, we could certainly party with the Haitians. And, in conclusion, may I please remind you it does not say R.S.V.P. on the Statue of Liberty. Thank you very much.

ANONYMOUS
employee since 2010

"Surround yourself with people who take their work seriously, but not themselves – those who work hard and play hard."

– Colin Powell

ANONYMOUS
employee since 2004

Another year has passed and it gets harder and harder to write about our Zappos Culture because people still can't believe a place like this exists. I am not good at expressing my feelings on paper so I am going to leave you with one of the most valuable lessons I've learned pertaining to my job as a buyer. It comes to you from an epic movie titled "Joe Dirt". Here goes:

"Joe Dirt: So you're gonna tell me that you don't have no black cats, no Roman Candles, or screaming mimis?

Kicking Wing: No.

Joe Dirt: Oh, come on, man. You got no lady fingers, fuzz buttles, snicker bombs, church burners, finger blasters, gut busters, zippity do das, or crap flappers?

Kicking Wing: No, I don't.

Joe Dirt: You're gonna stand there, ownin' a fireworks stand, and tell me you don't have no whistlin' bungholes, no spleen splitters, whisker biscuits, honkey lighters, hoosker doos, hoosker don'ts, cherry bombs, nipsy daisers, with or without the scooter stick, or one single whistlin' kitty chaser?

Kicking Wing: No... because snakes and sparklers are the only ones I like.

Joe Dirt: Well that might be your problem, it's not what you like, it's the consumer."

You're welcome.

ANONYMOUS
employee since 2006

Every year I try to come up with something profound to write in my entry. This year, I give up. Plain and simple, I love coming to work every day. I find that I get excited on Sunday nights when I come to realize that I get to go back to work the next day to see my friends and family. I even get paid for it. Unbelievable. I feel completely blessed every day that I get to do something that I love with people that I love.

ANONYMOUS
employee since 2007

I have never experienced a culture like the one we have at Zappos. Every one of us brings something special to the workplace every day. I have worked here for almost five years now, and I can say that I feel blessed to be able to experience all of this!

ANONYMOUS
employee since 2010

The Zappos Culture is not only about the environment, it's about the people, the personalities, and the family atmosphere that has been created. The "culture" takes care of people, looks after them and ensures they are fulfilled and following their passion. We work in a very unique culture that allows people to speak freely without fear, to voice their concerns without resentment, and to follow their passions with the support behind them. If you are lucky enough to be part of an environment like that ... it's pretty amazing.

ANONYMOUS
employee since 2007

Thank you, Zappos, for another amazing year! I have an amazing team and feel so fortunate to work for a company that promotes pursuing your passion.

ANONYMOUS
employee since 2007

From a man with great passion and even better hair, this little gem sums up Zappos culture for me. "You do your best work if you do a job that makes you happy." – Bob Ross

ANONYMOUS
employee since 2010

The Zappos Culture is pretty amazing, let's be honest! Since I have started at Zappos, I have been given the ability to make my own decisions and have had so much trust instilled in me. I love that we are able to be ourselves every day, and it is celebrated and embraced. I think it is unbelievable that our culture has become world famous and we have so many people touring our offices every day. It is something that inspires me on a daily basis and makes me proud to say that I work for Zappos!

ANONYMOUS
employee since 2010

The family at Zappos has so many different personalities and styles; this is exactly what makes our culture unique. The culture makes the day-to-day fun and makes time fly by. I enjoy the "work hard, play hard" attitude that employees at Zappos have. Working here has been an adventure, and I cannot wait to see what happens next!

ANONYMOUS
employee since 2010

Another year here at Zappos means another great year for me. I still cannot believe how amazing it is to be at a company like Zappos. Over the past year there have been many challenges for me, my team, and the company, but all have been overcome because of the amazing culture we have here at Zappos. This past year my team lost one of our members, which caused us all to take on a heavier workload during one of the busiest times of the year. But because we all love what we do and enjoy being in each other's presence, we were able to come up with a plan of accomplishment. And now, only five months later, we all feel like everything is back to normal. This, to me, shows how awesome my team and this company are. Nowhere else would you get a group of people that all come together for the good of the group and company, instead of looking out for themselves. To continue on a company level, I have never seen such a large group of people come together to form a "family-like" feeling as I did after the security breach in January. This incident was in no way a great event, but to see every person from every department across the entire company come together for the greater good of our customers and to help CLT, was one of the most amazing things I can say I have ever seen from a company. Witnessing the impact of these two events over the past year has really given me a new perspective of what the Zappos culture means to me — and I love it!

AARON T.

employee since 2005

I've done quite a few of these entries, so I won't ramble this year. The Zappos Culture, to me, means the freedom to express myself. Whether it be performing an actual job description, interacting with vendors, peers, subordinates, or managers, we're all encouraged to be ourselves. I spend a third of my day (sometimes more) with my coworkers, and that kinda makes them my extended family, so I'm blessed to be able to come to "work" and act as if I'm among my own family. We have a unique, amazing culture here that continues to evolve, and I'm thankful I've been allowed to contribute to it.

AILA M.

employee since 2009

For me, the best thing about Zappos is "Embrace and Drive Change." I've been in retail for many years, and this is by far the most entrepreneurial company I've ever worked for. Zappos is always open to new ideas and everyone reacts quickly to changes. Here, we really own our own destiny! Not to mention it is absolutely the most fun company I've ever known :)

ALESHA G.

employee since 2004

This year will be my eighth year at Zappos and the culture means more to me now than ever before. I am going to have my first children while working for Zappos. Yes, I am part of the twin epidemic! But to me, culture is being part of a family. A family that supports you, that is happy for you, and that wants to see you succeed. My extended family lives in Northern California, so they won't be here to help raise my kids. But I am so grateful to have my Zappos family to be a part of their lives. I feel as if I have grown up here, even though I was 26 when I started. Growing up in this culture has given me a sense of security that I never had before working here, a sense of family outside of my family, and a sense of purpose. What I do is so much more than a job. I know I am not saving the world. But I am so proud of who I have become working here. And I don't think it would have been possible without the culture we have grown here.

ALEXANDER C.

employee since 2011

To me, the Zappos Culture is all about helping one another. Someone just starting out in a new job might feel awkward or afraid to ask assistance, but that is not the case at Zappos. Since my first day with the company I have been amazed — and still am today — at how many people are willing to go out of their way to help one another. I have never worked for a company that has had a focus on making sure that, no matter who you are or what your title is, you can always ask for help and someone will always be there to help you.

ALISON D.

employee since 2011

It may sound clichéd, but working at Zappos really changed my life. Here I have made wonderful friends, found my life partner, and reignited my passion for fashion. I know as I travel through my life, the time I have been at Zappos will always be with me, and I am reminded daily of how fortunate I am. Thank you for the opportunity to achieve my dreams.

ALLISON B.

employee since 2010

The Zappos culture, to me, means embracing the company's past and bringing it into the future. We always strive to be the best – whether that is the best retailer, best employer or best culture.

AMANDA W.

employee since 2012

My favorite part of the Zappos Culture is the fact that it is what makes me wake up excited every day to do my job. Being able to get excited about your job on a daily basis is completely priceless, and something I'm so grateful for. I owe it all to our culture and the people I'm surrounded by!

AMANDA W.

employee since 2011

There aren't many places where you can walk in and have people hold the door for you and smile. I can't think of many places where people will ask you how you are and wait for your response because they genuinely want to hear. What Zappos has created inside and outside of these walls continues to amaze me and I have a difficult time putting into words how I feel about the Zappos Culture and the people who bring it to life. I am coming up on my first year, not only at Zappos, but in a real career. I came here straight out of college prepared to hide my little bit of weird, don a suit and join the corporate world. Instead, I was hired at Zappos where T-shirts and shorts are accepted and beer pong is just one of our versions of a coffee break. I moved across the country for the job, but I gained so much more. I found friends and family here.

ANDREA L.

employee since 2007

Zappos is ever-changing and I'm very lucky to see what is to come and to be apart of it. It's exciting to see it unfold. The culture will only grow stronger as we see these changes come together, not only downtown, but as a company too. Our culture is family and we all support each other. I wouldn't want it any other way.

employee since 2011

The Zappos Culture means being surrounded by incredible people, loving your job, laughing a lot, learning something new every day, inspiring the community … and plenty of happy hours! :)

ANN S.

employee since 2011

The first time I walked into Zappos last year, I thought I was dreaming. All of the smiles and greetings and conversations were like nowhere else I had ever worked. I thought, "This could not possibly be what it is like every day." But now, almost a year later, I can say without hesitation, that Zappos is just as amazing, if not more so, than it was the first day! I feel like part of the family coming home when I walk in the door every day. Coming from another retailer in the industry, I can honestly say Zappos is the most amazing company I have had the privilege of working with. Not only is Zappos great to its employees, it is great to its vendors, the community, and Las Vegas as a whole. I feel so honored and privileged to work at such an amazing company. I am one lucky girl!

ARLENE J.

employee since 2011

The Zappos Culture is what made me decide to move away from my family and friends in Virginia and come to Las Vegas almost six months ago. What the culture means to me is an environment where you are surrounded by the most welcoming, friendly, fun, and caring people. I'm inspired every day to be a better person, to challenge myself, and to share what I know with others. I feel like this all sounds so cheesy but it is so true. The culture here is amazing!

BERNADITA B.

employee since 2007

The Zappos Culture is really great. Lots of people are envious of Zappos employees. We are working and having fun at the same time. "Zuperb" customer service is our key to success. Go, go, go, Zappos …

BEVERLY R.

employee since 2011

It is amazing to me that I am now celebrating my first year here at Zappos! I moved here from Westchester, New York, the land of trains, planes and automobiles! I have not looked back for a single moment and this has been a tremendous experience, far beyond my wildest expectations …

The culture at Zappos is special and magical. It allows everyone to exist within a structure that has no boundaries or limitations. I have met some tremendous individuals from all walks of life and with exceptional talent and ability. I also have worked and interfaced with people who are incredibly genuine and sincere. I often say that Zappos has restored my faith in humanity! Every day, I look forward to a challenge, knowing that I am destined for fun and laughter in the same breath.

BRADEN M.

employee since 2006

To me, the Zappos Culture is ever-evolving. However, as large as the organization grows, our culture has always been routed by the same basic belief: Treat your employees well and success will follow. Zappos encourages us to grow, to be social, to think, and to question. The company created a pipeline to cultivate leaders from within. Zappos provides classes for personal and professional growth. We have a life coach to help us achieve our goals. Zappos takes care of us and we take care of Zappos. We all work together to create an environment that is welcoming and inspiring. I feel blessed to have a home at Zappos and to be part of the melting pot of talent, creativity, and style that is our culture.

BRIDGET D.
employee since 2011

If I could sum up my year at Zappos in ten words or less, it would be "Life is short. Live your dream and share your passion." That's one of my favorite quotes from "The Holstee Manifesto." It has been an amazing ride filled with parades, happy hours, and theme parties. Can one even call this "work?" I'm beyond grateful that I am a part of it.

BRIDGET D.
employee since 2009

"The future belongs to those who believe in the beauty of their dreams." – Eleanor Roosevelt

BROOKE J.
employee since 2005

This best explains our culture:
"Culture is a little like dropping an Alka-Seltzer into a glass – you don't see it, but somehow it does something" – Hans Magnus Enzensberger. You almost cannot put our culture into words, but you can always feel it.

CALEN B.
employee since 2011

The Zappos Culture, to me is the ultimate mixture of working hard while having a great time. Each employee here is empowered to help the company succeed in one form or the other. This empowerment allows each individual to find purpose in what they are doing on a daily basis. This purpose propels us to do WHATEVER it takes to make Zappos a better place for the consumer and our Zappos Community. I am beyond grateful for the opportunity to be working here, and excited for Zappos and its progression towards the future.

CAMERON G.
employee since 2005

This will be my seventh Culture Book entry. It's difficult to believe it has been that long! However, I think that says something great about the legacy that is Zappos. How can so much time pass, so much be experienced and accomplished, with Zappos yet to lose its luster? How can every day still feel as exciting and new as the first? The reason is that Zappos has never felt like a JOB. When I leave my house in the morning and walk though the doors at Zappos, I am greeted by friends; long-term relationships that have made my life enjoyable and meaningful. The Zappos Culture is a way of life, and for many of us it has been one of the best we could possibly imagine.

CARLA L.
employee since 2006

This is what the culture at Zappos means to me:

– Doing a scavenger hunt with the clothing team at the mob museum while dressed as mobsters or the authorities. It was a really cool experience and we got a lot of fun looks from the other patrons at the museum, mostly because they were jealous of how authentic we looked. ;)
– Zappos sponsoring the Color Run and getting the company and community involved in an extremely fun and colorful event. I had pink and green ankles and a pink skull for almost a week ... but it was a blast!
– Doing a parade around the office when Under Armour launched! We all wore UA and cheered, and had our clothing kingdom trumpets to make everyone aware that UA is on the site.
– The ZEndurance team encouraging a healthy lifestyle by creating a reimbursement and reward program. My own personal goal this year is to run a 5k per month. So far, so good! There are a lot of fun races to get involved in and it's a great time to meet coworkers that you may not see often. Plus, since it has encouraged people to participate in every race I run, there are more and more Zappos people involved to cheer each other on!

These are just some of the recent examples that showcase the elements that make up our company culture. All of the examples involve bonding with our coworkers, meeting new coworkers and generally being FUN and HAPPY!

CARLOS J.

employee since 2011

To walk through the doors here at Zappos is to walk into another world. Everyone you encounter is oddly cheerful. Every room you walk into is unique, weird, and lively. After only an hour or two of being here, you begin to wish you never had to leave.

That is exactly how I felt when I took my first tour at Zappos prior to being hired. It's been seven months since I became a Zapponian, and I'm submerged in our culture. Everyone here is unique, friendly, and respectful. We all work because that's what we get paid for, but we also have tons of fun while working ... How is that even possible? Although hard to believe, it is a reality here.

Out of the many other places I've worked at before, no place compares to Zappos. Not only do we have a solid set of core values, it is obvious every day that we all live by them ... not just here at work but in our personal lives as well.

In all honesty, I'm a happier person since I've started working here. Here's to many more years at this amazing company!

CARON O.

employee since 2007

The Zappos Culture provides me with the comfort of knowing that every day I come to work, I can always count on smiling and laughing! That makes me happy! :)

CASSANDRA C.

employee since 2008

I love the Zappos Culture! It means that I never know what to expect when I get to work! It could be a barbeque, a parade, or even a team building! It is really nice to know that everyone is surrounded by friends who have become like family and that we will be supported and encouraged on a daily basis.

CATHY T.

employee since 2007

The Zappos Culture is unique and ever changing. I think as each year passes (I have been here for five years), my outlook on the culture of this company is always a little bit different, but the foundation of it remains the same: Every day when you walk through the door, you're allowed to be yourself, express ideas, and show your own unique personality without judgment. I think this is pretty cool since I spend more than 40 hours a week here. It's my second lovely home!

CATIE ST. AWESOME-O

employee since 2008

Things that I can do at Zappos that I cannot to at other places:
1. Yell at my computer without ridicule (a daily event).
2. Bribe people to like the Bulls by buying them doughnuts when the Bulls win (a weekly, fattening event).
3. Drink a Brooke amount of Perrier and not get judged. (I will out drink Brooke in Perrier one of these days.)
4. Have a Cheetos taste test. (I think regular won.)
5. Scare people when they come into the office. (Terry was my favorite scare of the month.)

CHELLE C.

employee since 2011

Even though I have only been with the Zappos family for seven months, I have seen and experienced some interesting, zany, unorthodox, and amazing things! I think that the Zappos Culture is not for everyone, but it has allowed me to be myself, explore my abilities, gain confidence, and meet some great people that have become great friends. I'm so happy to come to work every day and that means the world to me; it allows me to be more productive at work as well as a happier person outside of work.

CHRISTINA Q.

employee since 2010

The Zappos Culture, to me, is being able to be myself, not only at work but at home as well. I have really grown a lot here at Zappos in just a year and a half now and it has changed my life completely.

CLAIRE S.

employee since 2007

I love Zappos for all that I have learned and the lifelong friendships I have made ... and I love the Zappos Culture, which made both things possible. <3

COURTNEY B.

employee since 2010

Oh my dear, sweet little Zappos. Thank you for being my veritable haven of a workplace for over two years. Thank you for introducing me to amazing people. Thank you for letting me do my job without having to throw people under the bus. Thank you for the respect I receive from my peers and superiors. Thank you for pressuring me to do great work, while letting me take chances that don't always go as planned. Thank you for trusting me and cultivating my talents.

I like you, I love you, I thank you.

CRYSTAL R.

employee since 2010

The Zappos Culture is nothing short of awesome. We're a company that recognizes and celebrates passionate people; it's not just about the technical abilities we possess for the job we're here for. There's definitely an X-factor at Zappos and a greater purpose than just "work." Once again, it's nothing short of awesome. I'm so lucky and grateful to be a member of the Zappos family.

DANA Z.

employee since 2009

So, it's been almost three years now since I have joined Zappos, and as unbelievable as it may sound, it keeps getting better each year! It is so nice that I get to talk about all of the wonderful opportunities that have opened up for me from working here. After being in the retail industry for 18 years, I was pretty happy to be out of the retail segment until I found Zappos. It was truly an instant family for me. I have met such wonderful people in such a short time and I immediately bonded with them. We also have such amazing relationships with our vendors, who are now part of that instant family. One of my closest relationships and partnerships is with Eric from Eagle Creek, who is closely aligned with our culture here at Zappos. As I sat with Eric and Paul talking about business and how our companies are so much alike, Eric had this to say ... "If Zappos was some sort of object, it would be a quilt. Each time I visit, I realize that I have more friends than I had before, each connected in their own way, creating a unique patchwork of personalities. Together they add up to something even bigger. I know I always have a couch to crash on and something to keep me warm at night. Now, that sums it all up!"

One other thing that I am excited about right now is being part of creating history for the downtown area of Las Vegas. So imagine working in a company that encourages its employees to get involved with activities outside of their job responsibilities. Crazy, right? Not possible, right? WRONG!!! Zappos has really been life-changing for me. Wouldn't have it any other way. :)

DAVID S.

employee since 2012

Day three at Zappos. What a whirlwind of great fun!

Thus far, the Zappos Culture means one thing to me: friendship.

Everyone is so open to helping me get set up and teaching me the ins and outs of Zapponia ... It's amazing how awesome everyone has been. I've met so many wonderful, friendly people. I feel most welcome.

To me, the values here are all driven from being friendly. For three days, everyone has proven that Zappos lives it ... I love it here and I'm proud to be part of this amazing place. Thank you, everyone.

DEE C.

employee since 2007

Another amazing year has come and gone. I will be hitting my five-year mark this year and it truly has been fantastic. I have grown so much and gained so much. My team is absolutely crazy and I love them all, because each person is so different. The downtown project is now well on its way and we are excited to see what creative ideas evolve. Let's see where we are next year, as we get closer to the official move. Here we come, Vegas!! Hope you are ready for the craziness!

DEREK F.
employee since 2008

I'm so stoked to be part of a company that has continued to keep its culture at the forefront of its business. It's been four years, and I am still happy. I get to do what I love and I've made some of the best friends I've ever had here. I'm grateful every day when I wake up that I get to come work for a company like Zappos. I'm so excited for what the future holds!

EDDIE W.
employee since 2011

"It is very important to generate a good attitude, a good heart, as much as possible. From this, happiness in both the short term and the long term, for both yourself and others, will come." – Dalai Lama

This quote describes the atmosphere at Zappos perfectly. When I first started working here I was blown away by the genuine happiness; I have come to know this feeling as the norm. I am truly lucky to be working for a great company and working with so many amazing people.

EILEEN T.
employee since 2002

Zappos is a work hard, play hard company! Everyone is empowered to do their own thing to develop and encourage our culture. We are a marriage of merchants and techies, which makes a perfect union. Our Zappos Culture is the hardest thing to maintain as we grow, so we all must share with each other how Zappos started and the great stories that have kept it going so that we never lose it. The Zappos Culture means that, even though you are always working, you don't feel as if you are, since we're all in this together living our passion and focused on the same goal.

ELISA MORACHE.
employee since 2009

Zappos Culture. It is something that all of us create. And it wouldn't be what it is without each person contributing. I love this place and feel that it is part of me, as I am part of it! I am excited to see what the future holds. Viva Los Zappos! :)

EMILY B.
employee since 2009

There is a quote I love that goes a little something like this, "There is a certain happiness in being silly and ridiculous." This sums up what Zappos and our culture means to me. I don't think I could be as happy in my job and life without being silly and, at times, a little ridiculous. It's great to have a company culture that gives us the chance to just be ourselves, silliness and all.

ENOCH W.
employee since 2011

To me, the Zappos Culture means finding happiness via personal growth and service. In order for one to find lasting happiness and satisfaction in life, one must continue to improve. There are many ways to grow, but one of the best ways is to serve others. To extend a helping hand to those who are in need or facing challenges in life brings great joy and satisfaction.

ERICA S.
employee since 2009

"... This is for the possibility that guides us
and for the possibilities still waiting to sing
and spread their wings inside us
cause tonight Saturn is on his knees
proposing with all of his ten thousand rings
that whatever song we've been singing we sing even more
the world needs us right now more than it ever has before
pull all your strings
play every chord
if you're writing letters to the prisoners
start tearing down the bars
if you're handing out flashlights in the dark
start handing out stars
never go a second hushing the percussion of your heart
play loud ..." - Andrea Gibson; Say Yes

ERICA W.
employee since 2004

The Zappos Culture is what we make it, how we create it, and how we interpret it. To me, it's a breath of fresh air; it's home away from home – or, what I write home about.

I remember when I was a kid and we'd sing, "If you're happy and you know it clap your hands ..." I high-five my coworkers, friends, partners and Zappos guests multiple times a day. As an adult, I am still clapping my hands, with a team, to let everyone know that I am happy!

ERIN G.
employee since 2011

The Zappos Culture is a place where you are accepted for who you truly are on the inside!! Being a part of the Zappos Culture is truly an amazing privilege. It always brings a smile to my face. :)

FRED M.
employee since 1999

A lonely city,
Unloved and unattended,
Empty lots and empty buildings,
A city yearning for life.
A company full of life,
Culture of sharing and passion,
Four C's "Community"
Entering the heart of a lonely city.
A loved city energized and alive,
Buildings full of people and motion,
Happy community learning from each other,
The city is the beating heart of a thriving community.

GALEN H.
employee since 2004

Our culture continues to amaze me. The Zappos Culture is something that most people and companies never have a chance to experience. It has created a place where individuals can be themselves. A place that allows people to be creative and imaginative. A place that allows for individual growth while naturally creating company growth. A place that allows people to create their own paths, not only at work, but also in life. It's truly amazing and it's the number one thing we all need to cherish. I feel extremely lucky to be part of the Zappos Culture.

GRAHAM M.
employee since 2006

As I write this, I'm completing my sixth year at Zappos. This place has changed my life and I am forever grateful. I'd like to take this opportunity to thank Galen H, who was the first person I met at Zappos. He gave me my first tour, introduced me to the Zappos Culture, hired me, and continues to be the benchmark for what the culture should and can be to this day. I'd also like to thank my team – the 6pm Team – a group of people often overlooked, but who never allow themselves to forget that they are a valuable part of the Zappos Family, and who constantly remind me that hard work and passionate determination is sometimes the only thing that keeps this crazy place together.

HEATHER C.
employee since 2007

The Zappos Culture is knowing who you are, enjoying who you work with, and loving what you do. Oh, and everything is better when a monkey is involved.

HEATHER E.
employee since 2010

Zappos is truly a wonderful place! I love that I'm eager to get out of bed every morning and get to the office to work with such great people. You never know what the day is going to hold and that's what makes it so amazing. I'm extremely fortunate to work for such a great company!

HEAVEN T.
employee since 2006

These past six years have really flown by. Thank you, Zappos, for helping me grow and molding me into the person that I am today. Not everyone can say that they look forward to going to work or hanging out with coworkers. I'm definitely one of the lucky ones. Here's to more wonderful years to come!!

JARED F.
employee since 2009

The Zappos Culture is not something you can define in words. Each department has its own unique culture, but as a whole, we all come together with our own shared belief of who we are as a company and where we want to go. My favorite part of this culture is the fact that we don't have to change who we are when we come to work.

JARETT A.
employee since 2008

At Zappos, you never know what you are going to get, do, feel, or be. One day you get to go to a happy hour with all your coworkers and dress up in costume; the next day you are flying to sit through shows at Fashion Week; but then you are filming a skit and jumping out the back of an SUV in your underwear, and THEN you find out the company is reviving downtown Las Vegas, starting by buying the Las Vegas City Hall.

The Zappos Culture is indescribable, effortless, unfounded in the fashion industry, and ground-breaking. You feel a purpose while wearing a Superman cape and blowing a horn as a tour passes by. You do things that you never thought you would get to be paid for or considered part of your job, like creating classes to share your knowledge of anything at all, or even visiting the

Mob Museum. The Zappos Culture can only be described as special, and the only thing more you really wanna say about it is just that you thank your lucky stars you are a part of the movement that is Zappos.

Four years ago, when I left Seattle for a bigger opportunity here at Zappos, I wasn't truly sure what to expect, where exactly my career was going, or how this really was going to affect me as a whole. Zappos changed my life … The people are unique, open, passionate, loyal, caring and fun. Every encounter feels genuine, every experience feels abnormal, and every progression feels like it should have been impossible. I have always felt supported in every endeavor, always felt that my voice was heard, and always felt I was accepted for who I am without judgment. I have grown significantly (*and I'm partially referring to the Zappos 15 lbs.) to appreciate life in and out of work, understand that work-life integration can translate into a corporate family, and now know there is more to life and a career than just making money. For those who are no longer at Zappos, those who are now at Zappos, and those who are on their way into Zappos, thank you. Zappos is not just a culture; it's a life-changing movement and I am so honored to have had this experience. I love you, Zappos! xoxo, JareBear

JAY A.
employee since 2009

Well, this is my third Culture Book entry, and WOW, time flies! This year, instead of talking about my amazing Zap-friends and Zap-experiences, I am going to talk about an even more meaningful experience that I had this year.

In May 2012, my mom was diagnosed with cancer … for the third time. I am extremely close to my entire family and this hit us hard. I went through a variety of emotions, but the first thing I thought was that I wanted to be with her and to try to help with whatever I can. Everyone at Zappos was amazing! They said go – go now – be with her! And I did! When I was home with my mom, looking at the flowers that 6pm had sent her, I realized that I had two families. And my Zappos family was watching over the Alexander family. It felt good … it felt very good. I am very thankful to be working at such a great place with such wonderful people! Thank you and love to Zappos and to all of my Zap-friends! Your caring, support, and love did more than you will ever know!

JEANNE M.
employee since 2006

My team inspires me every day,
We work like crazy, but then we play,
The building's full of my closest friends,
Their excitement and passion never ends
Boundless opportunity, transforming a city,
And the Downtown Project makes me giddy!! ?

JEFF "JEFFY 5 BTLZ" B.
employee since 2006

The Zappos Culture, to me, is being able to smile all day at work. Not to put up a front, but because you are really happy to be here. It is just so different here than it's been at any other office. I've visited plenty of other offices in the past few years and I would have to say that ours is the most vivacious. We celebrate our wins and work through our losses. And for customers who may come across this entry, buy boardshorts!

JEFF E.
employee since 2010

It is such a pleasure and honor to work for such a good company. I would like to say that we really treat our vendors with the upmost respect. It is truly a partnership, and when we have these relationships with vendors, great things happen. We have to continue to build these strong relationships to help our business grow at the rate we are expecting. We do this and great things will happen.

JENNIFER S.
employee since 2007

The Zappos Culture, to me, is every day with my team! We have so much fun together, no matter if we are in the office, on buying trips or just hanging out having some cocktails. It is an amazing bond that we have, even though most of the team is new and we have not known one another that long. I feel so lucky to have these people in my life and I am so lucky to be working with every one of them.

JESSICA C.
employee since 2010

I have been here for almost two years now, and I still can't believe how fast time has flown! The relationships and memories I have made in these past two years have been amazing. It's always easy to learn from or be inspired by someone or something at Zappos on a daily basis. I not only can incorporate it into my work but into my personal life as well. It's so exciting to be a part of a place that is so passionate about not only its customers and employees but the community too.

JESSICA M.
employee since 2009

The Zappos Culture allows us to be who we are, but still get the job done. It allows us to be creative, to not to have to "fit in a mold" and this leads to greater personal success.

JESSICA R.
employee since 2009

The Zappos Culture means never-ending changes; newness; tons of opportunity; new people; good people; involvement; evolution; passion; drive; dreams; commitment; trust; individuality; friendships; hard work; grinding out the hours; celebrating the accomplishments; building new relationships; corporate challenges; Z-endurance events; amazing benefits; making someone's day; having my day made; expansion; reaching new people/customers; community involvement; downtown – old Las Vegas; music; restaurants; the arts; trendsetting; start-ups; tours, tours, tours!!!

JEWELS C.
employee since 2011

The Zappos community and Zappos Culture have changed my entire life. Before being hired, I had a job; now I have a career and a life and a new family. At no other company can you stop what you are doing to go play a quick game of basketball, or grant a wish for someone, or have a water balloon fight. The sense of family at this company gives you really makes you feel you are part of something bigger than yourself. I wake up on Monday ready for my day, not dreading the beginning of the week.

JOEL G.
employee since 2010

Chris Farley: I think we got time for one more question. Uh … remember when you were in The Beatles? And, um, you did that album Abbey Road, and at the very end of the song, it would … the song goes, "And in the end, the love you take is equal to the love you make"? You … you remember that?
Paul McCartney: Yes.
Chris Farley: Uh … is that true?
Paul McCartney: Yes, Chris. In my experience, it is. I find, the more you give, the more you get.
Chris Farley [ecstatic, starts to point at Paul and mouth "AWESOME!"]

KARA T.
employee since 2010

It's so refreshing to wake up every morning and be able to work at a company that has this thing called "culture." Prior to working at Zappos, I knew the definition of it, but a company culture … well, that was just absurd. Mission statements, yes; a company's philosophy, of course; but the Zappos Culture is in a realm of its own. It's unique, inspiring and influential. It not only defines what Zappos is as an organization, but also who we are as employees. I feel very fortunate that I get to be a part of it, learn from it and continue to grow it every day.

KARRIE M.
employee since 2006

Haiku For You
Zappos lives downtown
One with the Community
Innovation WOW

KATE C.
employee since 2010

"In seeking happiness for others, you find it for yourself." Anonymous

KATHLEEN J.
employee since 2008

Every year that passes here at Zappos HQ brings me to a deeper understanding of my true purpose in life. I've found a place where I am free to do what brings me personal and professional fulfillment and allows me to use my creativity to bring happiness to others. I know that this couldn't happen anywhere else and I'm thankful every day to be able to say that I am a Zapponian and take nothing for granted. I'm happy with what I have been blessed to experience so far and look forward to the opportunities to come!

KATHY K.
employee since 2006

What a great feeling to come to work daily and know that you are not only working with your coworkers, but with your friends. It truly is a wonderful place to work, where you can be yourself and grow professionally and personally. The relationships I have built within the company and with my vendors are very special and they mean so much to me.

KATIE D.

employee since 2011

I celebrated my one-year anniversary here at Zappos a couple months ago and I could not be happier. The Zappos Culture is like nothing I've ever seen or experienced in the "professional" world. The Zappos Culture creates an environment where creativity, innovation and entrepreneurship can flourish. I am so grateful to be a part of such a wonderful organization.

KELLY R.
employee since 2006

I am excited to make my contribution to the amazing Zappos Culture Book for the seventh time! I am about to head out to a Red Sox game with New Balance and, seriously, how lucky am I? I can only thank Tony, Fred, and my Zappos family for their part in participating in and embracing the Zappos Culture. Because of that, I get to have some once-in-a-lifetime experiences at a once-in-a-lifetime job. Our culture is what drives us! At the New Balance meeting several of us had today, they told us it was great to work with people that are so happy and passionate about what they do, that we are a breath of fresh air. Wow! That is our culture that has been passed on for years, and I can only thank those before me and around me for making that happen. I love you, Zappos!!!!

KEVIN B.
employee since 2011

The Zappos Culture is like nothing I have ever experienced before. I have never had a job where I look forward to coming to work each and every day. The friendships, opportunities and experiences that Zappos has given me are amazing. The culture here is something that I do not take for granted and will continue to involve myself in for years to come!

Thanks, Zappos!

KIMBERLY H.
employee since 2012

I was so excited to come on board and be a part of such a strong culture. After moving away from home to come here, it has been more than comforting to find such a great work family. No matter what the title or the department, everyone is so eager to lend a helping hand. I think that being a part of the Zappos Culture is to not be afraid to put yourself out there to meet new people and learn new skills. I love that we are encouraged to develop meaningful relationships that will help us all continually grow as an employee and a person. I look forward to creating more experiences and contributing to our unique culture.

KRISTIN C.
employee since 2009

5 Things:
1. That time I ran eight miles in a flamingo costume with my Lucky Footwear rep.
2. 4pm laugh sessions on "whatshouldwecallme.tumblr.com."
3. Whiskeytown.
4. Joining a bike gang.
5. Cat lovers.
I like you. I love you. Thank you.

LAUREN E.
employee since 2011

The Zappos Culture is unlike anything I have experienced in my previous work. Zappos has set me outside of my comfort zone, and has let me try new things I never thought I could accomplish.

LAUREN G.

employee since 2006

L.O.V.E.
I love Zappos.
I love the people who work here.
I love the culture.
I love being inspired by my surroundings.
I love my team.
I love the craziness.
I love it all ...
 ... all you need is LOVE.

LAURIE B.

employee since 2010

"Every man's ability may be strengthened or increased by culture." – John Abbott
Our Zappos Culture and Ten Core Values help us be our very best each and every day. We are all committed to holding true to these in our own way. I believe this is the ONLY way we can succeed at staying true to what Tony's original vision for the company was.

LAUREN H.

employee since 2011

Working at Zappos has truly been an eye-opening experience. I don't think you'll find another company full of such passionate, motivated, and intelligent people anywhere in the world! Recently, I got the chance to perform with other talented Zapponians, in the "All Hands" meeting, on stage in front of the whole company. Instead of being nervous, I was EXCITED, because I knew that this family would be proud of us for our talents and hard work, no matter how the performance went. We ended up getting a standing ovation that day, and it was a great feeling to know that we positively contributed to the culture.

LAWRENCE R.

employee since 2011

Zappos...
Where to begin? I wake up excited to go to work every day. I have the best friends anyone could ask for. A friend told me: "You are the company you keep." Zappos has nothing but good company. There is never a dull day in the office and I couldn't be more thankful for anything. In the past year that I have worked here, I have seen myself grow. Remember when you were a kid and your third grade teacher had you make a time capsule? And you had to write where you would like to be in ten years? I am exactly where I hoped I would be: working for an incredible company, working with great mentors, happy as can be, and having no regrets. Thank you to every single person in the company because we all contribute to the culture that is Zappos.

LEEMARIE S.

employee since 2006

When I describe a typical day at Zappos to people – the amazing things we get to do, our passion for revitalizing downtown, how much fun we have, how no two days are the same – they usually stare at me in awe and say how much they wish they worked for a company like ours. I feel truly blessed to able to flourish in this kind of environment and I really get a kick out of telling people about it! My life would be so different and less fulfilling if I were just another drone at another company – Zappos allows me the rare opportunity to truly enjoy myself at work. Not many people can say the same!

LINDSAY E.

employee since 2006

After almost six years at Zappos, my definition of what culture means to me has definitely changed. My family made the transition to Vegas from Kentucky last summer, and while it was one of the hardest decisions we have ever made, it was the right one. I know that it was the right decision because I have never felt more in control of my career with a team that is not just my team, but has become my family. Most people do not understand what I mean when I say that Zappos is my family, but I always say that you can't know it until you experience it for yourself.

LYSANDRA H.

employee since 2011

I am coming up on one year here at Zappos. What a whirlwind! I have made so many great friends and happy memories. This company has been nothing but amazing to me and I am so blessed to be part of something this beautiful. I love waking up in the morning and going to work. I have had jobs that I dreaded before. Loving what you do and being excited to go to work is a huge part of having a happy life. I am HAPPY!

MANDY R.

employee since 2011

Albert Einstein was quoted as saying, "Everything that is really great and inspiring is created by the individual who can labor in freedom." If I had to sum up what the Zappos culture means to me as employee, it's just that … freedom. Dreams and aspirations can mean so little without the freedom to pursue them, and I feel that Zappos gives us the freedom to chase our dreams. I love that I'm given the opportunity to run my own business within Zappos, and that I am able to make decisions and respond to the business as needed. I've worked in merchandising for several other, very corporate companies and it was difficult at times to respond to the needs of the business due to the number of people involved in every decision. I love that I'm trusted to run the portfolio without being micro-managed, even if that means I am fully responsible for all my failures and successes. I'm not only given the freedom to explore ideas and possibilities, but also encouraged to work toward making them happen. As if that wasn't enough, I love that I have the freedom to wear what I want to work and have flexible hours. I am so grateful and never want to take this freedom for granted.

MANON B.

employee since 2009

I'm in my third year here at Zappos and I continue to wait for the other shoe to drop. It hasn't. I doubt it ever will. This thing that we've got going on here is the real deal. I'm not sure how Zappos does it, although I sense that the intense application and hiring process probably has much to do with it. This company has managed to collect a plethora of insanely talented people. It's almost as though the dreamers, artists and innovators of the world who realize they should probably have a "real job" end up here. Company meetings where entertainment is featured let you forget for a moment that these people are in accounting, or merchandising, or customer service. This blissful moment of forgetfulness is enhanced by singing, dancing, and performing at a quality so high you'd swear you had paid for a ticket to witness … or better yet, participate in … all of it.

When people ask me how I feel about Zappos, I often say, "I'm a lifer." This place has ruined my sense of reality. Where else could I work after working here? With how many hours most people spend at work, it's so important to not only love what you do, but love where you do it. Why not have the place where you spend the most time feel like a second home? Blanket for when the air kicks on: Check. Picture of my honey on my desk: Check. An exorbitant amount of glitter on my desk, left over from recent birthday activities: Check. Delicious food within 20 feet at all times: Check. Coworkers who feel like friends, and even family: Check. All this while being encouraged to learn new things, move around within the company and openly share ideas on absolutely anything….

Yep, stick a fork in me. I'm done.

MATTHEW T.

employee since 2007

The Ten Core Values at Zappos really embody what the culture here means to me. Every decision I make, whether personal or professional, is guided by the Core Values. I've found that they are a great guide to living my life and increasing my happiness quotient. When I started working at Zappos, I had no idea about what I wanted to do or who I wanted to be. I just know I wanted to be happy. Now, I feel like I'm in the perfect position because Zappos has let me follow my passion.

MEGAN T.

employee since 2008

I've been with Zappos for over four years now, and each year it gets better and better. I can't image being anywhere else. I've built friendships here that will last a lifetime! I truly enjoy my work, coworkers and our vendors. We have an amazing and unique environment and I'm thankful to be a part of it!

MELANIE P.

employee since 2010

The Zappos Culture means everything to me. It means happiness in my business life as well as my personal life. The culture has led to lifelong friendships, amazing memories and finding my passion. Having my dream job wouldn't mean anything without the culture. The ability to do what I love and work with people who make me happy is why Zappos is home to me.

MELISSA K.

employee since 2010

To me, the Zappos Culture means empowerment. Each day we are empowered to make decisions, think for ourselves, and be who we are. There are not many places that allow employees to make critical decisions based on gut instincts. Zappos empowers their employees, which allows each of us to feel like we truly are part of growing the company and culture.

MICA M.

employee since 2007

The Zappos Culture means being able to walk into a building and see happy faces of people you actually know. It's about having friends to call on the weekends and for happy hour. It's about having a gym buddy to go to body pump with you every week. It's about seeing all your friends at the finish line of a half marathon. It's about a team that supports your goals and ambitions. It's about brainstorming the unthinkable. It's about cheering on your neighbor. It's about caring for each person. It's about building a family. It's a Zappos Family!

MICHAEL F.

employee since 2007

It is really not easy to put the Zappos Culture into words. We are truly a family here at Zappos and our culture is why it is so great to come to work each day. And with our move to downtown Las Vegas, I am certain that our amazing Zappos Culture and Ten Core Values will be the perfect platform to create a fun atmosphere for all of us and the community. It seems like our Culture has become what many other companies aspire to create. It is very special to be a part of it.

MICHELLE F.

employee since 2007

It still amazes me every day that I get to come to work at such an amazing place and work with incredible people. It truly is a family and I have come to build such great friendships here that will last a lifetime. To want to spend your evenings, weekends and vacation with the people you work with is such a great feeling. This is not a "job", it's my life and I love it.

MIKE N.

employee since 2003

Wow! Nine years now, and it keeps getting better. I just flew in from Los Angeles, and boy, are my arms tired! I was just married this year to a wonderful woman and work for an amazing company. How incredible is that?! I have lifelong friends here and an extended family. I care so much about the people I work with and get excited when changes come about. The Zappos Culture to me means so many different things. It's really a lifestyle. It's about treating people the way you would want people to treat you. It's also about getting a little crazy, then digging in the next day and making it happen. How many companies have a Zalloween-type event (where you can dress like a Samurai warrior and swing a golf club too)? That is always so much fun. And every year we team up and go for the gold during Corporate Challenge. Always an adventure, never boring. Looking forward to the next nine years.

MIKE Y.

employee since 2011

Culture is what defines Zappos. To me, it's not the name that makes Zappos a great company; it's the people. It's the energy and the passion around this place that makes it more than just "work." If Disney had not copyrighted the term "Happiest Place on Earth," I am sure Zappos would use that slogan.

MITCHELL N.

employee since 2011

At Zappos, our culture truly defines the company. Unlike other companies I have worked for, everyone actively plays an important role in creating and maintaining the culture. It is a catalyst to our happiness and successes and is present every day in many ways.

Simply put, our culture is what makes Zappos a great place to work.

MONICA D.

employee since 2011

The Zappos Culture is simple: This company is a place where you work with people you like and who become family. They invest in you the way you invest in them! I love this aspect of Zappos Culture, because after all, who doesn't want to spend eight-plus hours a day with their BFFs?

MUMMSIE.

employee since 2006

WOW, so many stories in the last six years at Zappos, and each adventure added a new layer of culture. A lifestyle that continues to evolve, full of laughter, family, travel, sales plans and more hangovers than I could ever imagine surviving! I'm extremely fortunate to work with such incredible people every day and know how priceless it is to enjoy what we do.

Carson or bust, baby!

MYRA T.
employee since 2008

The Zappos Culture is being greeted by all as you walk into the building. It's breakfast being served by Tony and Fred. It's watching a parade of people in HR go by dressed like barn animals and throwing candy. It's taking shots with people in cougar court. It's the Tech team showcasing all of their awesome inventions. It's being able to dance at the All-Hands meeting. It's a water balloon fight with the Finance team. It's meeting with a vendor to talk about how good business is. It's celebrating the birthday of a team member with cupcakes. It's dying your hair blue for a great charity. It's talking about merchandising to the new CLT training class. It's taking a hip-hop class at the company gym. It's cramming all your friends in the photo booth in the break room. It's giving someone an employee bonus and seeing the reaction on his or her face. It's watching the sexy sax man serenade the whole building. It's the feeling of when you exhale, knowing that this is where you want to work for the rest of your career. Yup ... and this was just Tuesday. :)

NATALIE F.
employee since 2011

One morning I had a brand rep visiting, and we had taken our rep to the Z-Cafe for a much-needed caffeinated beverage. We were sitting on the couches, sipping and chatting, when a parade walked by outside the window – complete with a person dressed up in a zebra costume. I viewed this, processed it, and continued on with the conversation. About three minutes later, the rep interrupted me and asked not only about the presence of a zebra on our campus, but our lack of reaction. That's when it hit me: nothing surprises me anymore. Our culture is the epitome of "Create Fun and a Little Weirdness," so while it seemed perfectly normal to us Zapponians that a zebra was wondering around, I had to admit that it probably appeared odd to an "outsider." Super heroes, jello shots, trumpets ... even zebras have just become part of my everyday life and I LOVE it. :)

NIC K.
employee since 2012

The Zappos Culture is in a class by itself! It's an ice cream sundae of creativity, common sense, and communication ... sprinkled with passion and drive ... and topped off with a healthy amount of community cohesion. And I'm George Costanza at the US Open!!

NICK S.
employee since 2011

"Every man's ability may be strengthened or increased by culture." -John Abbott
The Zappos Culture strengthens the roots of our company. It is meant to keep us together, but also to separate us from the competition. Zappos is special due to our culture and I am very proud to be a part of it.

NICOLE G.
employee since 2010

Thank you, Zappos, for the family, the friends, the ability to learn something new every day, and for all the support and love that anyone could ever ask for. Without our Zappos Culture, none of this would be possible.

NICOLE S.
employee since 2010

My friends, my family, my home ...
Happiness, laughter, joy ...
A home, a school, a playground ...
A way of life, my life, our life ...
HAPPINESS ...

NICOLE S.
employee since 2006

The Zappos Culture is something that can only be felt, not described in words. When you walk through the door in the morning ... which is held by a fellow Zapponian ... and you get an automatic smile and "Good Morning," you know that the culture is still thriving! All companies go through challenging times, but when everyone is still acting as a team and working together to provide the best service to our customers, vendors, and ourselves, it is truly inspiring and an honor to say that I am a part of the Zappos Family.

PAUL K.
employee since 2010

As my second full year of working at Zappos approaches, I still find myself amazed at what a transformative experience it has been. Although it's really only been a short time since I got here, it often feels like everything that came before this in my professional life (and in many regards, in my personal life as well) was a lifetime ago.

Before I came here, I remember waking up and dreading the thought of having to go to work each day. I remember how frustrating it was to wear a suit every day, only to come into a barren cubicle that nobody walked past. I remember the feeling of relief I got every day when the clock struck 6 p.m. and I could leave work as quickly as possible.

Zappos has been the opposite of all of that. I love what I do. I love my team. I love this company. I've even fallen back in love with my city.

Thank you, Zappos.

PAUL P.

employee since 2007

No matter what you're feeling before work, it can all go away as soon as you enter the doors. I like working with friends and people I like and care about. The Zappos Culture has provided me with the opportunity to do this every day. It's amazing what you can do professionally when you work so closely with people you care about. It pushes you to try harder and do more. You're not just working for yourself — you're working for the team and family at Zappos. The family spirit here is very contagious and I am humbled to be a part of it. Thanks.

RAQUEL R.

employee since 2012

In the short time that I've been a part of this amazing and unique company, I've learned that Zappos culture means:
- being surrounded by friends, not just coworkers
- never being bored! Bring on the happy hours, team outings, and more happy hours!
- mastering the art of holding open a door better than a bellman!
- always having someone to run a 5k with
- greeting new people, ringing your tambourine, and watching people stick their hand through the bullpen "walls" on a daily basis -
never stop learning! The training, continued education, and hands-on experience are all phenomenal!
- maybe finding yourself front and center on 6PM.com one day
- learning how to stay focused in the midst of a parade
- participating in a parade!
- Last but not least, waking up every day (yes, even on Monday) and being glad that you're going to Zappos!

REBECCA K.

employee since 2004

The Zappos Culture means I can come to work and feel relaxed, supported, and excited. There aren't many out there who can say they love their job. But I do! I feel so fortunate to be part of a company that tries to make every employee love their job by giving them the basic elements to be happy. These basic elements may be different for each individual, but Zappos has enough of them covered so that every person can find something to be happy about and proud of while at work. Those little things add up to making Zappos a really enjoyable place to be – and for that, I say "Thank you, Zappos!"

RICHARD Z.

employee since 2008

Zappos means a smile ... a smile leads to happiness ... happiness leads to adventures ... adventures lead to a gecko ... a gecko leads to an ear ... an ear and a gecko lead to a smile ... Ava and Tony, The Ninth Ward, New Orleans ...

RIMI G.

employee since 2012

Zup Zup Zappos! I will never be able to work for another company again. Zappos means wings to me; Zappos gives you wings to fly and if you're lucky you will get free wings from the Bistro!

ROWENA D.

employee since 2006

The Zappos Culture, to me, is working with an extended family, where we all get to learn and experience new and exciting things together. It's a weird family dynamic, where people genuinely care about others in the Zappos family, even the ones we haven't met yet.

RUDY R.

employee since 2005

Zappos continues to amaze me every year. I am so excited about our company. The fact that we are moving to downtown Vegas so we can help our community grow is amazing to me. We want to build a community in which we all help each other grow and be happy. I love being part of this. I see our company giving back to the people of Vegas and allowing our community to get involved in the progress and happiness of downtown. I love my team, and my job continues to challenge me to be better every day. Everything happens for a reason, and as we accept our responsibilities and do our best, we are presented with more to challenge ourselves with.

SAMANTHA L.

employee since 2010

Everyone always has creative ideas to grow Zappos to the next level and to have fun at Zappos!!!

SANDRA S.
employee since 2011

The great thing about the Zappos Culture is that it is contagious. That makes Zappos such an amazing place to work!

SARAH V.
employee since 2009

The Zappos Culture gives everyone the opportunity to be who they are. It allows us to be innovative and creative in our work, while also having fun doing it!

SCOTT J.
employee since 2002

This will be my tenth year at Zappos.com. Count 'em! Ten. Mike, my fearless director, was just showing me pictures of days long past and hair styles long regretted, and the man jewelry. When not looking at old pictures, it very rarely feels like a decade has gone by. We're still evolving, still growing, and still learning. And I still love the crap out of you, Zappos. Can't wait to be in downtown LV full time.

SHARRIS H.
employee since 2010

Focus on the journey, not the destination. Joy is found not in finishing an activity, but in doing it. Give a girl the right shoes, and she can conquer the world! I think it's safe to say that I've got the right shoes. Thanks, Zappos!

SHAY T.
employee since 2010

The Zappos Culture is being surrounded by (and doing) crazy (and sometimes questionable) things with amazing people ... people that I wouldn't be able to find anywhere else in the world! Each day when I walk through that front door, I feel so incredibly blessed and can't believe that I get to live this life. :-)

SHILOH M.
employee since 2011

The Zappos Culture, to me, means taking a variety of personalities and incorporating them into a tightly knit team. It is all about being who you are and embracing others for their individuality.

SHYLOH W.
employee since 2007

I can't believe this is my fifth submission to the Culture Book! Time flies!

It is always so incredibly hard to articulate or write about my feelings for Zappos, as it has literally become intertwined with my being.

Zappos is my family. Like any family, Zappos continually challenges me, coaxes me, overwhelms me, questions me and (most importantly) loves me. They keep me on my toes and never stop reminding me of all I can do professionally and personally. I can't, nor will I ever imagine life without them. I hope you will take the time to get to know us. I promise we will open your eyes to all you are and can become!

STEPH P.
employee since 2011

That warm tingling sensation when you sit down ... and no, I'm not speaking of urination. ;-) I'm talking about Zappos Culture. It's that feeling every time you sit at your desk, team lunch, happy hour, or any other event with fellow Zapponians. Pure happiness and comfort in knowing you're part of something greater than monetary profits. Words can't really do our culture justice, but memories can.

Trust me, even though I've only been here for a little over a year, I have plenty of memories that will last far beyond my professional career!

I <3 Zappos!

STEPHANIE C.

employee since 2010

Zappos gives us the freedom to be who we are, thus making us the most productive and fulfilled versions of ourselves. We're all able to speak our minds and let our voices be heard. I love being a part of this ever-growing and ever-evolving company!

STEPHEN C.

employee since 2011

To me, the Zappos Culture means being a part of a large, extended family. My experiences so far have been unlike those at any other company that I've worked for. There is camaraderie here where I feel like we all work as a strong, unified team in an effort to provide the best possible experience to our customers (internal and external). There is also a strong personal bond that we all share that goes beyond the walls of the offices.

STEVE H.

employee since 2004

The Zappos Culture holds us together and helps align us behind our company vision of Delivering Happiness. It's been great to see everybody embrace the move downtown in the last year and all the excitement about sharing Zappos Culture beyond our four walls. I've seen people from all departments get involved in different projects and it's awesome that teams were lobbying to be among the first to move downtown. It's a great testament to the strength of our culture that our teams look at the move as an opportunity to grow individually, professionally, and as a company. I don't know of another company where you could take folks from so many different backgrounds and have them align so quickly around a change as big as our move and a project as exciting as the downtown project. Zappos Culture truly sets us apart. It's up to all of us as we grow to over 2000 Las Vegas employees in the next year to make sure all our new folks understand the value, richness and unique qualities of our Zappos Culture.

STEVE P.

employee since 2008

You might as well remove the word monotony from your vocabulary. Every day here offers a new challenge/experience!! You truly never stop learning!!

SUNDAY P.

employee since 2010

The Zappos Culture means "family." I have been lucky to be on the clothing team for over two years, and I definitely consider this my family. We celebrate the good times and the successes, and we help lift one another up during the down times (whether personal or professional). I don't know where I would be without my team. Not only does this family spirit include my immediate team, it definitely encompasses other people that I interact with. I truly am blessed to have this family!

TERRA E.

employee since 2007

The Zappos Culture has made work fun, and also somewhere I am excited to go everyday! It has become my second family, and not only to me, but to our community. I'm so proud of all of our support to local charities.

TERRY I.

employee since 2007

The Zappos Culture allows its employees to be themselves and to be passionate about subjects they want to support.

TIFFANY B.

employee since 2011

I have been at Zappos a little over a year. I still remember my first day of work as if it were yesterday. Some of the best friends I now have were the people I met in my first day at New Hire Training. I moved across country by myself, but by the end of my first week at Zappos I had formed a new family. Before working here, I used to be very reserved and kept to myself. That may seem crazy to anyone who knows me now, but it's true nonetheless. Zappos has brought me out of my shell.

TORI B.
employee since 2011

Keep your heels, head, and standards high and don't chase anything but drinks and dreams. It's only taken a little over a year and I've fallen head over heels for Zappos!

TRACY G.
employee since 2012

The Zappos Culture has really changed my perspective on what a workplace should be. Instead of having coworkers and colleagues, I am now building friendships within my New Hire Training class and family spirit within my team. I've really seen a different side of how people interact with one another. Whether it's a simple greeting to another Zapponian, or keeping the door open for others, all these small gestures have really inspired me to be a more positive person, not only at work but also outside of work. Although I've only been here for less than a month, I've fallen comfortably within Zappos due to all the warm welcomes and treatments I've been given. I feel extremely fortunate to have been selected to work at Zappos and I am excited to continue to build more friendships along the way. I really hope that this becomes a permanent home for me!

VANESSA B.
employee since 2011

The culture here at Zappos to me means waking up in the morning and being excited about going to work. There's never a dull moment at the office and I always get to interact with happy people. Cheers!

DOUBLE DOG
TECHNIQUE
FRONT VIEW

Wienerfest 2012

Wienerfest 2012

2012 WEINERFEST

HOT DOGGONE GOOD TIME

LLAMA
LLIP LLOCK
PROFILE VIEW

COMO SE LLAMA

ME LLAMA LLAMA

BALLET STRETCH
BENT VIEW

2012 ROCK AND ROLL MARATHON

RUNNERS ROCK THE STRIP

OVERACHIEVENATOR
FRONT VIEW

Z MASQUERADE BALL

EYES WIDE COVERED

TWO-FOR-ONE FRAME
DISPLAY MODEL

WELCOME
AFTER-SCHOOL
ALL-STARS!

WESTERN ATHLETIC CONFERENCE
BASKETBALL CHAMPIONSHIP

WCC
KIDZ DAY
Zappos

WEST
COAST
CONFERENCE

BALLOON
THINGIES
FRONT VIEW

2011 RANDOM FUN

WCC KIDZ DAY

ZCLT
LOVEBOT
COWBOY
MODEL

2012 ZCLT ALL HANDS

WILD, WILD WEST

DAISY DUKELUKE
KNEE BADGE OPTIONAL

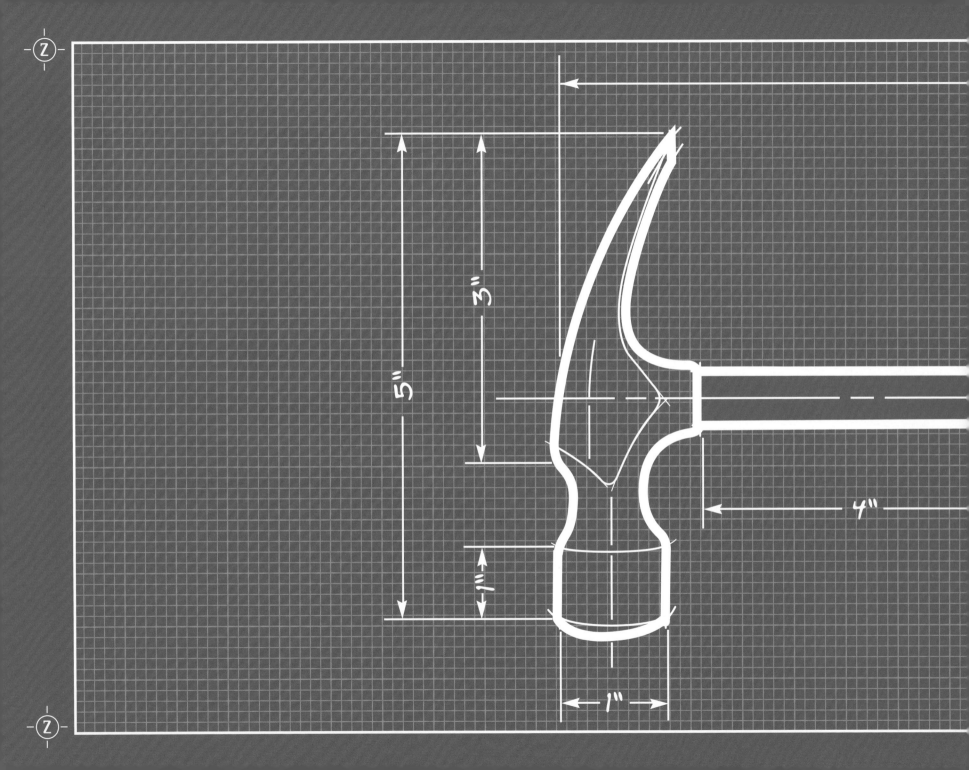

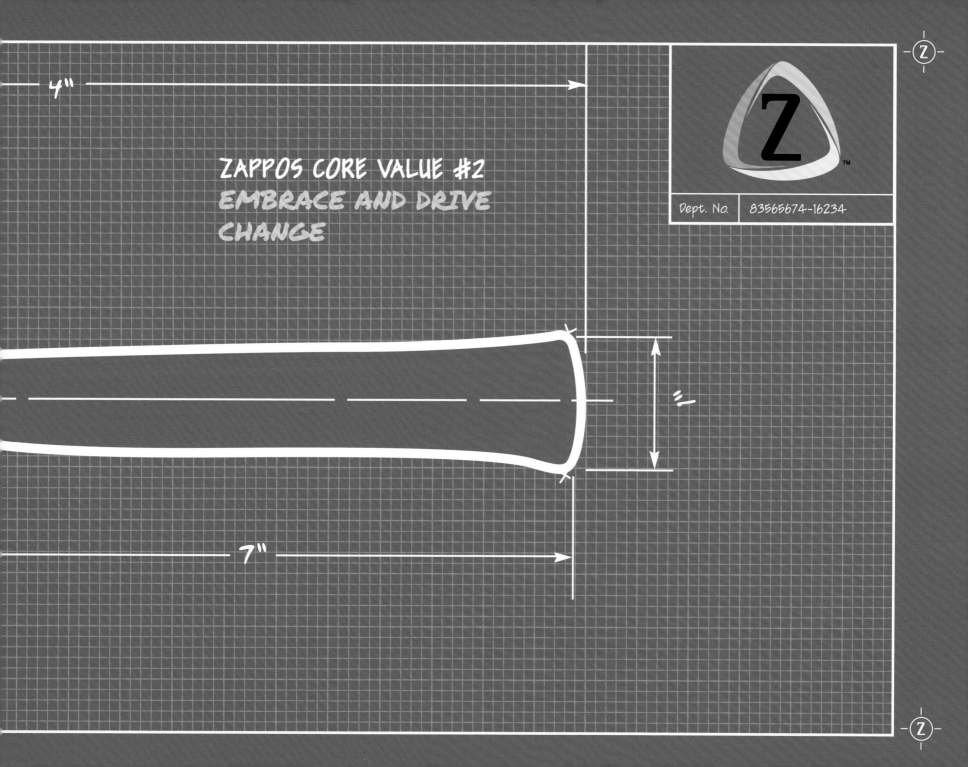

ZAPPOS CORE VALUE #2
EMBRACE AND DRIVE
CHANGE

Dept. No. | 83565674-16234

4"

7"

1"

ANONYMOUS
employee since 2012

"Zaikus"
Embrace the chaos
To work hard is to play hard
No suits on my block
Self-expression reigns
Progress follows your passions
Smile factories
It's good for your soul
Success should not yield to rules
To rock and to roll

ANONYMOUS
employee since 2009

It's about obsessively taking care of our customers, from fixing the edge case bug that might impact just one customer, to making sure that we're always thinking outside of the box to give our customers the most incredible experience, no matter how they touch us – on the website, our mobile channels, social channels, chat or the phones! The only way to do this successfully is by having a team whose members truly care about one another and our customers, and who constantly think about how to do things better.

ANONYMOUS
employee since 2011

The Zappos Culture is unlike any other that I have experienced. The fun, entrepreneurial atmosphere allows for unlimited growth and development in both our professional and personal lives.

ANONYMOUS
employee since 2001

The Zappos Culture, to me, means being happy . This applies to employees, vendors, contractors, customers, and anyone else we might interact with.

ANONYMOUS
employee since 2012

The freedom to think outside of the box to change old habits and to make the company better.

ANONYMOUS
employee since 2012

The Zappos Culture is family . I feel accepted and valued for what I can offer to the community . I know that I can voice my opinions and suggestions, and they will be listened to and considered . Zappos is a place where I can make a difference.

ANONYMOUS
employee since 2011

The Zappos Culture, to me, is being independent and responsible, which leads to a greater sense of control in life. It also means working with friends instead of colleagues, which means I can be myself and don't have to pretend to be someone else. Finally, the Zappos Culture gives me the feeling of being part of a community in a foreign country that provides a greater sense of security than just being employed. All of it adds up to a happy, satisfied life.

ANONYMOUS
employee since 2009

I don't go to "work" each day –
I go to "Happiness" !

ANONYMOUS
employee since 2010

It makes for a fun and exciting atmosphere in the workplace!

ANONYMOUS
employee since 2010

To me, the Zappos Culture means a lifestyle. The Ten Core Values are something you can use in your daily life. Since I have been at Zappos, I feel more appreciative of things . I don't sweat the small stuff as much. Zappos has taught me to be a better person. Life is too short to take too seriously.

ANONYMOUS
employee since 2010

<('.' <) <(^.^)> (> '.')>

ANONYMOUS
employee since 2003

Working at Zappos is like a wild adventure where you meet crazy people you can come to call lifelong friends.

ANONYMOUS
employee since 2010

The future's so bright, I gotta wear shades.

ANONYMOUS
employee since 2011

The Zappos Culture, for me, is being myself, working hard and having fun with it, every day.

ANONYMOUS
employee since 2008

Zappos means daily challenge; challenge to grow as a professional, as a friend, as a mom.

ANONYMOUS
employee since 2011

It means meeting real friends.

ANONYMOUS
employee since 2003

Year-over-year, so many things change, but one thing stays the same ... the people. The people make the company. The people are the culture. We drive each other crazy, yet we can't stop laughing and enjoying each other ... even rude, inappropriate uncle Larry.

ANONYMOUS
employee since 2006

The Zappos Culture means several things for me. It's a lifestyle, it's a place where I'm accepted, it's an environment that allows me to be myself.

ANONYMOUS
employee since 2004

Work hard. Make friends. Have fun.

ANONYMOUS
employee since 2008

The Zappos Culture is about being open and ready to embrace and drive change. We have a lot of changes and still all manage to remain a family. It is amazing, seeing how much we have grown and still being able to be a part of it all.

ANONYMOUS
employee since 2011

The Zappos Culture helps me to learn and grow. And people actually care about each other. Yes, really!

ANONYMOUS
employee since 2012

What does the Zappos Culture mean to me??!! Since coming to Zappos, I have been presented with many opportunities, including the opportunity to meet many different smart people from many different walks of life. For me, our culture would mean embracing the differences between you and others and swimming in a melting pot of ideas, challenges, helping hands, boosts when mistakes are made, and celebrations when triumphs happen. We have to be careful with the culture, though, by making sure that we do not use it to alienate others in any way. The positive aspects of the Zappos Culture should be presented to bring people into our fold and exposing them to something they would not otherwise be exposed to!

ANONYMOUS
employee since 2011

Once you become a member of the Zappos family, you are encouraged to be yourself. I find that this level of acceptance is different from that at other companies. I love the diversity and security that is fostered, resulting in happier and healthier people and relationships!

A.P.
employee since 2012

Dedication + determination multiplied by attitude = Zappos Culture.

AARON R.
employee since 2011

Zappos Culture allows you to "absorb what is useful, discard what is not, and add what is uniquely your own."

ABBIE M.
employee since 2005

I believe this is my fifth Culture Book entry, since I started right after one year's entries were submitted, but this process never gets old to me. It's my favorite thing that happens all year. I journal personally, and I'm familiar with the value of getting a snap shot of the "now" to look back on. In six and a half years, I've seen a lot of things happen at Zappos. Good things, not-so-good things, inspiring and motivating things, groundbreaking things, and all-around happy things.

There are some common elements in each of these: teamwork, motivation, vision, and determination. Most importantly, they all involve our Zappos Family.

There have been SO MANY times over the last six years where tears of gratitude have fallen from my eyes for having this place, and these people to look forward to seeing/working with. Moreover, they've looked forward to seeing/working with me. That, to me, is more valuable than pay, recognition, or a multitude of other forms of compensation that most seek in a career (even though we're spoiled and enjoy most of those anyway). It makes ALL the difference.

Thank you, Zappos. For all that you've given me. There is no page long enough to list out everything I've gained personally and professionally from experiencing Zappos first hand, so again, I say thank you from the bottom of my heart. My life is forever different, and better, because of you.

ADAM A.
employee since 2010

There once was a firm that sold shoes,
and had many from which one could choose.
We've grown in number and size,
and have clothes on the rise,
yet humbleness remains our muse.

ALANE C.
employee since 2006

I am grateful to be a part of the Zappos family. It is a great place to work. I have made so many friends and I love the people I work with. They are an extension of my family. I have been amazed at the kindness and the generosity of others who work here. There are so many people I work with that I have grown to love ... people I would not have met any other way. Thanks, Zappos, for enlarging my family.

ALEX A.
employee since 2010

The Zappos Culture is like none I have ever witnessed or been a part of before. Culture, to me, is a big part of life. Being from the south of France, coming to America was a big change in my culture, and throughout all the years that I have been here, I have witnessed and been a part of so many other cultures, but none can compare to the Zappos Culture. It is truly a big family with new relatives you meet every day as you walk around. We're all loving and helpful towards each other, the way a family should be. So many things that I see and have learned at Zappos have stuck to me and have become a natural part of my daily actions outside of work, from simple things like holding a door open for people to using more courtesy on the phone when helping someone. My dad always told me to find a job I love doing so I will enjoy going to work, and that will let me live a happy life. Well, I love being a part of QA, and I enjoy coming in to work every day and being around my Zappos family, and you know what? My dad was right. I may not have some of the things I want in life, but I am living a happy life right now because I have the things and people I need in it. :]

ALEXIS P.
employee since 2011

You will read the same testimonials over and over about how great Zappos is, and how everybody just loves it so much. But please don't mistake that for show. It's truth. People wouldn't say they love this place if they didn't mean it, nor would they even stay working here. It's not the kind of place where people just have a "job." This is a place where people have a home. Thank you, Zappos, for making it easy to wake up every day and be truly thankful that we have the most incredible place to go to.

ALICIA J.
employee since 2009

Zappos Culture, to me, means being driven, encouraged, and pushed to step outside of my comfort zone. And I do, on a daily basis. Whether it's summoning up the courage for a simple "hello," or giving a presentation on something I'm passionate about in pursuit of a new position. Not only do I have goals, but I have a clearly defined path to reach them. And I have people to help me hold myself accountable to that path. Zappos Culture also means charity. I am so excited to work for such a giving company. And I don't just mean the company itself, but the people within the company. I don't think I have ever been surrounded by such positive, generous people. It seems like everyone here is ready and willing to give the shirt off their back to help a fellow teammate. It's just one reason I still get warm fuzzies when I come to work.

ALLISON S.
employee since 2010

I'm not quite sure how I got so lucky with Zappos. Maybe it was some odd force that pulled me in this direction, but whatever the case, it wound up being a life-changer. I have finally found a (work) family where I can be accepted and grow. I can be the person I was meant to be, and for once, not be looked down upon for my low-key attitude or my random quirkiness. We're all a little different here, and that's what makes us work. There's a huge sense of respect that I have had a hard time finding at other places, and I'm forever grateful for it. If only there were a little more Zappos in the rest of the world.

ANDREA W.
employee since 2007

The culture at Zappos is unparalleled. Our culture accepts each individual's unique personality, with different backgrounds, coming together as one big happy family. I feel honored to work in such a fun and exceptional work environment!

ANDREW P.
employee since 2009

I like the Zappos culture because it is a great way for people to express themselves at work.

ASHLEY K.
employee since 2010

There are many things I love about our culture, but our family environment and being free to be ourselves are the ones that stand out. I have never worked at a place where everyone feels like family. No matter how bad a day you're having, there is always someone to make you laugh and cheer you up. The people here inspire me every day to be a better person.

Zappos is one of the few places where you are allowed to be you. I love coming to work knowing that I can just be me and not have to pretend to be someone else. Thanks, Zappos for being the best place to work!!

ATRELL L.
employee since 2005

This will be my seventh Zappos Culture book submission and it feels really good to be in a position to do so! The Zappos Culture means working amongst some of the most creative, talented, gifted, weirdest people that I've ever met in my life. It means discovering things about yourself that you weren't even aware you could do. It means taking risks and not being afraid to make mistakes. It's also truly awesome to have the Ten Core Values as a guide. What's even more awesome is that these core values are not just words that we talk about. We live and breathe them. And in a lot of ways, these values were already ingrained in us. So would I trade it for anything in the world? ... Naaaah! Not now or anytime soon :)

BEVERLY S.

employee since 2005

Recently, I went on an eight-mile, five and a half hour hike in Zion with some friends from Zappos for Memorial Day weekend. I had had no idea what I was getting myself into when I said yes to this. If there was a word that was the opposite of hiker, that was me. When we got off of the shuttle and walked to the start of our trail, I looked up to see what we were hiking up to, and I couldn't believe what I was about to do. Fifteen minutes into the hike, we realized what we were originally looking at was not our destination. We were going to hike to something much higher – Observation Point, 2,147 feet high. My legs were already on fire, and we had just started. (Did I mention I have a fear of heights?) I felt like turning back, but they encouraged and cheered, "We came together, and we are going to finish together." When we got to the top, it was one of the most empowering moments I've ever had. I was on top of the world, literally. I am so thankful I had the support of my friends to complete the hike. Not only did I accomplish something I never would have dreamed of, I had the opportunity to experience the wonders of Zion with the caverns, red sandstone walls, and even lush plant life. Looking back at my Zappos journey, there have been challenges. But just like the hike, I was able to overcome them and become a stronger person because of the support and encouragement from my teammates.

BHAWNA P.

employee since 2010

After almost two years of working here, I still feel very lucky to be a part of this culture! Corporations try to define it, mimic it, mandate it, or justify it with "return on investment." Some organizations strive to offer a great culture but make the wrong hiring decisions – putting profits over people. Fortunately, we have a very stringent hiring process and make every effort to hire individuals who will help us protect the culture we have so carefully cultivated. This translates into employees holding each other accountable and making sure that we don't allow the culture to slip. Without the right people, an organization may never be able to attain the culture it desires. After all, you can't grow culture in a test tube. (Well ... not yet at least!). So, I guess I still didn't answer the question of what Zappos Culture means to me. It means everything! It is what keeps me coming to work every day and enjoying every minute of it. It is knowing that I am respected, that I work with a fantastic group of talented individuals (shout out to HR!) and that I am given the autonomy and responsibility to make our workplace even better. Why do I love the Zappos Culture? Because I am allowed to be myself.

BRAD B.

employee since 2010

Zappos is an amazing place that never ceased to WOW me each and every day.

BRUCE R.

employee since 2006

It's been five and a half years. That's the longest I've ever stayed at one company. Throughout this time, I've made a lot of friends, and learned a lot, both technically and personally. Zappos has afforded me a lot of opportunity and I look forward to continuing to grow with the company.

CARRIE A.

employee since 2011

Zappos is a place where the distinction between family, friends, and coworkers is no longer necessary.

CELINA E.

employee since 2009

The one word that comes to mind when I think about my experience at Zappos is "grateful." I am grateful for many reasons. I am grateful for all the dear friends I have met over the years. I am grateful for my daily experiences that have taught me a lot about life. I am grateful for all the great benefits. But what I am most grateful for is, if you're in a bind, the company will come together to help get you through it.

CHERYL L.

employee since 2010

I have now worked at Zappos for two fantastic years! I have learned so much in this time and I look forward to growing and progressing within the company for many years. Working here is always an adventure – one I look forward to continuing every day. :-)

CHRIS N.

employee since 2010

One of Zappos' greatest strengths is its resilience. Some combination of the core values of "Embrace and Drive Change" and "Be Passionate and Determined" motivate this characteristic. Over the past year, we have collectively dealt with some challenging situations, and on every occasion I have been inspired by the commitment of our teams to do the right things for each other and for our customers. It is a privilege to work with you all and be a part of Zappos.

CHRISTA F.
employee since 2004

"To invent an airplane is nothing. To build one is something. But to fly is everything." – Otto Lilienthal.

First, there was an idea of what company culture could be. Then the foundation was built – structure and freedom put in place where that culture could exist. But ideas are nothing at all if they are not executed.

Collectively, we have executed an amazing idea. And that is everything. :)

CHRISTAL T.
employee since 2007

FREEDOM ... I think George Michael said it best!
I won't let you down
I will not give you up
Gotta have some faith in the sound (aka:Zappos)
It's the one good thing that I've got
I won't let you down
So please don't give me up
Because I would really, really love to stick around ...
All we have to do now
Is take these lies and make them true somehow
All we have to see
Is that I don't belong to you
And you don't belong to me
Freedom
You've gotta give for what you take
Freedom
You've gotta give for what you take ...
I'll hold on to my freedom
May not be what you want from me
Just the way it's got to be
Lose the face now
I've got to live

CHRISTINA B.
employee since 2011

Wow! My very first culture book entry!
I can't tell you how much Zappos has changed my perspective on life. I am truly blessed to be part of the Zappos family. I've gained so many valuable friends and have had wonderful experiences while working here. I strive every day to live up to our ten core values inside and outside of work. If it weren't for Zappos, I'd probably be somewhere lost in the abyss of a horrible company culture. So I truly want to say "Thanks, Zappos" from the bottom of my heart!

CHRISTINA K.
employee since 2010

It's complicated. But worth checking out.

CINDY P.
employee since 2011

My feelings about Zappos Culture have evolved over the two years I have been here. At first, they were more about how the culture affected my work and personal life directly. Now I feel as though they are about being a part of something much larger and more important than myself ... the charities we contribute to and the lives that get affected by employees' generous donations, and Tony's vision being spread all over the world. I am very proud to tell everyone I meet that I am part of the Zappos family.

CYNTHIA T.
employee since 2008

You take the good, you take the bad,
you take them both and there you have
The Facts of Life, the Facts of Life.
There's a time you got to go and show
You're growin' — now you know about
The Facts of Life, the Facts of Life.
When the world never seems
to be livin' up to your dreams
And suddenly you're finding out
the Facts of Life are all about you, you.

DANESE D.
employee since 2011

Working hard. Playing hard. And enjoying the work/life balance, finally!! Thank you, Zappos :)

DANIEL E.
employee since 2010

Zappos, to me, is being supportive in everything you do, like a great pair of underwear. :)

DANIELLE D.
employee since 2011

Zappos is about giving a little extra effort to make a big difference to someone else.

DAVE S.
employee since 2010

Oh, the Zappos Culture's magic –
It wears a magic hat,
and when it saw the chance to thrive
it said "I'm havin' that."
It's not like working elsewhere,
nor easy to describe.
I love it here at Zappos 'cause
it's freaking dynamite.
@shakefon URZ

DEBRA J.
employee since 2007

I love Zappos!! Where else can you work, go on vacation and be excited to go back to work?. We work really hard, but in such a great atmosphere that it makes you want to do your best. I hope I never take this place – this awesome place – for granted.

DENNIS L.
employee since 2008

The Zappos Culture is like a giant family reunion every day. Everyone here is like your cousin. You may not chill, hang out and drink with all your cousins, but they're still family. That's the difference between other companies and Zappos. We treat everyone like friends and family, where they treat others just as business.

DEREK F.
employee since 2007

Hello! and welcome to CULTUREBOOKENTRY! If you would like to hear CULTUREBOOKENTRY in English, press 1!
(1) How many years have you been employed at ZAPPOS DOT COM?
(6) Wow, SIX is a great number of years! Press ONE if you love your job:
(1111111111111111111111111111) I'm sorry, I didn't get that. You responded ONEONEONEONEONEONEONEO-NEONEONE.
Please re-answer, do you love your job?
Press ONE for yes.
(1) Great! How many of those days out of the SIX years you've been employed have you awoken and been excited to get to work and face the challenges of the day? Enter number of days and press POUND
(1823389382#) I'm sorry, you entered ONE BILLION, EIGHT HUNDRED AND TWENTY-THREE MILLION, THREE HUNDRED AND EIGHTY-NINE THOUSAND, THREE HUNDRED EIGHTY-TWO. This is not a valid number of days for SIX years. Please re- ... Actually, you know what, we'll take it.
Are you excited about the downtown move and the challenges it will present? Press ONE ONLY ONCE for yes.
(1) Great! Do you enjoy the culture and the people you work with? Press ONE for yes.
(1111!! ONEBATMANSYMBOL) I'm sorry, ONEONEONEONEEXCLAMATIONEXCLAMATIONO-HENNEEEBATMANSYMBOL is not a valid response.
Please re-enter your answer:
(1) Thank you for using CULTUREBOOKENTRY!
Please have a great day!

DIANA G.
employee since 2005

I have been with Zappos for six and a half years. Looking back at how small we were and how big we are now, I can't help but wonder where the future is going to take us. One of my favorite things about the Zappos Culture is that it's not only about us, it's about the community as well. Zappos puts their employees, partners and customers first, but also has a great sense of social responsibility. I am extremely proud to be a part of this amazing company and can't wait to see what the future holds.

DON N.
employee since 2010

Reflecting on what the Zappos Culture means to me this year, two things come to mind:

Teamwork – When the data breach occurred, it was impressive to see how the whole company rallied together to get customer emails answered as quickly as possible and help diffuse issues in a stressful situation.

Fun and Weirdness – I have not dressed up for Halloween in many, many years, but in my first Halloween at Zappos, I was the Ghost of Henry VIII at the Finance Haunted House, Caddyshack Assistant Greenkeeper Carl Spackler at the Zalloween Golf Event and St. Louis Cardinal World Series star Albert Pujols at the Halloween Costume Contest – all within three days! Not bad for an old Tax Guy.

Looking forward to see how things evolve this year...

DREWSKI

employee since 2010

The Zappos Culture is unique because it lets everyone be themselves. Zappos doesn't say, be yourself one day, then tell you to change the way you dress the next. It's be yourself, EVERY DAY!

DURON P.

employee since 2007

It only gets better ...

We're about 16 months away from relocating to Downtown Las Vegas! The amount of change that I've witnessed over the past five years that I've been here is indescribable. I'm excited for the amazing things that are going to transpire in the next five years. Like, how much of an impact we'll have not just on the surrounding community, but on the entire city of Las Vegas and possibly the world. Until next year ...

P.S.: Shout out to the entire ZCON/HR Squad! ;-)

EILEEN K.

employee since 2010

When I first came to Zappos, I heard over and over again that we work hard and we also play hard. Our number one priority is our customers — they are always first, no matter what. So during work, we work hard to make sure that our customers are taken care of, first and always. After work is when we play hard. When we are done working for the day, teams get together a few times a year so we can work on the core value of building a positive team and family spirit. We have an amazing group of people here who love Zappos, love our customers, but mostly we love each other. When we spend so much time together at work, it's really nice that Zappos realizes that it's important for all of us to be friends outside of work also. We are encouraged to get together after work to bond with our team and other members of our Zappos family. This is the reason why I love the core value of building a positive team and family spirit.

ELYSE' (GRANOLA).

employee since 2010

The Zappos Culture is deciding you want to have an "instant dance party" button in the front lobby ... and doing it! The Zappos Culture is wildly entertaining.

I love everyone.
"Granola"

ERIC K.

employee since 2008

Cinnamon-raisin bagels.

ERICA J.

employee since 2007

To me, the Zappos Culture is the love I have for the HR Team. We're a dysfunctional family. We make fun of each other, know how to push each other's buttons, constantly laugh together, and truly value our friendships. Camaraderie like ours is what makes me grateful to come in to work every day. Oh, and Johnny P. That guy is "culture" — all day, every day.
Om

ERICKA L.

employee since 2007

Culture at Zappos is enjoying a warm cup of cappuccino in the morning.

FIONA B.

employee since 2010

I've been with Zappos for two years now and I've loved every day of it. Normally, at my previous jobs, I would get this "two-year itch," and always wonder why I get bored working at my job and leave. Now I realized that most companies do not offer anything like our Core Value #5, "Pursue Growth and Learning." Every day when I come into work, I am learning something new and growing as a person. Due to Zappos, I am a better person for my coworkers, family, friends, wife, and new mommy.

Zappos is more than just friends. Here, we are family. I know I can turn to my team members and they are there for a shoulder to cry on, a sounding-board to rant on, or someone to tell exciting news to.

I love working here and never have a "case of the Mondays" anymore. Thank you, Zappos, for all the love you give!!!

GAGAN A.
employee since 2010

Zappos is like a mini-world where you find people from all walks of life – artists, dancers, singers, and even magicians. They excel in what they do but still they work towards one big goal – making Zappos a world of wonderful people, the happiest place on this earth. It has been a great experience to be part of such an amazing adventure.

GAYLE H.
employee since 2011

The Zappos Culture, to me, means working for a company that cares about its employees, customers, and the community. I feel lucky to work for a company that offers so much flexibility and opportunity.

HAO Z.
employee since 2012

Zappos is the best … not one of the best, but the best. Everybody keeps telling me that it's not good to get the first job from Zappos because it will be very hard to get used to any other job. Well, in that case, let me just stay with Zappos forever! It is the Zappos Culture that makes the company alive. I honestly like to wake up every morning, ready to work. Our culture makes me feel like part of a big family, not just a corporate entity. I love Zappos!!

HHH.
employee since 2010

I have been here a little over a year and I still love every minute of my job at Zappos. I couldn't imagine debiting and crediting numbers anywhere else while also perfecting my ping-pong game!

HOLLIE D.
employee since 2006

As always, Zappos is the best place to work, has the best people, and provides the best work environment possible. But over this last year it provided me a lot more. Let me start at the beginning.

In March of 2011, I decided I was going to start living healthier. I weighed 260 lbs. and was not active at all. I was tired of being fat and tired. I was also worried that I would start to get sick. I was borderline diabetic and had high blood pressure and cholesterol. It was time for a change. I started my journey by eating better and accepting and admitting what the problem was. I joined Weight Watchers and posted my weight and goals on Facebook to help hold me accountable.

How does this relate to the Zappos Culture? Well, as I started this journey, many people at Zappos talked to me about it and took the time to listen to my story and what I wanted to do, including Tony, who encouraged me to share my story at an All Hands meeting. This gave me an even larger pool of people to help hold me accountable. My coworkers also encouraged me to participate in the Zappos Rock'n Roll Half Marathon. When that happened I thought to myself, "They are crazy. I can't even walk 13.1 miles." But I decided to try, so a Zappos employee gave me a training program, answered the questions I had, and recommended shoes for me to use. I started, and the first day out it took me about an hour and ten minutes to finish three miles. I was worried, but my coworkers continued to encourage me not to quit. Some even trained with me so I didn't have to do it alone. So I kept going. By the time the half marathon rolled around, I was not only able to complete it, with my coworkers by my side, but I was able to run about four miles of it. It felt amazing.

As of today, I've lost about 70 pounds. I am running three half-marathons this year, and am going to attempt to complete the 8,000-meter challenge. And I am not doing it alone. Several people at Zappos continue to help and encourage me. As I sit here and write this, I still cannot believe this is me. I want to say thank you to all the people that helped and encouraged me along the way, and thank you, Zappos, for being the kind of company that encourages employees to support each other. You helped me change my life.

ISRAEL S.
employee since 2010

It's Zappos. Need I say more? I'm so grateful that I work for a company that expresses the care it does for its employees. We are truly given so many great things and each day I remember to be thankful for everything that is given to us. Not to mention — where else can you find friends that are closer than family? I'm very happy to be able to go to work each day at Zappos and hope that it lasts forever. Thanks to everyone for making the company, family and friendship what it is today.

JACKIE W.
employee since 2010

My two-plus years here at Zappos have been great. It's my home away from home! I love coming to work and experiencing the love, hugs, laughter, bonding, experiences, knowledge, advancements, and positive vibes from my second family, and especially the CUSTOMERS! I always tell my Zappos family I will be 105 years old and saying, "Please don't send me home, I can still see the screen and the keyboard!!!" LOL! Thank you, Zappos, for everything!

JACOB P.

employee since 2003

What the Zappos Culture means to me is pretty much the same as it meant to me nine years ago when I started here: "Wow! What an amazing group of people I work with!" I still have the same passion and the same excitement. And I still have the same love for what I do.

JAMES H.

employee since 2010

I tried to dig down deep and think of something new to say this year that would crush what I wrote last year and I couldn't. That is the best part about our company. No matter how many people come and go, no matter how big we grow, no matter how many different workers we know, we are still the same company down deep. I doubt that any other company could say the same. That is what makes the Zappos Culture unique.

JAMIE N.

employee since 2004

The Zappos Culture is about family. Your coworkers become your best friends. In good times and bad, the family atmosphere keeps you going. It's about knowing who you are and being valued for the things that make you weird or different. It's about freedom to do your best work and apply your talents regardless of your department or job description. Zappos allows you to find out what you are passionate about and pursue it through your work. In all these ways, it's easy to find purpose in what we do. Every day things change, new challenges are presented, and more work needs to be done. It's hectic and crazy, but it's what I love most about Zappos.

JEN B.

employee since 2010

:)

JENNIFER L.

employee since 2010

Les détails de ma vie sont sans importance. Très bien, par où commencer? Mon père était propriétaire d'une boulangerie, un homme originaire de Belgique en quete perpetuelle d'amélioration, atteint d'une narcolepsie modérée et avec un penchant pour quelquechose que je ne peut pas mentionner. Ma mère était une fille française âgée de quinze ans du nom de Chloé, elle avait les pieds palmés. Mon père courait les femmes, buvait, et avait des revendications scandaleuses telle que celle d'être l'inventeur du point d'interrogation. Parfois il accusait les châtaignes d'être paresseuses, le genre de malaise général que seul le génie possede et la fou deplore. Mon enfance était classique: étés à Rangoon, leçons de luge. Au printemps, nous fabriquions des casques de viande. Quand j'étais insolent, j'étais placé dans un sac de jute et battu avec des roseaux, assez standard vraiment. A l'âge de douze ans j'ai reçu mon premier scribe. À quatorze ans, un Zoroastrien nommé Vilma entrepris le rituel de raser mes bien amis. Il n'y a vraiment rien de tel qu'un sac tondu, c'est à vous couper le souffle, je vous suggère de l'essayer.

JENNIFER S.

employee since 2010

Cinderella is proof that a new pair of shoes can change your life. Or an outfit. Maybe even a handbag, too.

JENSKI S.

employee since 2008

My job may be stressful sometimes, but it's more than rewarding. I'm so lucky to have coworkers who are like family to me and who are always there for me. I couldn't ask for a better job.

JERALD T.

employee since 2005

Se7en years ago, I joined Zappos and thought this was a really cool company and that just might make it. WOW!!!!!!! As I look at my se7en-year pin, all kinds of wonderful memories come to mind. I think some of the best are all the people, both famous and not-so-famous, that I have been able to take on a tour and a shuttle ride, and to share the Zappos experience with. It truly is a magical time in all of our lives, and as I wish upon a star, for se7en more years as special as these:)

JESS N.

employee since 2011

My table tennis skills have improved immensely.

JESSIE M.

employee since 2010

The Zappos Culture, to me, is thoughtfulness. You can see it in everything that people do, say, pass on, donate, contribute, and attempt. Imagine an entire planet based on thoughtfulness! :)

JIM D.

employee since 2011

True culture is hard to find. Sometimes you think you have true culture and then you catch the early flight home from San Diego and a couple of people jump out of your bathroom, blindfolded like a magic show, ready to ... What I'm trying to say is that true culture is blind.

JIMMY A.

employee since 2005

Nine mile skid
on a ten mile ride
Hot as a pistol
but cool inside
Cat on a tin roof
Dogs in a pile
Nothing left to do but
smile, smile, smile
-R. Hunter

JONATHAN S.

employee since 2011

My feelings on the Zappos culture boil down to three examples. I always went to my prior job with a feeling of dread, thinking about all the things I would do once the clock hit 5 p.m. After working at Zappos for only a month, I was driving to the office and I was genuinely excited to get to work. Like the Seinfeld episode where Jerry starts crying and says 'what is this salty discharge?' I had no idea what it actually felt like to look forward to going to work. Second, is that I've never been to a place where I've laughed so much. It seems that whenever things are getting stale, someone will break the mood with a joke or silly comment. Lastly, Zappos is a place where you can bring your whole personality to work. I'll admit it, I like quoting stupid 80's movies or talking about the Macho Man Randy Savage. I can do that at work and it actually makes the environment better. We all bring our personalities to the job and it makes for a more interesting/fun/connected place. Oh, and one more thing. Where else would I be able to bring a giant, inflatable, remote-controlled shark to work and have it be awesome? Nowhere but Zappos.

JUSTIN H.

employee since 2009

It's hard to put into words what I think about the Zappos Culture, because it's really a way of life now, more than anything else.

It's doing the right thing. It's believing in people. It's helping each other out. It's ideas ... so many ideas! It's inspiration. It's follow-through. It's family. It's really the basis of making anywhere feel like home.

KACHINA K.

employee since 2011

A few serendipitous encounters led me to Zappos and let me know that this was the right place to be. Although I was initially hired as a temporary employee, I was "passionate and determined" to become a permanent part of the Zappos community. My anxiety over the possibility of not being hired haunted my dreams. It wasn't just about getting a job or a paycheck. It was about being a part of something bigger than a place to work. It was and is about cooperation, ideas, support, inspiration, community, laughter, fun, balance, humility, friends, and family. Ultimately, it's about believing that we are changing the world through customer service. I take pride in where I work and what Zappos stands for. I am honored to be a part of this team and consider this one of the best experiences of my life.
Temp EE 12/6/10-10/23/11
Perm EE 10/24/11 to present. :-)

KANDIS Y.

employee since 2010

This is my second year at Zappos and I am as happy, if not more so than the first day I joined the team. I do not think I knew what I was getting myself into when I joined Zappos. I was joining something I didn't realize I was missing. Today I work for a company that truly makes me happy. I work with people I not only consider my friends, they are my family. I am so thankful, and feel so lucky to be a part of Zappos and to have the relationships I have been fortunate enough to build over the last two years. I cannot wait to continue to learn and grow with Zappos.

KAR T.

employee since 2010

A place like home, where everyone accepts you for who you are.

KARI C.
employee since 2010

Things that make me smile-
- Cold Mint Milanos cookies
- A pair of jeans that fit just right
- A smiling baby
- My family
- My Zappos Family
- My job
- When there is leftover pizza in the Bistro.
I am truly blessed to be working for such a wonderful company.

KATHY A.
employee since 2011

Ever since coming to work at Zappos, I have looked forward to coming to work every day. The fantastic people I work with treat each other like real family. We have fun, work hard and play hard every day. All the different activities, parades and changes keep the workplace exciting and energetic.

KATRINA J.
employee since 2006

Time for another entry into the Zappos Culture Book.

Here we are on the verge of another transition – the "Downtown" move. I was not with Zappos when the company packed up and moved from San Francisco to Las Vegas, with Tony leading the way. No one knew what was ahead. But they had trust, faith and braved the unknown.

Here we stand on the verge of another poignant moment ... some may have doubts, some have already laced their shoes and have embraced the challenge head-on. I myself have my head held high with pride in my heart as Tony leads us not, into the unknown, but as he leads us "Home."

KEITH C.
employee since 2008

He who never made a mistake, never made a discovery.

KELLY K.
employee since 2011

Our Zappos Culture is the most important thing that I love preserving here at Zappos. That is what makes us different and sets us apart from other places. Being able to come to work and enjoy my coworkers and have a personal relationship with them is something that I value greatly. I work with friends, not just coworkers. I trust and love the Zappos Culture. This is the only place I want to be and I miss my team when I'm not here. Even if we did not have the rockin' picnics, happy hours and parties, this would be the greatest place to work. Those are just bonuses to being here. The people of Zappos make its culture one of a kind, and I am so happy and grateful that I have them to come to every day. I have created lifelong friendships that I will cherish forever.

KELLY W.
employee since 2008

"I alone cannot change the world, but I can cast a stone across the waters to create many ripples."
—Mother Teresa

KENNETH B.
employee since 2011

Always being challenged.
Learning to adapt to change.
Never dreading going to work.
Having tough days here and there, but no bad ones.
Graphs. So many graphs!
VPN and wireless ... :)

KIERSTEN S.
employee since 2010

Culture is a smiling face when you pass by. Culture is someone opening the door when your hands are full. Culture is jumping out of bed because you are excited to get to work. Culture is laughing so hard at work that you almost pee in your pants. Culture is going above and beyond to make a coworkers day. Culture is working extra hard because you want to do a good job for your team. Culture is becoming a better person because the people around you are amazing!

KIMBERLY G.
employee since 2010

Zappos is an amazing company to work for. I enjoy coming in to work each and every day!

KMAC.
employee since 2007

"Perfection is not attainable, but if we chase perfection we can catch excellence."
— Vince Lombardi

KRIS O.
employee since 2005

do good.
work hard.
make good choices.
be brave.
grow.
be good.
measure twice, cut once.
repeat.

KRISTY M.
employee since 2007

I *heart* Zappos and our culture! Our culture is why I'm here. Zappos has sooo many good people, and being a good person is what I feel we're about.
Our people, good people:
~Are positive
~Are always happy and excited for a chance to help someone
~Smile :)
~Never judge
~Never take part in silly rumors or gossip
~Are conscious of their rectitude
~Care about the whole, not just personal gain
These are just a few of things that I see around me that remind me that we are a family of good people.

LISA M.
employee since 2004

Fun, engaging, spontaneous, rewarding, interesting and zerendipitous.

LISA S.
employee since 2010

I am a recruiter here at Zappos and get asked almost daily by candidates what our Zappos Culture means to me. The culture here means so many things to me but our Ten Core Values come to mind when I am asked this question. Here at Zappos, it is not about being just like everyone else; we are valued/appreciated for our differences. At Zappos, it is all about stretching yourself and making the most of each day in a positive way and supporting and encouraging others as they do the same. At Zappos, everyone suggests new ways of doing things and our ideas are embraced and welcomed, imagine that!! It is also about having some fun along the way ... did I mention we have parades!?! It is about having a higher purpose than your own and sharing it with everyone you meet and speak with ... did I mention I recruit at Zappos and speak with a lot of people!?! Did I mention I love my job :)

LIZ G.
employee since 2006

The Zappos Culture is more than what goes on in the office. It is the relationships we form and the friendships we make. You can't find that anywhere else. I never have.

LOREN B.
employee since 2004

By the time this Culture Book is released, I will have been part of the Zappos family for over eight years. Defining the Zappos Culture has become harder in some ways and easier in others. Ultimately, it is the people that define the culture of our company. I have watched Zappos grow from 80 to 800 to over 1,300 employees in Las Vegas alone. The growth in KY is another story. (A story most likely told in these very pages.) Change naturally comes with growth of this nature. Change in systems, procedures, buildings, services, desks, coworkers, products, benefits, carpets, bistro food items, team names, department names, tour points, company logos, and more. That's a lot of change, and I have barely scratched the surface. This is why I want to recognize that we are a culture of change. Change can be f'ing scary; I have been scared of some changes around here myself. Looking back, however, it has made us a stronger family and a better company. Here's to driving and embracing change! I applaud the Zappos family members that face change head-on and break through to the other side.

LOUIE M.
employee since 2006

The Zappos Culture is what it is because we allow people to be who they are. We allow them to express their individuality in their own creative ways. This means the boundaries of what our Culture can be is constantly being pushed by new ideas. I feel this is what sets Zappos apart. It is much easier to cultivate a relationship with someone when you know who they really are. I think this gives Zappos such a great team and family quality and ultimately what makes our Culture unique and special.

MALLORY M.

This year has been the best year for me at Zappos. I have moved departments to the ZCON family! They have really shown me what the true core values of Zappos are. They brought me on as one of their own and have treated me the way my own family does. Every company has good times and bad times, but it is the people that make up the company that truly make it a successful and happy place to work. And Zappos has those people. I am truly blessed to be a part of a culture that lets you be you, never looks down on you, and always treats you like a person, not just an employee. I am truly happier than I have ever been and I have Zappos to thank for that.

MARA B.
employee since 2011

Becoming part of Zappos has been a huge change in my life. The Zappos Culture pushes all the boundaries of traditional employment. I've been at many companies that preach work/life balance, but at Zappos you feel they really support the idea. Here at Zappos you are always thinking, "How would this make me feel?" I think it's important to blend both business practice and the human element to be successful. The thing that strikes me the most, day after day, is just the common thread that you see in all employees at Zappos. You never feel alone when you are walking through the building. There is always a smile, nod or hello just waiting. And the best part is that everyone really means it.

MARCELA G.
employee since 2005

The Zappos Culture = Happiness!
I have never worked in a place where you can be yourself and are encouraged to be yourself. I feel extremely lucky to be part of the Zappos family :O)

MARCIE A.
employee since 2007

"Gimme a whiskey, ginger ale on the side, and don't be stingy, baby."

MARITZA L.
employee since 2006

The definition of happiness: a state of well-being characterized by emotions ranging from contentment to intense joy. Yup, that's Zappos :)

MARK G.
employee since 2009

"I'm talking about someplace warm. A place where the culture flows like wine. A place where the women instinctively flock like the salmon of Capistrano ..." Mark G

MARTA D.
employee since 2011

If I had placed a bet that I would never leave my hometown of Seattle, I would've lost, because I would never in a million years believed in a million years that I would move away. But Zappos came calling and I took a leap of faith and moved here last summer.

If I had come to work for any other company, I think my experience so far would be vastly different. This goes to show what Zappos has done for me. I have met and befriended so many amazing people, work with an incredible team, and done a myriad of fun things. I feel so lucky to be welcomed by everyone and have the opportunity to do so many things, and I don't regret my decision for one second.

MEGAN P.
employee since 2006

"Most folks are about as happy as they make up their minds to be." — Abraham Lincoln

MICHAEL B.
employee since 2010

The Zappos Culture means that there's still fun to have, even when you have the following to fix:
root   15608   1 6 May03 ?   1-22:52:49 [gw.x] <defunct>
For example, typing about the culture while I still have a defunct process to fix. General good times are to be had in between some real, hard, important work.

MICHAEL R.

Waffles.

MICHELLE F.
employee since 2010

The Zappos Culture, to me, means a complex web of interrelations and support, much like an ecosystem. We're all entwined, and anything that affects one of us trickles down to affect us all. Culture for a Zapponian is something that surrounds, supports, and affects us.
This year, as tragic an example as it is, the best example I can think of is when we lost Amber. That affected everyone, at least a little. Even those who didn't know her were affected by the loss felt by those who did know her. We all banded together for support, not just for ourselves, but also for her family. We were surrounded by a community of our peers in healing from the loss and looking forward to the future. Our "ecosystem" of culture is one of the blessings of being here. I'm grateful for it. I see it every workday, and usually on my days off as well. I feel like I'm a piece of something powerful and encompassing.

MICHELLE V.
employee since 2012

It only took a week (my first week) to realize how amazingly special Zappos is. It's UNBELIEVABLE! Only at Zappos can you do crazy things all day and somehow get a ton of stuff completed. I still don't understand how we do it! The people here are absolutely ZA-mazing. I'm so excited and proud to be the first-ever HR Intern! So blessed! <3

MIKE A.

employee since 2006

The Zappos Culture is about passionate employees who aspire to make our company a world-class organization. There is no one way to achieve this – it's up to each individual to determine what the culture means to him or her, and to then work hard to make Zappos the company we all want it to be.

MIKE B.

employee since 2010

For me, the Zappos Culture begins even before I get out of bed in the morning (insert "that's what she said" joke here). Until I started with Zappos, I never experienced a company that made me actually excited to get up for in the morning. This is a testament to the environment and the people that work here. We truly are a family and will support each other and help each other just like a family would. The culture continues on throughout the day by giving employees autonomy and creative freedom. You never know what great ideas will pop up and what each day will look like. We aren't constrained by typical "corporate America" rules and red tape. Zappos is truly special and I'm so happy to be a part of it every single day!

Oh, and Johnny P. IS the culture! Alexander Hamilton - Boom!

MIKE W.
employee since 2011

At this time, I have been a part of Zappos for just over a year. It's incredible how fast the time has gone, and how much I have learned. Zappos is full of great people who are always available to lend a hand without thinking twice. I couldn't imagine myself being anywhere else.
... and now, instant dubstep!
yes "wub" | xargs say

MIKELL G.
employee since 2011

The Zappos Culture is one of a kind. To me it means: sharing a simple smile with a stranger, randomly meeting someone at a Zappos event or even in the hallway, adding a personal touch to all that you do and delivering happiness in every way possible! I love being a part of the Zappos family and am so grateful to be surrounded by such Zaptastic people! Can't wait to bring the Zappos Culture to downtown Las Vegas!

MIKI C.
employee since 2006

I often hear from people about how unappreciated they feel at their job and how they don't feel they can really be themselves or speak up. Working at Zappos I sometimes forget there are still workplaces out there that can be this way, and then I feel both thankful to be working for a company that really values their employees' individuality and encourages them to speak up if they have an idea for making something better. I wish more companies would understand the value of a happy work environment.

MILLIE C.
employee since 2006

The Zappos Culture means that I get to do the following every day at the office:
1. Work with the nicest and most generous people;
2. Laugh;
3. Help someone;
4. Teach someone;
5. See my friends and family;
6. Talk about clothes and shoes; and
7. Wear blue jeans and sandals.

MISS PATTI C.
employee since 2005

I just celebrated year number seven with Zappos. And I still love coming to work every day. Our culture continues to grow with each new person. "Embrace and Drive Change," one of our Ten Core Values, is ongoing. I've seen a lot of changes since I started and with our move downtown I'll see many more. I'm excited to be a part of this company and to be involved with all the changes. Here's to the future!

NICH H.

employee since 2011

For me, the Zappos Culture is a bit hard to define simply. It's an ever-evolving structure that builds and grows with every new addition to the company. I see, though, that we surely keep our core values close to heart. I've been able to grow, learn, and develop more rapidly here than at any other place where I've worked. I've been here just under a year at this point, but I'm having a great time and look forward to a long time helping the company, and its culture grow as best I can.

NICOLE L.

employee since 2012

To me, the Zappos Culture means the opportunity to be creative and not have to fit myself into a predetermined mold of what I should be while I'm at work. At past jobs, there's always been a set of guidelines of what I should look like and what I should think that was determined by someone else. Here I get to decide myself.

NICOLE M.

employee since 2011

The Zappos Culture means coworkers who are more than work buddies ... they are like the family you actually like. You are all working towards to the common goal of making Zappos an amazing place to work!

PAM T.

employee since 2003

It feels fantastic to be inspired every day by so many people and ideas. This is what drives me to want to do more, to deliver my best every day. This is an example of why our culture is so special. And now we have an opportunity to share our culture with the local community through the revitalization of downtown Las Vegas. We're setting the stage and investing in a future that will significantly and positively impact the Zappos Culture, as well as renew the downtown community. This is exciting and we're fortunate to be a part of something so mammoth!

PATI V.

employee since 2006

ZAPPOS? What more can you say except it is a fantastic company, from the peeps to the CEO, Tony. We are one big, extended family. Even our vendors get in on the action. We get them so involved in the Zappos Culture and they love it. Our move downtown is also a great way to get involved with Las Vegas, as we can make a difference in our community and spread our culture. Tony is making such a personal impact on the Las Vegas community, it is unreal. I love our company and I wish more companies would see how our culture could make their employees more productive: We have fun, but we also work hard. LOVE ZAPPOS!!!!!!

PATRICK O.

employee since 2010

I feel very lucky to be part of a company that takes such great care of its employees and has an amazingly strong culture. Most of my best friends are also my colleagues, which makes going to work a pleasure. We work hard, but play even harder!

PATRICK S.

employee since 2001

The Zappos Culture, to me, means that you are allowed to be yourself at work. Go, Ducks!

PERI G.

employee since 2006

I've been with Zappos for almost six years now, and every day is better than the last! It's true what they say, Zappos is as unique as it gets! There isn't another company out there that has provided — and will continue to provide — the opportunities and experiences I've been able to be a part of during my time at Zappos. I love being able to walk up and down the halls each day and say hi to people that have honestly changed my life for the better. I feel so lucky that I am encouraged that the company I work for continues to help me grow and learn in both my personal and professional life. It is such an amazing feeling to wake up every morning and feel excited to head into work, and not to feel like I'm headed into a mindless job where I don't make a difference and where my opinions, thoughts and feeling won't matter. I can honestly say that I love Zappos and am proud to call myself a Zapponian!

RACHAEL B.
employee since 2005

Our culture to me:
Coming in to work every day, being myself –
usually in flip-flops & hoodies :)

Throwing out ideas with people & always
finding ways to make the 'impossible', possible
Being truly supported like a family member &
having the opportunity to do the same with others

Always looking for new ways to be inspired &
helping others be inspired Being passionate
about what I do & having the opportunity to be
surrounded by passionate people & ideas

Our culture to me = Happiness

RACHEL R.
employee since 2007

If Zappos were a pair of pants, it would be jeans.
Everybody knows that jeans are infinitely better
than slacks.

RAN G.
employee since 2009

The Zappos Culture means fun and excitement. I
am really grateful to be part of the Zappos family. I
definitely wouldn't be this happy anywhere else.

RAVINDRA A.
employee since 2011

The Zappos Culture truly has changed me in many
ways and made me better at what I do. I'm really
fortunate to work at a place where I learn every
day from everyone around me.

ROBIN C.
employee since 2007

I would like to say that at Zappos. you are never
bored. Not only do you interact with amazing
people during the day, but during your free time,
there are always coworkers to hang out with. So
many of my coworkers have become friends I will
have for a lifetime. There is a kinship amongst
Zappos employees that is very difficult to find at
other companies, and I am truly grateful for it.

RON C.
employee since 2011

Having just finished my first full year at Zappos, I
am still in semi-disbelief at how great this place is
to work for. I have never worked with more people
that I enjoyed being around so much. Such a great
environment for work, as well. I love what I do and
the people I work with.

RONN S.
employee since 2011

I came to Zappos with the hope of finding some
place that I did not dread going to every day.
Luckily, I was not disappointed! I have only been at
Zappos for nine months. The time has flown by and
I feel privileged that I have had the opportunity
to work with everyone here. The people I've met
truly have changed the way I look at a lot of
things in life. I feel challenged constantly and have
continually learned, and seriously cannot believe it
has been almost a full year!

ROOT.
employee since 2012

I love my job. Zappos is an amazing company to
work for. The culture is so cool that sometimes it
feels unreal, like a story. I have seen some of the
craziest things here! Everyone is really helpful. I am
so thankful to be here.

ROSANNA V.
employee since 2007

I'm going into my fifth year at Zappos and we still
hold the values that have reinforced our bond, not
only as coworkers, but as family and friends. As
days go by, I'm grateful to be part of such a great
company and because of that, I can contribute to
the culture as my way of saying thanks.

ROWELL M.
employee since 2011

The Zappos Culture means to do your best, have
fun, work hard and play harder.

RYAN R.
employee since 2010

Culture means so many different things in so
many different ways that it's hard to pinpoint
exactly what makes the Zappos Culture such an
amazing thing. It's a friend to share the good times
with, as well as a friend to lean on in bad times;
it's the drive to chase and achieve your dreams;
it's diversity on a grand scale; it's a tight-knit
community; it's a passion that continually grows.
But most of all, it's people. Without the friendly,
diverse and passionate people we would not have
the Zappos Culture.

SANDRA H.
employee since 2008

I love that I love coming to work ... nuff said! :D

SCOTT I.
employee since 2011

I have been working at Zappos for about eight months now and I think it has been the fastest eight months of my life! I never truly enjoyed coming to work until I started working at Zappos. The people who work here are some of the nicest people I have ever met. Everyone is super-friendly and I actually enjoy spending time with my coworkers. Also, everyone is always willing to help you with something if you need it. I feel as if I may have learned more since I started here than I did in five years at my previous job. It's really nice to not only have fun at work, but also feel like you have accomplished something at the end of the day. For the first time in my life, I truly love my job!

SCOTT S.
employee since 2008

The family culture at the Zappos is a truly unique phenomenon. It is a living, breathing organism that you feel the moment you walk in through the front doors. It allows you to be the person you want to be and facilitates the free flow of ideas that transcend departments. I am proud to be part of a company that supports employees and creates an environment that promotes the best in all of us.

SHANNON R.
employee since 2007

Our people are our culture. We come to Zappos based on our expression of the Ten Core Values. It is how we displayed those core values during the interview process that gave us each the opportunity to work and play in the land of Zappos. Because we were provided this amazing opportunity, it is up to each of us to protect, preserve, and promote our culture. We should never take the great things that come our way for granted because they are a direct result of everyone's daily efforts to create the best place to work ever. I am indeed thankful for the chance to help the company to grow and prosper, for the chance to meet and make lifelong friends, for the chance to display my one true self, for the chance to assist others in their growth and development, and for the chance to bring happiness into my life and the lives of others. Thank you, Zappos!

SHAWNA M.
employee since 2010

Another entry? I cannot believe another year went by so quickly! You know what they say, time flies when you're having fun!? This past year was definitely a challenge, but I know that my Zappos family is always up for a challenge. No matter what obstacles we had to go through this year, we ALWAYS pulled through together. A lot of companies may look at the hurdles we had as something bad, but leave it to Zappos to accept it and make it into something great that unites the company and brings us all together for one common cause. The Zappos Culture means so much to me that I cannot really put it into words. The world is filled with so much negativity, but when I am here with everyone, I feel that we can push all that aside and just keep moving forward with a smile.

SIDDHARTH P.
employee since 2010

The Zappos Culture means having the liberty to be myself, having amazing opportunities, and working with bright, crazy and passionate people!! I think every person works best when he is happy and enjoying the work that he is given, and no other company understands this better than Zappos!!!!

STEPHANIE H.
employee since 2010

The Zappos Culture means coming to work and being yourself. It means not being afraid of making mistakes, because with risk comes the biggest reward. The Zappos Culture means growing and progressing, and finding passion for things you never even knew you could do. Working at Zappos creates a shift in perspective that will last a lifetime. I am so grateful to work here ... so much so that I could never express it in words. Thank you, Zappos!

STEVIE B.
employee since 2010

The Zappos Culture is like a fellow employee ... it's is there to support you, grow with you, learn from and be taught by. It may sometimes be vague, yet has a deeper meaning. It helps you meet others and make new friends. It challenges you and is with you wherever you go!!!

Our culture is like no other and it is what keeps me excited to come in every day. I have met a ton of great people since I started here and have seen them do great things along the way. Even today, I see new employees able to contribute because no matter how large the company grows, the ability of the culture to grow with us is in the hands of each person, all of us at the same time!!!

P.S.: Shanadoo – I bet we will have had many more "ohhhh Sh$#*(@" moments from the time I write this till the time you read this. Maritza – I really do love your fanny-pack. And Kathleen – I forgive you for killing my monkey. :) And to any new additions to the department, I'll get you next year!!!

Love you all,

SUSI P.
employee since 2007

The Zappos Culture is like no other. I have been here almost five years and I have grown and changed so much along with the company. The one thing that remains the same is the fun we have when we are all together! Go, Zappos!

TARA J.
employee since 2010

The Zappos Culture here means many different things to me, but now the one word that comes to mind is family. I recently had a baby and during my entire pregnancy, I had so much support from my Zappos family. Every day I had a new, clever, pregnancy-related sign on my computer monitor, which was so fun! My department threw me a huge baby shower, giving me enough wipes that I still haven't had to purchase any, even now, when my baby is four months old! And the love continued after the birth of my baby – flowers, gift baskets and more presents arrived. People got together to make and deliver meals to our house so that we didn't have to worry about food for the first few weeks. My husband and I were blown away by the months of love and support we got from my Zappos family.

TAYLOR S.
employee since 2012

Roses are Red
Violets are Blue
Sugar is Sweet
And Zappos is Too.

TEAM DERRICK
employee since 2011

Zappos creates a great family atmosphere without the little brother that you want to kill at times. Shout out to my family Kachow!!!

TIFFANY L.
employee since 2011

The most intriguing thing about the Zappos Culture, to me, is that it has taught me so much about myself – things I never knew. Joining the Zappos family was like opening a new chapter in my life that brought positive things as well as challenging moments. I am so proud to be part a family that gives the saying "home away from home" true meaning. There are no words to describe the feeling of being able to laugh, cry, learn, fail, and grow with the same group of people by your side. Zappos, you rock my world!

TIFFANY T.
employee since 2011

In a world ...
Where miniature tubs drag race in the parking lot,
And fire-breathing dragons forge through offices,
Where people from all walks of life from different departments join together to create music from their hearts,
And friendly ping-pong battles challenge the core of one's determination,
Lies a family of brave individuals, boasting talents strong and unique to rise up to the challenge of protecting their company's values,
All while remaining open to the infinite possibilities of its ever-changing nature,
This world is unheard of.
This world is Zappos.

TIM G.
employee since 2012

Double culture shock! I was lucky enough to have been hired by Zappos from across the globe (Sydney, Australia) and had my first exposure to living in a new country (VEGAS, baby!) and working for Zappos.

WoW! I have never worked in such a charged environment, with so many passionate people. I have only been working here a month and I find the positive atmosphere here contagious ... work is no longer a chore, but something I actually look forward to and I have found this attitude spilling over into my personal life.

What is the best part about Zappos? For me the answer is simple: The people! It is amazing how they take the time to form personal connections and are genuinely interested in what you have to say. I have always been made to feel welcome ... even if they do make fun of my accent. :)

TIM K.
employee since 2008

I feel so lucky to get to come to Zappos every day and to work with some of my closest friends. So happy to be on my fourth year at here at Zappos!

TISHA D.
employee since 2006

Six years later, I have been thinking a lot about what Zappos Culture means to me! Some things that came to mind are the fact that I work with amazing people in a place where there is the set of shared attitudes, values, goals, and practices that characterizes Zappos! The Zappos Culture, undoubtedly, has had a significant effect on Zappos' success, and mine as well! Culture is Johnny P!!!

TRAVIS M.
employee since 2011

If my firstborn, Felix (established 2012!), grows up to get to work in a fulfilling environment that possesses the cerebral bandwidth and richness-in-culture that Zappos does, it would be superlative.

TYLER W.
employee since 2011

The best way to describe the Zappos Culture is ... my wife gets to drop me off at an adult daycare where I get paid to play with my friends! I know it sounds crazy, but every day, I am challenged to accomplish something new, and every day, work is an adventure. Love my job.

VANESSA L.
employee since 2007

Six years and I still love every day, every laugh, every new experience, every moment I'm grateful for this place. I'd like to express my feelings for Zappos through the power of song. Zappos ... You are the wind beneath my wings. You raise me up, to more than I can be. At Zappos, I believe I can fly ... I believe I can touch the sky. Oops, I did it again. Now I had the time of my life, no I never felt like this before, Yes I swear, it's the truth and I owe it all to you. 'Cause I had the time of my life ... MmmBop.

VICTORIA B.
employee since 2007

"One way or another, everyone goes down the aisle with half the story hidden."
—Dowager Countess Grantham

VINCENT C.
employee since 2010

The Zappos Culture is about positivity, respect, honesty, supporting one another and succeeding as a team. It's about rediscovering yourself through others and through your work, as well as maintaining your own individuality. It's not about being the best at what you do, but being the best of who you are.

VINCENT V.
employee since 2010

Zappos Culture is where boy meets girl, east meets west, north meets south, Europe meets America, interpunction does not necessarily meet Culture Book submission, customer meets CLT team member, food meets eater, pizza grotto meets red robin, yum bacon meets filet mignon, and last but not least, red velvet bundt cake meets whipped cream.

WARREN C.
employee since 2012

The Zappos Culture promotes unity in the workplace and a sense of family. It means looking out for one another and making everyone feel welcome. As a new hire (less than two weeks, as of this posting) I really appreciated this sense of belonging from day one. I'm glad to have found a place here.

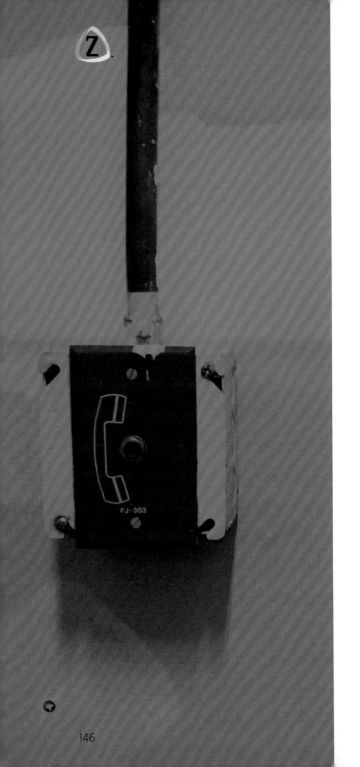

WILL B.

employee since 2009

The Zappos Culture is like the Force. Nobody can really explain why it works or how it works, but it can move X-Wings if need be.

WILLIAM A.

employee since 2008

Hi! Well, it has been four years and it's still a great job to have. A lot of people here are great to be around. It makes you want to come in and give your best. Zappos is a great place to work. Well, time to get back to work.

WILLIAM N.

employee since 2010

62 65 20 73 75 72 65 20 74 6f 20 64 72 69 6e 6b 20 79 6f 75 72 20 6f 76 61 6c 74 69 6e 65

ZACHARY Z.

employee since 2008

The person you are trying to reach is currently off saving the Milky Way Galaxy, somewhere in the Horsehead Nebula doing battle with a horde of intergalactic pirates. Please try again once galactic peace has been restored.

http://www.youtube.com/watch?v=QH2-TGUlwu4

ZACK D.

employee since 2006

WOW! Six years and still going ... Zappos and Zack are a match made in heaven. I am so grateful to be affiliated with such greatness. Everything in the course of my day is refreshing here at Zappos, from my relationships with our guests to public relations. I love it all ...

GETTIN' GONZO

IN-HOUSE CULTURE VIDEOGRAPHER

ANGEL L. 卢小君

employee since 2011

I have been a part of Zappos for almost half a year. It was strange at first, and then it became familiar, and finally, I became skilled. Everything goes smoothly. I can feel the passion of my dear partners and their enthusiasm affects me deeply. We help one another, whether we are at work or getting on with our daily lives. A great many funny stories happen after work.   "Create Fun and a Little Weirdness" Is one of the Ten Core Values that I think distinguishes us from other companies. This combination is a new concept for me; it also reflects the difference of our company. I can feel the happiness and passion in this big family. Cultural values are the embodiment of a company, and employees feel this influence silently. Our Ten Core Values are the essence of our company. I believe that under the guidance of the values, we will grow better and stronger in the future.

在Zappos已经快3年了，现在我对文化的理解已经跟上次一些文化书时的理解不一样了，不需要过多的言语来表达，我也没有那么多的词汇量。对于我来说，现在文化更像是一种习惯，例如每天要吃饭要睡觉一样，它在身体里面已经形成一种化学反应，食物和睡眠提供给你身体精力和能量，而文化能给你的精神产物，保证你每天激情四射、无限的搞怪、和善的对待你身边的每一个人等等，它就像食物一样，出口入，再进到胃和心、肝、脾、肺、肾里，最后深入到你的骨髓里。

AMY Y. 俞惠

employee since 2010

I love the Zappos Culture; that's why I stay here! I remember that our CEO said, "Money is not the only thing that we pursue." It's true. I think the value of our culture is to help us make progress.

ANN 马蕴文

employee since 2011

This is the first job I got after I graduated from university, and I will have been here one year this December. Here at Zappos, I have a really good time with my colleagues. I've learnt a lot, not only from the people I'm working with, but also from our Ten Core Values. You guys are sooooooo great! Zappos ROCKS!!

ANNA 赵一诺

employee since 2011

Being part of Zappos is my destiny. Anyway, it is true that I've chosen this way. More importantly, I have never regretted my decision. Everything demonstrates that I am right. This place touches me every moment of my life; we are partners as well as friends. Maybe we will be lifelong friends. We may even become lovers, get married and give birth to babies in the future. This is a big stage that allows everyone to share himself with all of us, no matter where we are from, no matter if we are ladies or gentlemen. I love the way we create fun; I have found that I can't live without daily humor. Actually, the Ten Core Values bring me a sea of things. In macrocosm, they give us the guidance in pursuit of success! I suppose that I'm trying to catch up with time, even though I know it goes fast. Everything I've done has been in pursuit of just one thing: Cherishing every minute with Zappos, cherishing every second with you! To be continued...

AVRIL H. 洪佳

employee since 2012

As mind is to body, so culture is to a company. If I were to describe the Zappos Culture in one word, that word would definitely be "WOW," I have been at Zappos for over four months now, but I feel as if I've been involved here for a much longer time and quite well. Zappos first Core Value is "Deliver WOW through service." I feel this value deeply. It WOWs me not only at work, but in my attitude to life. Zappos Ten Core Values have carried over into my personal life, which is something that I don't think it will happen at other companies. I like Zappos because it brings us a positive outlook on life. Meanwhile, I indeed appreciate our colleagues for being so kind, creative and energetic. We work passionately and live with enjoyment. I want to say how awesome you guys are. I love you, Zappos, and our big family. ^_^

ADA Y. 杨先仙

employee since 2011

On December 21, 2011, I became a Zapponian. I worried before coming here and almost gave up the chance, but finally, I decided to have a try. My first impression of the company was that it is young, enthusiastic and passionate. The so-called youth doesn't only stand for the ages of our colleagues; it also indicates that you can feel the taste of youth here. Enthusiasm is here no matter where you go; you see the kind smile of colleagues and warm greetings. The passion _ we are still young, so we need passion, not just enthusiasm. When I first started here, I asked myself what makes the people here so happy in their work and daily life. Now I know that it is because of the culture. I can feel the charm of culture here. Culture is our common goal. Our ultimate goal is the same, even if we pursue it in different ways. This is the reason why we love it here.

2011年12月21日我走进Zappos。在来Zappos之前，我有过很多顾虑，也差一点就放弃了这次机会，但是我还是抱着来试试看的心态。
它给我的第一印象是年轻，热情并充满激情。年轻不仅是指员工很年轻，还代表着这里洋溢着青春的味道；热情是无论你走到哪里，都会看到同事们亲切的笑容，和热情的问候。激情，我们都还年轻我们需要的不仅是热情还需要激情。当时我在想是什么让他们如此的快乐的工作和生活。现在我知道了，是文化，在Zappos，我深深的感受到文化的魅力，文化是我们共同的目标，也许方法各不相同，但是我们最终的目标是一样的，这就是我们聚在这里并热爱这里的原因。

ALICE L. 李彬

employee since 2011

I have been with Zappos for about half a year now. This is my first job and I like it very much. The working environment here makes me so relaxed; I feel fulfilled every day.

One of my favorite of the Core Values is "Create Fun and a Little Weirdness." Happiness is very important in our daily life. There is no doubt that I enjoy working here very much. As for "Instill happiness into the core of your company's business model," I think our company really has done a good job!

BELLA X. 徐园园

employee since 2011

Zappos makes me realize that an enterprise can also have family spirit. I feel the warmth of family here at Zappos. In the beginning I couldn't do anything; everyone was so kind, and so willing to help me and teach me a lot. Soon, I could do my job well. Now I've been here for half a year. Each day is a harvest and I am very happy! I really love Zappos!

BEGONIA L. 李莉

employee since 2011

I think the greatness of our company lies in the fact that we view service as our first priority, not only between the company and our customers, but also among our colleagues. Secondly, we experience freedom here. We are free of restraints, which helps us accomplish our tasks in a more comfortable way. Another great advantage of our company is that it is people-oriented.

CHLOE Z. 赵露

employee since 2012

Hello, everyone, my name is Chloe Zhao -赵露. I'm in the Images Processing team, and I'm very happy to be here. I joined Zappos in February 2012. The Ten Core Values have left a deep impression on me. First, I think the most important value is the seventh one _ "Build a Positive Team and Family Spirit." Our team gets together at work, and when someone has problems, we try our best to help them as much as possible. This makes the environment around us very relaxing, and I like it. Sometimes we are busy with projects and we unite to finish them.

Of course, the other values are also important to me. I think they are the soul of the company. They help us know what we can do and what we should do. We do our best at work to "Deliver WOW through service," and after work, we take part in many activities, continuing to put the values into practice. We also have an English corner where we speak in English, play games and laugh. We are so happy here, and we enjoy the happiness that our colleagues bring us. I enjoy the Zappos family, and I'm very happy to be part of the family.

COCO C. 陈珊

employee since 2012

Being a member of the Zappos community was my first choice after stepping into social life. I couldn't help believing that we are a family _ a big and great family with the same values and the same goals. What impressed me most was the first Core Value: "Deliver WOW Through Service." WOW is at the heart of our good service. And it comes from our customers naturally, from their hearts. That is the most important thing in our enterprise. More WOW means we will have more returning customers, and it makes us more successful! Hurray!

成为Zappos的一员是我进入社会生活后做的第一个最正确的选择。我不得不相信我们就是一家人，是一个有着同样的价值观跟同样的目标的大家庭。我们Zappos十条核心价值观中使我印象最深的是第一条"通过服务传递WOW。"WOW即是肯定我们优质服务的最好表达。并且WOW是来自我们顾客自己内心的感受，是自然而然表露出来的一种满足。赢得顾客的满意是我们事业上的最重要的东西。更多的WOW，意味着更多的回头客，然后意味着更多的成功。万岁！

CARL Z. 钟鹤年

employee since 2010

Zappos has been a positive experience for me. Thanks, all you nice guys! I learned a lot here and one of those things is that it is okay to be myself, even though it feels difficult at times. Also, I met a girl here at Zappos, who is so unique too! I am a lucky boy to be here. J

DAISY Z. 赵琼林

employee since 2011

It has been more than half a year since I came to Zappos China Office. All my colleagues are so enthusiastic and generous. We are very involved in culture activities. We never mind making mistakes when dealing with projects. All of these derive from our distinguished corporate culture.

The Ten Core Values guide us to be happy in both our work and daily life.

我来Zappos已经半年了。在这里，所有同事们热情大方。举办文化活动时，我們积极主动；學習项目时，大胆尝试不怕犯错。这些都源于公司文化的与众不同。这些文化带领我们在快乐中工作，生活。

DIRK Y. 杨志成

employee since 2012

I'm so happy to work at Zappos. It's just like a big family. We work together, live together, and the most important thing is that we are happy. I am a new member of Zappos. When I first came here, there were so many things I didn't know how to do, but my teammates were so nice to me; they taught me with so much patience and I have learned a lot. Thank you so much, I love you all.

ECHO W. 吴晨亮

employee since 2011

For me, the Zappos Culture is a manual for my present and future well-being. I love the Ten Core Values because they guide me and put me on the right path to achieve my dream. Simply put, I am truly humbled to be part of Zappos.

The Zappos Culture is different from others for many reasons. One reason for its uniqueness is its emphasis on personal growth and happiness. Zappos does not only pay attention to corporate growth, but also to each individual's career progress. Another reason for its uniqueness is the autonomy it gives employees. Zapponians here have a sense of ownership of Zappos and each of us can be leaders in many fields within the company.

The Core Value I respect the most is "Embrace and Drive Change," because I think it will have a far-reaching impact in my lifetime. After blending into the workplace here, I realize change is the norm. It is fabulous to change myself and even motivate my team to embrace and drive change. Every moment here is another chance for me to change and reinvent myself!

EVA L. 黎玲

employee since 2010

My journey with Zappos is full of happiness and joy. This journey has lasted two years, and I always keep in mind that the Zappos Culture means you can be who you want to be. Indeed, it is true. We are encouraged to learn, to grow, to step up and to be leaders. I am nearly at a loss for words to describe what I have learned during these two years, there is too much to say É I know I am growing professionally. To me, the Zappos Culture is a part of my life. Zappos always makes me become more passionate and determined. It also teaches me about teamwork and leadership. I would like to learn more and more, and I am sure my experience at Zappos will be a priceless treasure in my future, both in my personal life and in my career.

一路走来，与Zappos相伴的每一天都是开心而快乐的。转眼在这里两年，我始终觉得Zappos的文化就是让你成为你想要变成的样子……真的，事实就是如此。它鼓励我们学习，成长，进取并成为领导。如果想要用什么语言来描述我在Zappos学习的一切，真的是太多了……但是有一件事情是非常明确的，那就是我真的成长了。对于我而言，Zappos文化已经成为生活的一部分。它让我越来越有激情，越来越坚定。同时，在团队合作和领导力方面，它教会了我很多。我愿意在这里学习更多，而且我相信无论是生活还是职业生涯方面，在Zappos的这段经历一定会成为一笔无价的财富。

FRANK Y. 袁宏阳

employee since 2011

I'm really lucky to be part of Zappos! I think it is the best company _ one that can make all employees feel happy every second! At Zappos, we are not only colleagues, we are also close friends. People here respect and help one another. We share happiness and sorrows when living together. That's because we treat each person as family member. I love our company! Believe it or not, you can't help loving here!!

真的非常幸运加入Zappos！我认为没有一间公司能像Zappos这样让所有人每一秒都能感受到幸福！在Zappos，我们不仅是同事，更是朋友。我们互相尊重，互相帮助。在工作中我们会分享有用的信息，在生活中我们会分享所有开心和不开心的事情。我爱我们的公司！不管你信不信，你会情不自禁地爱上这里的！

FENDY F. 冯怡婷

employee since 2011

Zappos, I love you! In this big, warm family, everyone helps, befriends and learns from one another, and practices the corporate culture together! Zappos provides a relaxing and pleasant work environment in which we can talk, joke, create some weirdness, and join in various interesting activities. I'm very lucky that I joined the Zappos family.

Zappos，我爱你！在这个充满温暖的大家庭里，大家相互帮助，友好交往，积极学习，共同实践公司的文化！在这里，我们并不是单单只为了工作，工作之余，我们可以相互交流，说说笑笑，搞搞怪，参加各种有趣的活动，让每位同事在工作上都能够轻松，愉快的度过！所以说，能够加入Zappos这个大家庭是多么幸运的事！

FORREST W. 王源

employee since 2012

I've been with Zappos for more than three months. As a newbie, I'm glad I got an opportunity to work at Zappos. It is an awesome place for me to work and study. I learn a lot here. I not only grasp how to deal with our work projects, I learn how to better handle interpersonal relationships. Just be open and sincere with others. Be honest and humble in communicating with others. Try to respect different points of view. Then you will find this is a wonderful place, full of happy and positive family spirit. Indeed, all the Zapponians experience it.

GRACE G. 郭华玉

employee since 2009

Hello! I am Grace. I have worked here for more than three years. In this big family, every day is bright and alive; our office is full of laugher at every moment. I love Zappos. The atmosphere here is very good, and everyone is very friendly. Zappos is very different from other companies, so we always feel free to talk about everything here. That's really wonderful and amazing! Let's work together. After work, I like to play table tennis and surf the Internet. So do you like doing sports? It can make us healthy, ha-ha. If possible, you can follow me, and it must be fun and exciting! I hope you guys can be happy and I expect you to come soon. You know, China is a pretty country; her beauty is waiting for you all to come and experience. Thank you!

IVY L. 李娟
employee since 2011

It's very lucky that I'm a member of the Zappos family. The key reason why the Zappos Culture dwarfs others lies in that fact that each member of the Zappos family recognizes and practices the Ten Core Values. Zappos strength also comes from its innovation, flexibility, and the fact that it always puts people first. Our young CEO put the Ten Core Values forward to lead Zappos on the road to growth. Despite the twists and turns, Zappos will eventually achieve remarkable results and the recognition of customers will demonstrate the success brought about by insisting on those Core Values.

能够处在Zappos这个团队工作，正是因为我们这个团队里的每一位同事都十分认同并一直在实践我们的十条核心文化价值观，同时，我认为我们的文化之所以相比起其他公司有所独特，也是因着积极、创新、灵活并且更具人性化。这十条核心价值观也是我们年轻的CEO提倡，作为核心企业文化一路带领着Zappos的成长，而Zappos一路走来尽管过程中也摔倒过跟头，但最终所取得的成绩以及客户对我们的认可也同时证明了我们一直坚持的文化为我们带来的成功.

JADE L. 林洁敏
employee since 2012

Peace, love, unity and respect are qualities I want in my whole life. They are things that humanize people, make you understand who you are, what you can do, and what amazing things human beings are capable of doing. Working for Zappos, our culture and the Ten Core Values has really given me a fresh idea about the meaning of work and life. This is my first job, and I am glad to find that it is where I am encouraged to be myself. It is a place that creates your thinking and helps you seek happiness.

JANE H. 黄健雯
employee since 2009

I have been working for Zappos China Office for nearly three years. I have enjoyed this time because more and more colleagues love our culture and join in this big family. It's a pity that some colleagues left after spending some time with us. No matter what happiness or sadness I experience, I learn something here; our goal is not only to increase our professional skills, but also to improve our management ability.

6月，我在这工作将近3年了。在这段时间里有高兴的事—更多因喜欢文化而加入的家人，失落的事是相处过后他们的离开……不管是开心还是伤心，在这我学到东西—在社会上工作，如果只有职业技能的提升是不够的，还需要提升自身的管理能力。

JEFF L. 刘家昌
employee since 2009

I have been with Zappos for almost three years now, and I have gained a different understanding of our culture since the last time we wrote in our Culture Book, Now it's not necessary to use so many words to express my thoughts; after all, I don't have the necessary vocabulary. Now culture for me is more like a habit, just as we have to eat and sleep. The Zappos Culture has created a chemical reaction in our bodies, not unlike the way that food and sleep provide us with vigor and energy. Our culture can build our spirit, which can guarantee our emerging passion _ both infinite and wacky _ and make us nice to those around us, and so on. Our culture is not unlike the food we eat that passes through our mouth, and then enters our stomach, spreading life to our heart, liver, spleen, lungs and kidney, and finally penetrates our bone marrow to help us grow.

在Zappos已经快3年了，现在我对文化的理解已经跟上次一些文化书时的理解不一样了，不需要过多的言语来表达，我也没有那么多的词汇量。对于我来说，现在文化更像是一种习惯，例如每天要吃饭要睡觉一样，它在身体里面已经形成一种化学反应，食物和睡眠提供给你身体精力和能量，而文化能给你的精神产物，保证你每天激情四射、无限的搞怪、和善的对待你身边的每一个人等等，它就像食物一样，出口入，再进到胃和心、肝、脾、肺、肾里，最后深入到你的骨髓里。

JESSICA L. 廖丽芳
employee since 2009

I have been with Zappos for two and a half years; I still remember how I advanced from an ordinary team member to a team leader and then a project manager. Each small step created all my opportunities and advancements awarded by Zappos, as well as the mission given by Zappos. I feel quite proud and satisfied, because of the team I lead and our many projects. We have won lots of WOW. It is really the happiness what Zappos delivers to every individual person. Personally, the happiest thing for me was getting married a few weeks ago!!!!! I greatly enjoyed having this event take place while I was part of Zappos. The most miraculous thing is that my husband is also a member of Zappos. And now we are building a small, lovely family within this big Zappos family. Here I would like to share another miraculous thing: I am three months pregnant!!!!!! I guess every mother has the same feeling _ nervous but excited. After my baby is born, I will tell him what the Ten Core Values of Zappos are and let him keep them in his mind. I always believe that, in Zappos, happiness will surround us.

JOZIE W. 王昭
employee since 2011

Time does fly at Zappos. I have already spent almost 190 days here in Zappos China Office. I have always longed for a job that is enjoyable and delivers a sense of belonging. And then I found Zappos. With all my lovely teammates, I have fun and I experience joy. I find the Ten Core Values are guiding me to a better self. Our China Office delivers WOW to us all the time. We are setting records every day. A variety of activities take place all the time. With the coming of our American friends, we have thrown several wonderful, fabulous, and unforgettable Culture Nights. The luckiest thing is that I can be part of Zappos, like being a hostess for the Culture Night and even getting the chance to plan it. With the help of our American friends, we are becoming a better office. This big family is becoming a bigger and stronger one with every effort we make. I am so jubilant that I can be one point of Zappos timeline. I love all of you! Vive la Zappos!

JULIA H. 黄荣
employee since 2011

Nearly eight months have passed since I started working at Zappos China Office. I feel great about our company culture, which is really worth cherishing. In my opinion, the key Core Value of our culture lies in its people orientation, both from the perspective of our customers and our fellow employees. We try our best to deliver WOW to both our customers and employees through service. Zappos differs from other companies that pay more attention to the business than the culture; we put a lot of emphasis on culture. When we started to work here, the first thing we needed to learn was to accept the cultural training, which is an integral part of our work. Actually, each Core Value is equally important, although I like the seventh value best, "Build a Positive Team and Family Spirit." This helps you feel love and build a bridge between the managers and the staff, the senior employees and new hands. From the perspective of work and life, our team spirit stands out and plays an extremely important role. Each department of our company is closely knit. We don't have boundaries between departments. This helps each department accomplish its work in cooperation with the others. We are all, hand in hand, embracing our brighter future.

JUSTIN Z. 张秋茂
employee since 2012

I think our Zappos Culture makes us more loyal to the company, so that we feel like we are at home. This can help the company retain staff, and it can also make us work together more harmoniously. My favorite of the Ten Core Values is #5, "Pursue Growth and Learning."

KARRY C. 陈晓清

employee since 2011

I have been working in Zappos China Office for more than eight months. This is my first job, and it was lucky that I was able to pass the interview successfully. Thanks, Zappos, for giving me this chance.

I love Zappos Ten Core Values. The Zappos Culture has brought us happiness and freedom. After practicing our Core Values, all colleagues here live as friends and family members. We truly care about each other. In Zappos China Office, I have learnt a lot, not only at work, but in life as well. (For example, at work, I have been becoming more professional and learning to excel, which I had no idea about before. In my daily life, I have learnt how to communicate with others and my Mandarin has improved. (I speak Cantonese.) Zappos has also given me a big stage to develop my talents. I have participated in many cultural activities. I have danced with colleagues and gone to Karaoke in my spare time. I really enjoy working and living here, and hope the company can become better and better.

我在Zappos工作已经8个月了，这是我的第一份工作，我很幸运，能够顺利的通过面试。我很感谢Zappos给了我一个工作的机会。
我很喜欢Zappos十条核心价值：Zappos 文化给我们带来欢乐，自由的空间，带来了同事像家人，朋友之间的互相关心，帮助。在Zappos 学到了很多知识，不仅是工作上的，还有生活上的。（比如：在工作上我学到了更专业，对excel表格越来越熟悉，越来越了解。生活上学会了沟通，普通话也有所提高）Zappos给了我一个展现自我的一个舞台，我积极参加了公司的文化活动，跟同事们一起学习舞蹈，休闲时跟同事们一起去唱k。在Zappos我很快乐，很开心。希望Zappos越来越好。

JERRY L. 罗威

employee since 2012

Hello all, I'm Jerry. After three weeks of working at Zappos, I am coming to understand our firm's culture better and better. In the beginning, I was just attracted by Zappos material things, and I knew our firm's culture just as words on paper. Obviously, it's superficial and not deep. But after these three weeks, I can say to everyone proudly that it's my honor to join Zappos, a company that is full of joy, team spirit, and family spirit, which caught my attention in the beginning. I cannot forget the help given by Abbie, Melody, Amy, Krisy and Andy (among others). Without their help, I don't think I could have adapted to my new circumstances so fast. Work hard and help others with all our ability; send "WOW" to our customers through our service.

KEVIN F. 丰凯

employee since 2010

I have been asked many times, why do you want to work in Zappos China Office? Many words occur to me: CULTURE, FAMILY SPIRT, PASSION, HUMBLE, GROWTH, and so on. The most important thing I think is that I really enjoy the life here! We have our unique Ten Core Values, and no doubt we cherish them. Everyone in the office is willing to practice, and even extends them. We also have our 11th Core Value here: a bear hug. We want to deliver our happiness to everyone! Welcome to the China Office!!! J

KRISY W. 吴洪

employee since 2010

Hello guys, I am Krisy, the leader of China CLT. I am very proud of our team members. We are all positive and passionate, "Wohooo," and we like creating fun in our daily life. We think that we can only do our tasks well by maintaining a good attitude. How do you think of it? As for me, I like eating, sleeping, watching TV, singing and so on É but I am getting fat now!!! I don't want to be fat, so I must control myself to avoid eating too much! Aha! Welcome to China, my dear friends!

LINA L. 林俏萍

employee since 2011

I graduated in 2011 and then got my first job at Zappos. I never thought my first job would be like this, but it was not bad. Thanks, Zappos, for accepting me as a fresh worker and providing me with an opportunity to learn and grow. All in all, in 2011 I really enjoyed a happy life at home and at work for Zappos. Thanks to all the people I met at Zappos. They rock! They are patient, helpful and optimistic. I love Zappos and our Zappos Culture.

LISA Z. 张聪利

employee since 2012

I have been working for Zappos for just over four months. What drew me to the company was the chance to gain a deeper understanding of its culture. Initially, I chose to join this big family because I appreciated that culture. Now, the reason for me to continue to work at Zappos is my love of the Zappos Culture. We all are trying our best to create a big family and create a little fun for others; we have a common goal to pursue growth and learning. The culture is not intended as a system of constraints for employees. Rather, it is our common mission; we all want to be, first and foremost, Zapponians, so we have this special company's culture. Each of the Core Values is the crystallization of wisdom. I love the happiest call center in the world!

MELODY W. 王重阳

employee since 2011

I have been working here for nearly six months and I have learned lots of things. I not only learned how to deal with relationships, but also what I should do when I am at work. In this family, everyone is so simple, so warm and friendly. I can feel the warmth of home here. During this time, I have made people worthy of becoming long-term friends. My temper changed a lot, although sometimes I am still a little irritable. As a new graduate, I feel time flies and I have been improving step by step here. I believe I can have many precious memories here. Looking forward...

MICHELLE J. 纪昀轩

employee since 2011

Frist of all, I would like to give a big WOW to my colleagues, as they keep serving their best and treating others with hospitality and kindness. It is said that one's first job after graduating from college is very important. I'm glad that I made a right choice by working here. I enjoy working here because it's just like a big family; we work and live together. Our days are full of joy and fun, and some simple moments really touch me deeply.

来到这里，先是对这里同事的服务感到Wow，然后是对他们的热情感到Wow。都说进入社会的第一份工作是很重要的，我觉得来这里是一个正确的选择。在这里工作很轻松很快乐，这里就像是我们的另一个家，大家就像是一家人一样在一起工作，生活，每天都有欢乐，每天都有感动。

MICKEY W. 王钢

employee since 2012

As a new graduate from college, I feel happy to have joined the Zappos family. Right now, we are just working in a small town, compared to those who work in some megacities like Beijing, Shanghai or Shenzhen. We just have an ordinary salary, compared to those who work in banks or IT companies. These are not things I should envy, because one day I can have these through my hard work. I also have a precious thing that they do not have _ the family spirit at Zappos. That is why I came here and what I cherish.

MIYA W. 翁艺瑜

employee since 2009

Each company has its own unique corporate culture, which is the essential core and power source of the company. Compared with other companies, it is Zappos Ten Core Values that distinguish it, and makes it a superstar of online shoe selling. What has impressed me most is the openness and creativity demonstrated by the Zappos Culture. Here, we attach importance to building a pleasant, relaxing work environment in which each person can be a little weird and our family spirit takes shape. What's more, our services always "WOW" our target customers. All of the above elements contribute to the constant growth and development of Zappos.

每家企业都有自己独特的文化所在，它是核心，也可以是力量的源泉。而我们Zappos的十条核心价值与别家企业的文化相比，也正是因着这些独特，而成为鞋业网上零售的巨头。另外，我更加喜欢的是Zappos文化的创新和包容，我们这里强调欢乐搞怪的氛围，塑造家庭精神，而更重要的是我们的团队服务WOW到了我们所服务的客户，这些作为我们文化里不可或缺的因素，使得Zappos一直以来都在不断得到成长和发展。

NANCY T. 谭思思

employee since 2010

I have been working in Zappos China Office for more than two years. To me, Zappos is my warm family. Whenever I encounter difficulties, Zappos always stands by me. I started my career here as an undergraduate and began my first romantic relationship. Then I got married and pregnant. I cherish this a lot; I share sorrows and joys with my friends here. It's the ride of my lifetime; my memory of this great family will never fade.
As the manager of the Pipeline team, I am both lucky and honored to witness the rapid growth of our China Office, from just one colleague to more than 70 colleagues. It's a challenge for us to recruit talented people who fit our culture. Our persistence in our culture will never change. We will never make any compromises in our Core Values. They are what draw us together. We will always follow our culture and we practice it in our daily lives all the time!

NICK Z. 翟子为

employee since 2011

The first day I came here, my manager told me a lot about the Zappos Culture, starting with the Ten Core Values. Zappos is so unique. I really love the environment here! Have you ever seen a company keeps you relaxed while you work? Have you ever become part of a group of nice people with whom you can enjoy working overtime to finish today's stuff together? Does your partner volunteer to help with your cases? I cannot say with certainty that this doesn't happen outside Zappos. But I don't think other companies put such emphasis on working together. I mean servlce.   Yes, the Ten Core Values are not just a decoration on the wall; I have all ten of them in my heart. And more important, they are part of my behavior. The seventh Core Value really impresses me. "Build a Positive Team and Family Spirit." At Zappos China we have a PS team, a PO team, a CLT team, a Mac team, a PPL team and an ACKI team. Why so many teams? It's a big family! Sometimes CLT needs to OT; PO or MAC would rather lend a hand than hang out. WHY? This is how I know these Core Values are not just empty words. And this is what the family spirit of Zappos is. This is Zappos China. How lucky I am to be one of you!

Zappos文化，来到呢度第一日就开始强调文化，10条核心价值可以话系第一必修课。

呢度同其他地方真系好唔同，唔讲其他，就系呢度工作环境就已经同其他地方天差地别。你有无见过一间公司上班系可以处于甘轻松既状态？有无一班人为左做好今日既工作一齐努力加班？有无可能你因为自己份内事搞唔掂又有同事主动过来帮手？我唔敢讲话其他公司呢D情况完全无，但系人地公司绝对唔会用呢个来作为自己既一个宗旨咯！

10条价值观已经系熟读熟背，当然10条文化价值唔系话挂系墙度日日叫人背就算，系真系有人做出来先有用，如果唔系既话就只不过系一张废纸，以我感受最深既一条来讲，建立积极的团队，塑造家庭精神。系Zappos，有好多分组，PS组，PO组，CLT组，分类组，但系我来到呢度之后，原来一个组完成唔到工作，要加班，好正常，但系真

正令我觉得10条文化价值唔系斋讲既就系当时其他组可以话只要系识做呢个项目既都会过来帮手，点解距地唔落班去玩？可以话因为大家都系因为有个精神系度，呢个就系家庭精神，呢个就系传说中既团队。可以系一个甘样既工作环境中工作，我好幸运！

RAIN Z. 钟荣勋

employee since 2010

Zappos is full of family atmosphere. It is the Zappos Culture that supports our progress and development all the time, and you will find this is what makes us different from other companies. The culture makes us want to do better and work harder, and we do so under relaxed working conditions. I love the culture here, that's why I love Zappos. I believe Zappos will become better and better in the future. I love Zappos.

Zappos是一家充满家庭气氛的公司，公司的文化就是推动进步和发展的不懈动力，和其它公司不同的是你会很快感受到这里的家庭气氛，文化的渲染使每个人都感觉到自己在进步。你可以很投入地去工作，非常轻松的工作环境。我喜欢公司文化的底蕴，所以喜欢ZAPPOS.看好ZAPPOS。我仅仅是喜爱ZAPPOS，没有吹捧ZAPPOS的意思。

RICHARD H. 谢传刚

employee since 2004

The Zappos China Office is where my heart belongs. Having built it from scratch with the help of so many people, I'm amazed with the explosive growth of the office in the last 12 months, not only in the number of employees, the floor space of the office and the employee dormitories, the facilities, etc., but also in its culture. Here, our version of the Zappos Culture builds on the Ten Core Values that every Zapponian is familiar with, blends in Chinese values and reflects the fact that all the employees work and live together 24/7. In a way, the Zappos China Office has become a family away from the family for all of its employees, who come from almost every corner of the country. To further strengthen the bonding among this passionate group of young men and women, I jokingly introduced "bear hugs" as the 11th Core Value of the office last year. I am surprised how well it's been received and practiced by everyone ever since, not just among our coworkers, but also towards all the visitors — especially those colleagues who came from the States! What a happy family! I'm definitively happy. :)

RIVER J. 江颖颖

employee since 2011

I was attracted by Zappos Ten Core Values when I saw them for the first time! Great! Genius cultural values! And they are part of all members of Zappos in America. A grand and humanistic measure!

Maybe other companies have analogous ideas and want to put them into practice, but they don't do so as thoroughly. I haven't seen another company that has come close to what Zappos has done. So I want to say I am so lucky to join this big family.

Here, we can express ourselves sincerely and approach others honestly. We share things with one another, care for each other, and help each other. It feels like this is another beautiful college life. Of course it's supported by everybody here because it's not one thing or a separate individual. Spirit and atmosphere are important and they are shared by all. Not everyone can possess those ten values. They reflect our goals and dreams. And it's just like when the ocean meets a stream. I think it requires everybody's strength to make the whole family rich and varied, and live longer.

I hope our Zappos family will continue to grow and progress, and that we will be able to live in perfect accord with one another. I believe the harmonious air is the basis of our lives here.

SAM Y. 游陈麟

employee since 2011

Zappos Ten Core Values deliver many unexpected benefits to us. Like the family spirit, every Zapponian is ready to help the newcomers. Another wonderful thing is that we often have interesting activities that draw for everyone in. At Zappos, everyone is dedicated and humorous. We are a big family indeed!

SHELLEY C. 陈清

employee since 2012

WOW! It's been just one week since I joined Zappos, and already I have the honor to express my ideas in Culture Book. Everything at Zappos makes me say WOW. The office environment, the friendly co-workers and the enthusiastic atmosphere, all make a deep impression on me. I love the spirit here myself.

What attracts me most is Zappos Ten Core Values. Each value is so lovely. I am a person who does not like intrigue; I embrace harmony. While I was at university, I required myself to be diligent and keep learning, avoiding laziness. In our company, I appreciate that each single day is bright with sunshine and every person around me is so open-minded and so favorable, so that my heart is always sanguine. The power of positive team and family spirit is mighty. During the circle of learning, I am increasingly growing.

I like English but I dare not to show myself as my level is still low. Sometimes I even cannot find a topic when I try to communicate with foreigners. Working at Zappos gives me a precious opportunity to improve my English skills. I am doing a job that I'm interested in. I'll cherish what I have. The culture of Zappos is my goal. If there is no change, there is no creativity. No passion and determination lead to little progress.

SOPHY L. 赖智慧

employee since 2011

I'm Sophy. I have worked here for more than seven months. I do have a happy team these days, both at work and in my daily life. Since our team members are about the same age, we share many of the same interests, which makes it easier to communicate and understand one another. Whatever, the most important thing is that we persist in following Zappos Ten Core Values. Among them, I like #7, "Build a Positive Team and Family Spirit," the most. Zappos is different from the last company I worked for; the relationships among people here make us stronger than just colleagues. We care about each other; we help one another when we're in need; we encourage one another when we are in trouble; we also argue and communicate with one another when we are at odds with one another. I do love the way that we communicate, since it makes us a big family!

STEVEN S. 苏京洲

employee since 2011

I have been with Zappos almost six months, and I think that our Ten Core Values have changed me in this half a year. I can remember when Nancy gave us new employees our training in the Zappos Culture, and let us describe how the Core Values combine with our work and daily lives. What impressed me most was # 9, "Be Passionate and Determined." Although the department I am in related to my major in college, I performed very badly when I was doing the PS training. The employees who came on board with me started to do the PS project. I felt down and I couldn't believe how poorly I had done at that time. Finally, I started to process the images, but I could not finish the task quickly because I had no self-confidence. Zappos is a big family indeed; with the help of my colleagues, I was able to figure out my problems at work one by one. What's more important, I realized I was a member of the Zappos family. Thinking about being passionate and determined not only helped me relax at work, but it helped me realize I can learn from my mistakes. Everyone here is a member of the Zappos family; the culture leads us to grow up.

来到Zappos之家已经有半年的时间了，细想这半年的时间里，我们的核心文化给了我怎样的变更呢，记得我们来到公司Nancy为我们做文化培训时，就有让我们每个新来的员工对自己认同的核心文化根据自己的工作和生活进行理解，而对于刚进入Zappos之家的我影响最深刻的就是充满激情与决断力.虽然我在这里的工作内容与我在学校学习的都有关联，但是在最初的工作培训的时候，我确表现的很不如意，同期来的同事都已经开始自己的项目工作了，但我自己的信心的也开始有了动摇，而当自己开始项目工作的时候，也不敢果断对那些图片进行快速处理。但是正如Zappos给我们的印象，我们是一个家庭，对于我工作上的问题，最后都在同事的帮助下一点一点的解决，最终适应了在这里的工作和生活。充满激情让我不在担心工作给我带来的紧迫感，拥有决断力而更让我懂得工作的完成度要从错误中提高的。来到Zappos的所有成员就是这个家庭的一员，我们的文化就是牵引着我们一起伴随家庭成长的动力。

TAYLOR J. 焦彤彤

employee since 2006

It is amazing that I have been working here for seven YEARS, since June 2006. I think I am lucky to have met and worked with Zappos in China, and to have come to think of all my colleagues just like my brothers and sisters. Our culture means a lot to me. Zappos is always focusing on improving me, both at work and in my social life. They do not treat others the way I dislike, but encourage us to be true to ourselves and to others; teaching us not to be afraid of change but to deal bravely with challenges. Learning new things, just like my Babe alwaysJ, etc.

I love Zappos, I love the Zappos Culture, and I'm proud to be a part of the Zappos family.

TINA L. 刘方方

employee since 2011

I think that Zappos is really a big family. When you come here, we are caught up in mutual recognition and understanding, even when we organize activities to promote everyone's well-being, like hiking, playing sports, etc. What's more important, if you have a problem and need help, you will find colleagues at your side immediately. All our coworkers are so patient, sincere and modest. The Zappos air is filled with warmth.

TOM C. 陈国青

employee since 2012

I'm new here, but everything here attracts me. You feel that work is fun since you are among such enthusiastic, young and dynamic people. Here, the relationship between colleagues is not only ordinary workplace relationships, but more like a family where people care about and help one another. Whether you are working or in meetings, you can joke with each other in a relaxing and enjoyable environment. If you worked here, I think you would love it.

WENDY H. 黄佳
employee since 2011

How time flies! I have been here for over one year.
During this time, some new coworkers came, some
left, and some are still here. All of them taught me
a lot, including knowledge, how to smile, and so
on. I appreciate them all the time. Moreover, we live
together very happily, in a home-like atmosphere.
We do many things and share ideas. Many positive
things can be found in our office, although some
disappear. But they have existed indeed. Ha-ha. We
want to make everything be funnier. We hope we
can live as a happy family, even though it is small.

WILLIAM H. 黄伟宏
employee since 2009

It has been almost three years, since July of 2009,
since I started to work in Zappos China Office. I
dare say that the ten unique Core Values of Zappos
have always been an indispensable part of our
work and social life. We are living a happy and
glorious life under the magic power of the values.
That's why I choose to stay at Zappos.

我是09年7月来到我们Zappos大家庭的，到现在
已经将近3年了，可以说Zappos文化就是我们生活
中不可缺少的一部分，我们在她的光环下开心的
工作与生活，这也正是我选择一直留在Zappos的
原因。

THE WHA?
HUZZAH
FRONT VIEW

2011 ZCLT OCTOBER FEST

99 BOTTLES OF BEER ON THE WALL

BEER BOOT
(UNWEARABLE,
BUT DRINKABLE)
SIDE VIEW

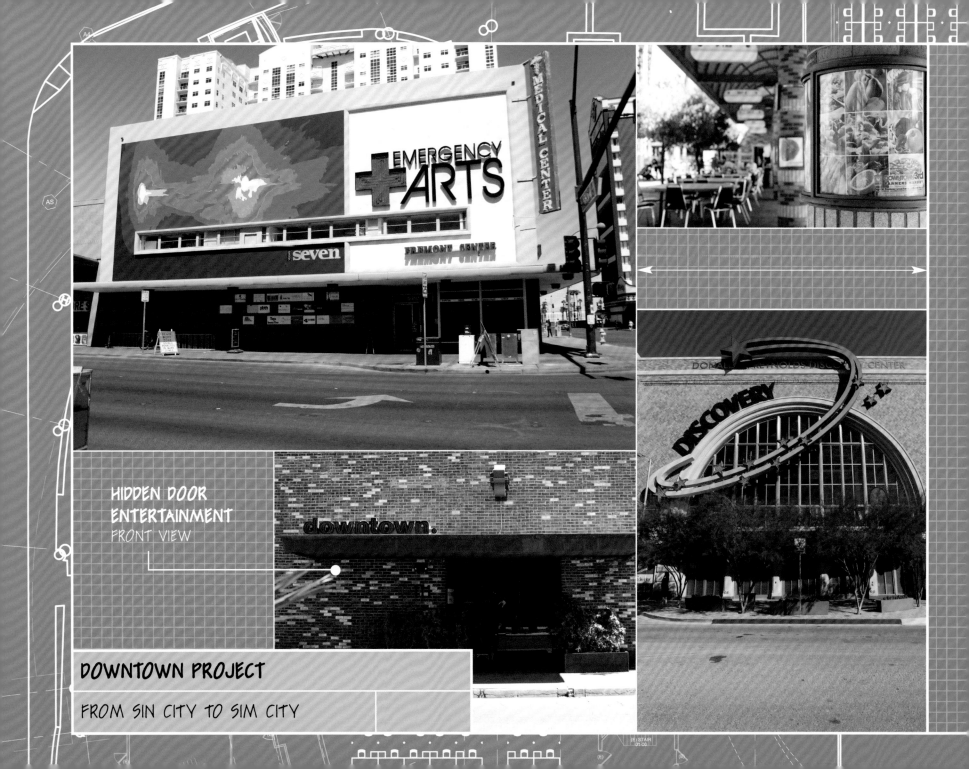

EMERGENCY + ARTS
MEDICAL CENTER
seven
FREMONT CENTER

HIDDEN DOOR
ENTERTAINMENT
FRONT VIEW

downtown.

DISCOVERY
DONALD W. REYNOLDS DISCOVERY CENTER

DOWNTOWN PROJECT

FROM SIN CITY TO SIM CITY

SMITH CENTER
FRONT VIEW

CAPTAIN
BLUEBEARD
STOIC VIEW

2011 BALD AND BLUE

BALD IS THE NEW BLUE

THE
EXPERIMENT
DEADTREE
MODEL

$E=mc^2$

ZAPPOS GRAND PRIX

WAVING THE TINY CHECKERED FLAG

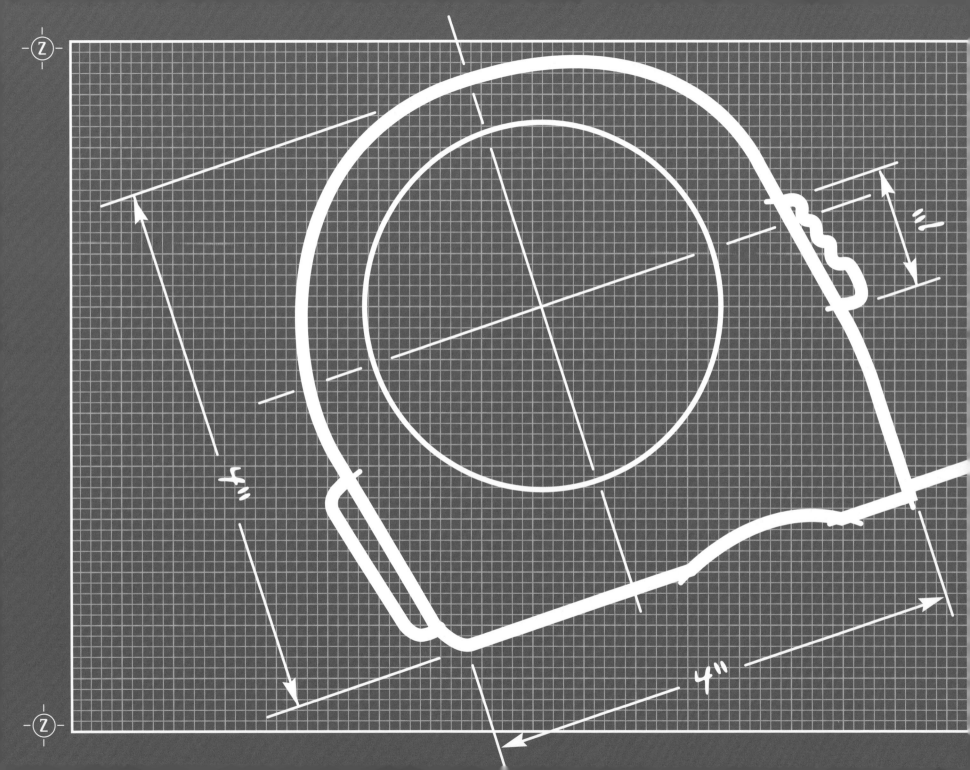

Dept. No. | 56789-098

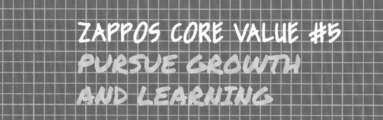

ZAPPOS CORE VALUE #5
PURSUE GROWTH
AND LEARNING

ANONYMOUS

employee since 2012

To me, the Zappos Culture really means family. I love coming to work and seeing each member of my team. We have so much fun together, but also accomplish so much. My Zappos family really encourages me to progress professionally and personally and to really go after my passions. Work will … and should … always feel like work, but it's a lot easier and more fun when you have a great supporting cast around you.

ANONYMOUS

employee since 2005

Live life and don't be afraid to make mistakes with grace. Be well and help others to do the same. Realize your potential and make contributions to your community. Be an unstoppable, yet humble force.

ANONYMOUS

employee since 2005

Maybe I could make more money, or have a fancy title, working in a similar position at another company. Those things become less attractive when you're part of a company that's trying to make a difference in the corporate world. Those aforementioned perks aren't uncommon, but the leadership that Zappos consistently exhibits is.

ANONYMOUS

employee since 2006

The Zappos Culture is unlike anything that I have ever experienced. Coming to work doesn't actually feel like coming to "work." It feels like hanging out with extended family and friends. I mean, sure, we do work, but enjoying where and who you work with is a great feeling. I don't dread Mondays any more; in fact, I can't wait for the weekend to be over so that I can see my co-workers. Name any other company that you could say that about! I bet you can't. Zappos is the best of the best, the cream of the crop, and I am happy – nay – honored to have been chosen to be an official Zapponian. Here is to many more years to come!

ANONYMOUS

employee since 2009

I'm not sure what to write. I like it here. It's awesome. The culture permeates every team. You feel like you're coming in to more than a job every day. You're coming in to see your friends, not just co-workers. It's very unusual in the corporate world, and the biggest reason why working at Zappos isn't soul-crushing.

ANONYMOUS

employee since 2006

The strong company culture that exists at Zappos makes working here special. Every email I write and every conversation I have with a fellow Zapponian is influenced by the company culture. Keeping the culture alive and well will ensure our continued success.

ANONYMOUS

employee since 2011

The Zappos Culture is great! We are working with others to create amazing things with our brands and our customers!

ANONYMOUS

employee since 2005

It seems like almost every year, we are faced with an incredible challenge to conquer as a company, and each time, we rise to the occasion. I don't think that would be possible without the Zappos Culture, which is essentially a strong family bond. We're constantly learning together, growing together and having fun together – all of which conditions us to take on those challenges together as a team.

ANONYMOUS

employee since 2011

The Zappos Culture is a day full of laughter with great people. :)

ANONYMOUS

employee since 2010

The Zappos Culture, to me, represents everything that the typical workplace ignores. Laughter, randomness, freedom of expression, team dynamics, innovation, creativity … These are things that are stifled in most other places, but here they are revered.

I am thankful every day for escaping a gray cubicle and being granted an opportunity to work with a team that lets me truly be me, no matter how weird that might be.

ANONYMOUS
employee since 2010

The only thing better than working here would be living on my own island!

ANONYMOUS
employee since 2005

Being a part of the Zappos family has allowed me to do just that – surround myself with family and friends. Every day is a new day, and is unlike the day before. I'm fortunate enough to be able to take risks, break the rules, and be able to do what truly makes me happy. Most importantly, every day is fun, which encourages me to come back for more the next day.

ANONYMOUS
employee since 2009

I don't know how to articulate this clearly, but essentially, to me the Zappos Culture means that even though some days are tough, it is always worth it because of the people. I am here because of the people and the family we have created. The people are everything, and without that the culture means nothing.

ANONYMOUS
employee since 2010

The Zappos Culture means customer service!! The point of being happy at work every day, having fun, feeling like I'm with my family when I'm here, is to provide our customers with the best service possible. People have always said that happy employees make happy customers, but Zappos takes that to heart with EVERYTHING we do … from our impromptu parades, to the various employee events, to the way we talk to our customers. Our customers love us because WE love us!!

ANONYMOUS
employee since 2011

What I love about the Zappos Culture is being in an environment where I can just be myself ,,, a little strange and all. It just makes it a joy to go into "work" every day knowing that I am walking in to be with friends and family, not just to work. And this extends outside of work also, into the social life that we share with each other. It is always amazing to be surrounded by such a great group of people.

ANONYMOUS
employee since 2007

Love this place!

ANONYMOUS
employee since 2007

Zappos is a fantastic place to work. There is definitely a family and team spirit. You can always depend on your team members to help you out with any situation, whether it is business or personal. The benefits are fantastic, and get better every year. I feel very fortunate to be a part of the Zappos family.

ANONYMOUS
employee since 2010

Be the change you want to see!

ANONYMOUS
employee since 2009

You know your company has a strong culture when you walk around the halls of the office and see many people who will be in your life for years to come. Zappos is more than a company … for those of us who have the privilege of working here, it's a family.

ALEX K.
employee since 2005

People, people, people. Despite the parades, happy hours, nerf wars, free lunches, vendor parties, goofy conference rooms, and cluttered desks, when I think of the Zappos Culture, I think of the people. Really smart and passionate people working together on projects, brainstorming the next feature and problem-solving things that occasionally go wrong. It's the people that are at the heart of the Zappos Culture.

ALISON C.
employee since 2008

Every time I give a tour of our offices, I find myself reflecting on the amazing culture that has developed here. As I share the history, stories and interesting facts about the company, I am reminded that the culture we have within these walls is very different from the culture of other companies. It is something we should all appreciate, treasure and pass on … Zappos is truly a special place.

AMANDA W.
employee since 2007

Culture has come in many forms throughout the years here at Zappos. As I close in on my fifth year here, I look back at how things have changed.

My team has grown, shrunk, disappeared, changed, and reinvented itself. My job itself has changed, been re-defined, molded and re-shaped completely into a long list of things that I have learned, unlearned, and rediscovered.

If I had one thing to say to anyone, it would be "Embrace and Drive Change," because change is inevitable. Learn to enjoy it, even when the future seems frightening.

AMBER O.
employee since 2005

A desk piled with books, notebooks, random papers, a foot-shaped fly swatter and a collection of birthday cards. Walls covered with photos, certificates, a winning BINGO card and a "Smooth Amber"-scented car tree. Emails littered with LOLCats, smiley faces and (I swear) work-related conversations. Coworkers who are friends. A company that actually cares. Yep, Zappos is a pretty amazing place to be, and I can't wait to see how many more memories I collect along the way.

AMY M.
employee since 2010

The Zappos Culture is about being able to grow while always staying true to myself. I feel fortunate to be able to come into work and do a job I find challenging while having fun with the people I work with. And what's not to love about a new position where your "Welcome to the Team" gift is a nerf gun?!

ANDREA C.
employee since 2012

It's only been four days since I started with Zappos, and I'm just incredibly happy and grateful to be here. In just a few days, I've seen amazing human interactions, genuine friendliness and kindness, ready smiles and hellos, as well as awesome energy, deep commitment and incredible depth of knowledge. I've heard about Zappos and its culture, but to see it in action, even just in these first few days, has been phenomenal.

ANGELA C.
employee since 2006

The Zappos Culture means that I'm able to come in each day and work in an environment that allows me to be myself, but challenges me to be better today than I was yesterday. I really enjoy what I do, and the people I get to share my days with. We are so spoiled at Zappos that sometimes it's easy to think that all our wonderful perks are the norm. It's not until you speak to other people who work in the "real world" that you realize what we have is special. It's great to be a part of a company that cares about every single human being it interacts with.

ANGELINA F.
employee since 2010

Rapid growth and change may make some feel that something essential about our culture has been altered or lost, but our culture cannot (and should not) remain fixed. I feel fortunate to work for a company that affords us the opportunity to question, contribute to, challenge, and drive the company we are a part of. At the end of the day, the Zappos Culture is what you make of it!

ANNE P.
employee since 2008

The Zappos Culture, to me is like a giant buffet of happiness. There isn't just one dish to choose from, but a variety of choices to suit each person's appetite. Some people need their happiness to be light and sweet, while others need something a little meatier. You're even encouraged to try samples of other kinds of happiness, just to see if you'd like it. The great part is that nobody's choice is wrong, and hopefully everyone finds a favorite brand of personal happiness.

ASHLEY M.
employee since 2007

Every year when we are asked this question, past years' responses immediately come to mind: "working with people I like and respect so much;" "an environment that encourages opportunities for personal and professional growth." But every year, there is a new element contributing to my perception of the culture. Those points are still a part of my explanation when asked about the Zappos Culture, but the new development this year is the commitment to the community. It is amazing to work for a company that cultivates strong relationships and growth, but also encourages us just as strongly to get actively involved in reinvigorating a city and community.

AZIZ B.
employee since 2011

Confetti. Lots of confetti.

And putting some good Karma back into the universe.

BOBBY M.
employee since 2010

It's a motivation and inspiration that drives me to get up in the morning and look forward to coming to work. Which never has a dull moment. It's always filled with fun, excitement and laughter.

CHANELE H.
employee since 2007

I recently celebrated my fifth anniversary here at Zappos, and I can't believe how fast the years have gone by. During the time since the last Culture Book, I've been even more impressed by the team and family spirit that we embody here. Before I worked at Zappos, I was working at a job where I was comfortable, but I didn't like it. I'm not even so sure it was the job I didn't like, but more my coworkers. I took a huge step outside my comfort zone when I came to Zappos. It was a weird transition, from working with people 30 years older than me to working with people who were actually my age, and people that I could relate to.

During my five-plus years here, I've made a lot of great friends and worked with so many great people. I always knew that I had a family here, but the last year was so full of ups and downs in my personal life that it really became clear that we care about each other here. From my first root canal to a car accident on the freeway, I had my Zappos family supporting me. When my dad passed away, I not only had my biological family, I had my Zappos family. When I got engaged to my boyfriend of seven and a half years (and now a fellow Zappos employee), there they were again with their support and well wishes. Then we bought our first house and our dog fell out a second story window, and once again, my Zappos family was there to offer their support. There's that saying about finding out who your real friends are when the going gets tough, and I think this last year has made it clear to me that the Zappos Culture is for real. Behind all the fun and weirdness, we're genuine people and we look out for each other. I'm grateful I stepped outside my comfort zone and came to this wonderful company. I'm excited for us to bring the Zappos Culture to the downtown community!

CHRISTOPHER G.
employee since 2010

When I think of the Zappos Culture, too many things come to mind. If I were to write them all down, I'd probably have my own Culture Book. I've seen some of the wildest and most amazing things happen at this place. Whether it's the smiles people have when they come to take a tour and see how wild we are, the happiness of a new hire graduating from ZCLT Training, or a much-deserved wish being granted by our amazing wish fairies, this place is my home away from home. Actually, it IS home. Though I love skateboarding and my friends from outside Zappos, I can honestly say I would not be as happy if I were not at Zappos. There are so many GNAR things I can go on about, but honestly, when I think about all the crazy fun and happiness that comes from this wonderful place I call home, all I can do is smile. :)

CHRISTOPHER P.
employee since 2004

Zappos means everything to me. Through challenges and opportunities, there is always something to look forward to. Although there are so many things that make this company amazing to work for, for me it always comes down to our people. We're surrounded by people that don't rest in making this company better and better year after year. Whether it's business, culture or everyday projects and initiatives, we see young leaders who step up and shine through adversity. We see people who don't make excuses … they just buckle down and get the job done. We see groups of people that come together to make things better. We see individuals who consider Zappos 'the last place they'll ever work,' people who will always focus on making this unique and crazy place something we're ultimately building for our grandchildren. We see people who consider their place here an obligation to our family and our customers to constantly improve, to deliver that extra 1% every day. I'm truly lucky to be in a company that gives us an opportunity to grow as fast we want to grow. We are all truly lucky to be working side-by- side with people who will never stop believing and working towards being the most amazing company in the world.

COURTNEY M.
employee since 2009

I <3 Zappos! Meow meow!

DANIELLE T.
employee since 2007

Well, this is my sixth Culture Book entry. While many things have changed over the years (in fact, more things have changed than stayed the same), the core of Zappos remains true. Zappos is still a company that cares passionately and deeply about its employees. It just occurred to me that Zappos may have an unhealthy crush on all of us - ha, ha. I know that I am valued here and the company wants me to succeed both personally and professionally. I have seen people here do amazing things inside and outside of work and Zappos was there to help in whatever way they could. So much possibility still exists. I also believe that every single employee has an impact on our culture. We have the power to build the culture or tear it down. Everyone is responsible. If you don't like what's going on, do something about it. Like He-Man and She-Ra, you have the power!

DARREN F.
employee since 2009

I have been with Zappos now for almost three years, and they have been some of the best years of my life. We truly are a family, and I wouldn't know what to do without my Zappos Family. The Zappos Culture and Ten Core Values have become a big part of my life. My favorite core value is number three, "Create Fun and a Little Weirdness." I get to do this every day when I walk into work and sit with my fellow A/V team members. My favorite thing about Zappos is that we're encouraged to do what we are passionate about. And that I'm given the creative freedom to express that in the videos I produce for the company. :-)

DAVID B.
employee since 2011

I moved 2,000 miles across the country to work at Zappos. Although I was optimistic, I was still filled with many uncertainties. What I've found is a second family, and I can't imagine being without them! I'm looking forward to the future!

DELANA M.
employee since 2009

When I first think of the Zappos Culture, I think of family, which rings true at Zappos. Since I started working at Zappos almost three years ago, I have formed bonds with people that will last a lifetime. I don't just consider these people friends, but more like extended family. It's our unique culture that allows us to express who we are, and we are able to see others in their true light. It's our culture that has brought us together and helped us be better people and better 'family members.' Basically, our company culture is our family culture. BTW, just want to add that Zappos WILL be the last place I EVER work because of the culture and family-like atmosphere.

DENA M.
employee since 2006

A breakdown of what "ZAPPOS" means to me in 2012:
Zany – I can't think of a day that wasn't filled with laughter!
Adventure – We take chances, shoot for BHAGs and enjoy the ride! Something we are encouraged to do every day!
Passion – Every single person here has it!
Perseverance – Our security breach was a true testament – together we overcame it!
Opportunity – Every day, more is created for employees, company, brands, and city!
Support – Zappos gives it to us, we give it to each other, to our industry and to our community!

DIANA R.
employee since 2009

The Zappos Culture means that you can come to work and spend time with people you consider your second family. It also means you can be yourself, and contribute to a bigger purpose. And it means you can have fun at your job, while working hard to succeed in your role. The Zappos Culture is amazing, and I love it!

DONNY G.
employee since 2011

Zappos is such an amazing place to work in so many ways ... let me count them:
1. I've had the opportunity to meet and create a life-long bond with friends.
2. The ability to do endurance events I might not have done if it weren't for the ZEndurance team (Marathons, Tough Mudder, Rhino Course, etc.).
3. Benefits that allow me to go get a massage with chiropractic work.
4. A culture that allows me to come to work and just be myself in how I dress, interact with others, etc.
5. The openness and collaboration everyone has with one another when it comes to ideas and projects.
6. The opportunity to work with an awesome UX team that creates experiences that delivers happiness and WOW!
7. The feeling of being a part of something special that embraces our customers!
8. Celebrating birthdays and anniversaries like a real party! (For example, my wife and I bombarding my boss's desk with Angry Birds!)
9. Ability to join a wonderful, fantastic, awesome family of Zapponians ... Zappos For Life!
10. In the words of our core value #10 – "Be Humble"... I humbly say, "Thank you, Zappos, for being so amazing and providing a lifestyle for me to be happy and deliver happiness!

EDDIELYNN T.
employee since 2007

Wow, another entry in the Zappos Culture Book. It just gets better and better, and there is no other place I would rather be! I <3 Zappos Culture. :)

EILEEN S.
employee since 2010

My time at Zappos does not feel like work; it is a great adventure and I never know what the day will bring me!

ELIZABETH B.
employee since 2011

The Zappos Culture, to me, means that when I look around at the people surrounding me, they are all smiling, interacting and being themselves. You do not have to be the most goofy or loudest person, but just being comfortable as yourself makes the culture unique and special.

ERIN J.
employee since 2010

The Zappos Culture is a virus worth catching. We should all be kindness zombies and spread the love.

ERIN J.
employee since 2008

I enjoy coming to work because I like everyone I work with!

GRAHAM K.
employee since 2009

Zappos is a place where dreams come true. I'm so thankful for the helpful, nurturing, one-of-a-kind culture that we have here. Where else would a company roll the dice on the downtown and make an area that many have counted out for years into the new tech hub of the West? I don't have to go to work. I get to go to work.

GWENDOLYN C.
employee since 2012

I HEART ZAPPOS! But I still love you, NYC!

HANNAH E.
employee since 2006

I remember my very first day here at Zappos. I was in my last semester of college, and had never worked in an office setting before ... so naturally, I came in with my Banana Republic blazer, thinking "Okay, it's time to put your 'big girl' pants on!"

Well, you can imagine my surprise when I walked in to see everyone dressed in casual tees and jeans. Some even had shorts on! What was even more pleasantly surprising was that everyone... I mean literally everyone... I came into contact with flashed a genuine smile my way, saying "hi" as I pass them in the hallway.

I thought, "What is this place? Why is everyone being so nice? They don't even know me!" My friend who used to be a buyer here (and was the one who referred me to Zappos) even introduced me to Tony on my very first day in the office. I thought to myself, "Wow, the CEO is wearing a T-shirt and he actually said hi to me!" That's just not what I expected ... but then again, I wasn't sure what to expect.

I talk about my first day because it's such an organic example of what Zappos culture is all about at its core. It's a genuine need to want to be better people every day, even if it means a simple "hello" and a warm smile to someone walking down these halls for the first time.

HEATHER T.
employee since 2005

To me, the Zappos Culture means fun and friendship. My coworkers are like my family, and they make coming to work every day fun and exciting. It's wonderful to know that if I'm having a bad day or hitting a rough patch, my team will be here to help me out and cheer me up. I love coming to work at a place where the people I'm surrounded by genuinely care about each other.

HENRY C.
employee since 2011

The culture at Zappos has inspired me in so many ways. It has taught me to be more thoughtful of others in the community. It has taught me to think outside the box in everything I do. It has taught me to appreciate all that I have and to try to 'do more with less' on a daily basis. But most importantly, the Zappos Culture has taught me to continually strive to be a better person and friend.

HOPE L.
employee since 2007

Only at Zappos – has been my mantra this past year. I was previously on the Pipeline team teaching and building classes for the company, which I loved doing. Then last year I was given the unique opportunity to apply for a style editor position, and I got the job! Only at Zappos would something like this happen! I am living my dream and am so grateful every day to come to work for such an amazing company that is so inspiring and so supportive of their employees. I'll never stop saying, "Only at Zappos!" :) xoxo

JACKIE M.

Zappos has become a huge part of my life, and I'm really thankful for that! For the past five years I've seen how much it's grown and can only imagine how far we will go. Not a lot of people can say that they look forward to coming into work every day, and I feel truly blessed that I'm able to do what I love most and get to share each day with my Zappos family.

JASON C.
employee since 2007

Over the last few years that I've been with Zappos, I've continued to watch us grow and mature as a company. Yet with that growth, it's still that same feeling of family within our company. It's simple things like holding doors open for other and saying 'hi' as you walk by everyone. At many places you don't really know a lot of people in the company, other than those in your specific department or with whom you work directly. Everyone here makes it a point to know and interact with others throughout the company, whether it's at work or in their personal lives. That bond with so many others really makes it a great place to be and keeps the culture strong.

JASON G.
employee since 2012

To me, the Zappos Culture is all about building relationships with the people inside the company, and allowing the culture to foster creativity, ideas, and innovation in both the company, and in our lives on many levels, professionally and personally.

JAY D.
employee since 2007

What does the Zappos Culture mean to me? Happiness! I'm genuinely happy to walk through our doors and acknowledge my coworkers – both old and new! I feel truly at home being myself around here. Typically, there's a fine line between work and personal life, but I'm happy to combine both. I honestly believe that if one has happiness, the culture basically takes care of itself!

JENNIE W.
employee since 2009

I don't believe in accidents or luck. The Zappos Culture didn't just magically appear, and doesn't just magically still exist. Our culture is a conscious act and a way of life. We all didn't walk in one way and change to suit the culture. We all walk in as ourselves, happy to be here and to be working toward the greater good of customer happiness. Who knew that helping someone else experience happiness would bring ME so much happiness?

JESSICA L.

employee since 2006

The Zappos Culture is unique because it's contagious. Everyone who comes into contact with us, whether they're taking our tour, talking to us on the phone, or running into one of us out in public gets to experience it and can then spread it on to others. It's made us world-famous and it's been awesome to watch it grow over the years. It's more than words on paper; it's alive and breathing. You can see it in interactions among employees, vendors and visitors, both in and out of the office environment. It's a sense of family and community, coming together as one for a higher purpose.

JESSICA S.

employee since 2012

I'm in my first month of employment at Zappos, so I'm still learning about the culture on a daily basis. So far, it seems very friendly and entertaining! In my first few weeks I've seen a unicorn/horse parade, enjoyed a Star Wars-themed potluck, and a really fun "All Hands" meeting. I can't wait to see what happens next!

JO C.

employee since 2008

Wowzers!!!

Is it that time already?! I feel like I always say the same thing for my entry. I love Zappos, Zappos is a way of life, my coworkers are my family. This is all still true.

This year has been tough. I have gone through some pretty serious family stuff and the one thing I could always rely on was the stability and understanding of my fellow Zapponians. My co-workers are like my family. I know without a doubt that I'm not the only person who feels that way This is the year I learned about true compassion from others ... My career at Zappos is always right at the top of my gratitude list.

Being here has caused doors to open that I never thought could open. I love my life and I love my Zappos life. I'll never stop being excited about coming to work here. I look forward to every new adventure that awaits me here at Zappos!

JONATHAN B.

employee since 2008

I love working at Zappos and with my team! Whether it's putting together a group outing or organizing a potluck, the people around me truly have become like an extended family. I always look forward to coming in to work because it's not just a job where I punch a clock; it's like my second home.

JONATHAN H.

employee since 2011

Where can you work doing something you love, follow your passion, be empowered to make customers and co-workers happy, dress however you want to and see friends every day? At Zappos! The Zappos Culture is the best there is. We celebrate birthdays and promotions and have team outings together. Zappos is different from any other place I have worked before. I feel truly blessed!

JOSELITO H.

employee since 2010

Every year when this question comes around, I have the hardest time coming up with the best way to describe how I feel about our company culture. Anyone that has read anything about Zappos already understands how crazy it can be here. But what is it like when you come in every day? Pretty awesome.

JOSEPH G.

employee since 2011

Zappos is constantly changing and evolving for the better. Every day I come in and feel privileged to work for such an amazing company. Every day I am challenged not only to better myself and my skills, but also challenged to have fun. I am surrounded by brilliant, funny people who make my day.

JUSTIN A 'JAY'.

employee since 2009

YOLO

KAREN S.

employee since 2010

I am so grateful to be part of the Zappos family. We are all given the opportunity to grow, voice our suggestions, and express our passions on a daily basis. We all have amazing tools to provide our customers with exceptional service in our own unique way... and to have fun while doing so!

KATIE G.

employee since 2011

The Zappos Culture means family. My coworkers aren't just teammates, they are great friends. And this isn't just a workplace... it's my home away from home.

KAYA F.

employee since 2008

The Zappos Culture, to me, is going to work every day with a smile on my face, and having fun at work all day. There are very few moments in my day where we are not laughing. I love what I do, I love the people I work with, and I love Zappos!!! And everyone I know here feels the same way.

KELLY T.

employee since 2010

Oh man, who knew you could have a blast at work every day?! To think I used to have jobs where I would roll out of bed in the morning and dread going in. How exciting to be part of a workplace that makes such a significant impact on their employees, as well as the community around them! You rock, Zappos!

KENNY L.

employee since 2007

I would liken the culture at Zappos to a delicious corn dog. No, wait, stay with me for a minute. On the outside, the cornmeal may seem like a fluffy and superfluous piece of the whole, but if you take it away...? You're left with just meat on a stick, which is pretty gross. In a similar way, the culture here at Zappos is the thing that binds everything together; it's the thing that helps make the eight-hour workday fun and enjoyable. I mean, I'd eat meat on a stick if I had to, but to make it more than just bland nourishment on a plank of wood, it really needs that warm and inviting cornmeal exterior. Now, does anyone have some mustard?

KRISTA A.

employee since 2007

Roses are red, violets are blue,
I heart Zappos and so do you.

KRISTEN W.

employee since 2010

The Zappos Culture, to me, means team and extended family. I am amazed every day by my work family and have developed lifelong friendships. The "work hard, play hard" mentality makes coming to work and performing tasks pleasurable. Being able to come to work every day in an environment that is enjoyable, and being offered the tools to be the best I can be and more, is a blessing! I am fortunate to have the opportunity to be a part of such an amazing culture.

KRISTIN B.

employee since 2011

The Zappos Culture is defined by the amazing people who work here. Unlike other places where I have worked, I really do consider my Zappos coworkers to be my extended family. We work hard, we play hard ... and at the end of each day I look forward to going into work the next day and doing it all over again. Zappos is a special, inspiring and empowering place. I am continuously WOWed.

KRISTIN R.

employee since 2012

I heard Zappos was an amazing place to work, but only when I officially became a part of the family did I really understand just how incredible it is. At my previous workplaces, I was used to people not opening doors and being unfriendly, so it took me a few weeks to get used to the exact opposite! Working at Zappos, I feel like I'm a part of something much larger that is striving to improve the quality of life for everyone. It's an amazing feeling!

LARISSA P.

employee since 2011

The Zappos Culture is like Jell-O ... colorful, fun and transparent. There is nothing to hide about our business or the way we have fun running it. We're a company of creative individuals – not unlike any other business! However, our company allows us to express our creativity rather than conform to a dress code or a rather bleak structure. We all work hard to acquire the amazing benefits and experiences here ... but like Jell-O, it makes it that much sweeter!

LINDA T.

employee since 2012

"You're smiling a lot more these days," someone told me the other day. Eight weeks ago I began my sixteen-week internship at Zappos, and I haven't looked back. Work is play and time runs differently around here, with hours and days flying past. Questions are always encouraged (and answers are provided!), rapport is easy, and opportunities that will spark your interest abound! To visitors looking in, Zappos must look like a giant playground. We strive for big hairy audacious goals ("BHAGs") with ideas as building blocks. We let our creativity run free in the way we dress, our spaces, and the way we express ourselves. We play knockout basketball games to help us re-engage and interact. At the end of the day, all the work still gets done, and maybe we'll go hang out and kick back with a beer or two.

LINDSAY B.

employee since 2012

The Zappos Culture is something you can read about, tour the offices, talk about among others, but until you are truly part of it, it's indescribable. When you are new to the Zappos family, you go into your first day wondering what this experience is going to entail, and after your first day you walk out knowing this is where you are supposed to be. To me, the Zappos Culture is family. You are there for each other, support each other through the good times and the bad; you laugh, make memories that you will never forget, and you create a bond. A bond that no one will truly understand unless they are also part of the Zappos Family.

LISA N.

employee since 2009

Our culture here at Zappos means so much to me. It has pushed me to grow, it has opened my eyes, and it has helped me remember that who I am and what I do matters. It's wonderful working at a company that takes an interest in your personal and professional growth and happiness. Thank you, Zappos!

LISA R.

employee since 2011

The Zappos Culture is like an explosion of rainbows, unicorns, cotton candy and warm towels right out of the dryer. It surrounds you during all moments of every day, whether you are at work or wandering around distant cities. It's a constant reminder to live life to the fullest with patience, kindness and an open mind. It shines light into the dark corners of you mind and leads you toward new and exciting opportunities you never knew existed. I am so grateful for all the amazing opportunities that Zappos has given me to help me grow, not just as an employee, but as a human being. I will always carry the happiness and knowledge that Zappos has brought to my life as constant reminder to never settle and to always strive for more.

LYNSEY B.

employee since 2010

From the planned, impromptu philanthropy opportunities we are given as employees, Zappos is a place to find yourself. This company encourages you to learn more about yourself, more about the world, and more about your coworkers. Every day I come into work, I am reminded of this quote: "Be who you are and say how you feel, because those who matter don't mind and those who mind don't matter." – Dr. Seuss. Thanks, Zappos!

MARCO B.

employee since 2010

I worry it's a mirage I kiss
Nothing here ever brings me down
Catapult me into a state of bliss
In tall grass, all the snakes hiss
Cans of doubt open across town
I worry it's a mirage I kiss
A comedy of errors, the occasional near-miss
Inside these walls I do not frown
Catapult me into a state of bliss
Excuses emboldened by a state of remiss
Rumors can never erase renown
I worry it's a mirage I kiss
A chance to grow, one cannot dismiss
No more will hope suffocate or drown
Catapult me into a state of bliss
Sky remains blue, nothing amiss
Upon my head sits this radiant crown
I worry it's a mirage I kiss
Catapult me into a state of bliss

MARIE K.

employee since 2010

I love my Zappos family. The relationships and memories I've made will last me a lifetime. I can't wait to see what the next year has in store for us!

MARIE M.

employee since 2010

I've found that Zappos is a place where you really have the chance to make what you want of it. That's something that isn't true of just anywhere. There are opportunities galore at Zappos and so many people around that are willing to help you achieve your dreams. The relationships I've formed and knowledge that I've gained here will last a lifetime! <3

MARISA B.

employee since 2011

The Zappos Culture is very much what you make of it. Like an awesome return on investment to the 'nth degree. Whatever you put in, you will most certainly get more out. Can't beat that math.

There are a lot of incredible micro and macro aspects that make the Zappos Culture what it is. From the positive, helpful tone in the e-mails we send (which has actually been a bit of a culture shock for me), to how everyone holds doors open for everyone (which is incredibly infectious), to the established Core Values, and even the importance we place on having an extraordinary culture (or even a culture at all), all lend to its "remarkability" (which isn't usually a word, but at Zappos, it works).

It means a lot to me to be a part of Zappos. I'm incredibly honored to have the opportunity to contribute to the culture and I feel like a very lucky recipient of its many, many splendors.

MARJORIE L.

employee since 2007

It's a great feeling to come to work and see smiling faces and hear encouraging words. The atmosphere at Zappos is very different from that at other places where I have worked. It's upbeat and positive. It's also great to give not just adequate customer service, but to go that extra mile for customers to make sure their needs are met and that they are very satisfied and will shop with us again.

MATT L.

employee since 2012

As a relatively new employee moving from a faraway land, I had a vague idea of what to expect at Zappos before starting and, to be honest, I was not really expecting too much. It was daunting to have moved here with no friends or family, but the culture of Zappos really shines in these situations. While it is up to YOU to take that step to find your social outlets, the Zappos Culture does everything in its power to give you the opportunities. If I wanted to, I could fill my social calendar with things to do every night, with different groups of friends and different departments within the company. I've had more dinners than I can count with people that I had never known but who are now great friends. Now I can confidently say the Zappos Culture really makes this company tick!

MATT S.

employee since 2009

Z – Zappos
A – A lot of fun
P – People
P – Pleasant
O – Organization
S – Sales

MATTHEW W.

employee since 2007

It's been five years ... five wonderful years. As I reminisce, I recall all the good times, being motivated, inspired and having felt very accomplished in everything/everyone with whom I've worked so far in this journey. The next 5-10-20 years will be a journey I am happily looking forward to with excitement and anticipation. Thanks Zappos!!! Thank you family!!!!

MEGAN V.

employee since 2012

The Zappos Culture makes this unlike any other place I have ever worked, in a great way! The open atmosphere creates constant opportunities for casual conversation, basketball pick-up games, and even friendly heckling of coworkers. I've only worked here for three months and have already lost track of all the fun events Zappos sponsors in celebration of its employees' dedication and loyalty, from company-wide picnics to pool party team buildings. It's clear that this company understands the value of great employees and exceeds expectations in rewarding innovation, hard work and any kind of comic relief.

MELISSA C.

employee since 2011

I fell in love with Zappos during my interview process and knew in my heart that I belonged here. My team members are some of the best people I've ever known and I can't wait to get to work just to be around them on a daily basis. We all laugh together so much that I forget I am even at work. On top of the amazing environment, I am fulfilled by my job and the challenges it provides me with. Zappos warms my heart every day and in turn, I share that happiness with the world.

MICHAEL B.

employee since 2011

What we have here at Zappos is something very special, and I doubt any other company in the nation has anything comparable. Zappos is my home away from home. Each day I look forward to coming to work to see those that I call family. People genuinely care about each other and are here for the highest of highs, and lowest of lows. We all pull together in times of hardship and party hard for our accomplishments. At any other company it's one against everyone. Not here. ... Not ever. That's what makes Zappos a true family culture!

MICHEAL E.

employee since 2010

Love, admiration, peace, acceptance, ingenuity and appreciation.

MICHELLE T.

employee since 2007

The Zappos Culture is simply a tool that keeps me in check, to continuously develop and improve my own state of being. Whether through personal connections or innovation of work, the culture is gently pushing each of us on a journey to be better, work harder, get smarter, be happier. :o)

MO M.

employee since 2007

There's not much I can add to what has already been said by my coworkers. The culture here is simply amazing! Friendly smiles, caring people, a fun atmosphere and the best happy hours ... What else can you ask for?

NATASHA P.
employee since 2005

Sometimes I need to step back from Zappos. After being here for a few years (and I say "being at" rather than "working at") I forget how fortunate I am. I get caught up in the day-to-day life until I start telling someone what it is I do for living and where I work, then all of a sudden it hits me! I work somewhere where ideas are applauded, new challenges are welcomed, and new hires are treated like gold, rather than threats.

But most important, I work somewhere where my daughters want to work someday! At ages five and eight, they think Zappos can do anything! They think possibilities are endless. At their young age, they have learned that I go to work because it's something I LIKE to do rather than something I have to do.

How lucky am I that not only do I get to work somewhere fabulous but I also taught my daughters a valuable lesson in life?!

NATE L.

employee since 2009

Two jobs diverged in a market, and I—
I took the one at Zappos,
And that has made all the difference
I like you, I love you, thank you.

NED F.
employee since 2001

The Zappos Culture is like Thanksgiving leftovers. Our flavor gets stronger as time goes on. Knibb High Football rules!

NICK F.
employee since 2011

Working at Zappos is like working with friends and family who care about each other. They work hard to make sure that each person is successful, challenged and happy in their job, and that they are recognized and rewarded for their accomplishments.

NICOLE E.
employee since 2011

The Zappos Culture, to me, is being able to express myself by dancing and singing whenever I feel the need to. I love how I can just burst into song or dance whenever the mood strikes me. The best part is how others on my team encourage me to entertain them.

In the past I have worked for some companies where this has been frowned upon. It is so liberating to be in an environment that accepts me for who I am and celebrates that it's O.K. to be different.

NOEL C.

employee since 2006

I almost forgot to submit my entry this year. Not because the Zappos Culture isn't important to me, but because I was so wrapped up participating in the culture that I almost forgot to write about it. In the past week: I pitched a Hackathon* idea, received a tech slow clap (probably most proud of this), got my Hackathon idea picked up, worked with my Hackathon group to come up with a working model, rallied everyone I know to come to the Hackathon, and organized and attended a team lunch excursion. This week has been exhausting, exciting, hilarious, amazing and fulfilling.

And I wouldn't want it any other way.
*Hackathon – a short time frame when development can focus on and create exciting new tools. These are projects that might otherwise never see the light of day.

PAT W.
employee since 2003

In short, Zappos.com has taken me places I never dreamed possible. I not only have a job that I love that gives me the ability to help others as well as learn new things every day, but it has also changed my life outside of the office. Recently I bought my first home in an area of town I've loved to hang out in since I moved here six years ago, and I will be working in the same area of town in less than a few months. Right now I'm extremely excited for the future, and I have a feeling that if Zappos has anything to do with it, I will yet again be amazed at where Zappos and my awesome work family will take me in the years to come. I am so very grateful to be involved with such an astonishing organization, and to be surrounded by great people every day. Last but not least, I would like to thank Zappos for introducing me to my beautiful and talented girlfriend Jackie M., who inspires me everyday to push myself and not just cruise through life like I did for so many years before meeting her. Thank you so much to everyone!

RACHAEL P.
employee since 2008

Every year, Zappos feels more and more like home. Every year, I meet new people who become friends. Every yea,r I'm growing both personally and professionally and I owe it all to Zappos. Without this company there's no way that I would be where I am today. Zappos changes lives for the better. I'm proud of what I've accomplished and I'm so excited to see where else I go with this company. I found my "forever job" at Zappos!

RAINA A.
employee since 2007

The Zappos Culture, to me, means taking care of your peeps and cultivating relationships! This is super important as we continue to grow. I've never worked with so many people that genuinely care about me and about what we're doing as a company. It is truly refreshing! We're all on the same team and heading towards the same goals. I think we'll get there together as a close-knit family.

ROBERT A.
employee since 2007

The Zappos Culture is the belief that it's possible to create a fun work environment, a successful business, and provide a positive experience for customers without the typical boring structured corporate environment.

If you are tired of playing "corporate hopscotch" and chasing "a new dog with a different set of fleas," Zappos is the best place to be!!!

ROBERT A.
employee since 2005

What I love about the Zappos Culture is that it's never dull. We're always evolving, changing, mixing it up, and never standing still. The amazing thing is that after seven + years of being here, it never ceases to amaze me. Bob Dylan had it right: the times they are a-changing, and we will all be the better for it

SAMANTHA S.
employee since 2009

To me, the Zappos Culture means loving what you do and the people you do it with. I've had some amazing experiences and met some equally amazing people working at Zappos. Not only are they my coworkers, but some of my best friends. I look forward to what the future holds, both personally and professionally.

SARA M.
employee since 2011

"All great changes are preceded by chaos."
– Deepak Chopra
Brought to you by Sara M.

SETH A.
employee since 2011

A Big Ole' Family. People who care about something bigger than themselves, uniting to create a world of happiness.

STACEY S.
employee since 2010

For me, the Zappos Culture refers to each moment that I can be my authentic self. It's about growing as a person and recognizing both my strengths and weaknesses, including the opportunity to improve. I relate it to being a passionate and determined individual in order to be the best employee, the best daughter, the best sister, and the best friend possible. And if that's what we each ultimately strive for, the "best" would be pretty phenomenal, wouldn't it?

Most importantly, Zappos is my home away from home, literally. Zappos has impacted me more than I've ever impacted the business, and Zappos is a friend I could never adequately repay. I am a happier, more confident, more patient, and more understanding person because of the experiences provided by Zappos.

My heart continues to be overwhelmed with happiness because of Zappos.

SUNSHINE J.
employee since 2010

I'm blessed to have a job that I enjoy. I am lucky to get to spend every day working with my friends. I am grateful that Zappos offers so many family-friendly after-work activities for my kids and I to be a part of. This place is 24/7 awesome.

SURBHI MAHENDRU.

employee since 2011

Taking an extra ten seconds out of your day to hold the door open for someone, even if they seem too far away. And then thanking someone who did the same for you.

Showing up at anyone's desk, whether it be an intern, director, administrator, or CEO, with the assurance they'll have two minutes to spare to answer your question, important or not.

Enjoying the jokes your coworkers crack about you and never let you forget, because really, it's just a sign of friendship.

Attending a coworker's dinner without invitation and finding they prepared a full bowl of delicious food for you anyway.

Knowing that there is no standard definition for the Zappos Culture, and it means something different to everyone. Hence, the creation of this book. :)

TAMI F.

employee since 2012

Zappos believes in the power of happiness. Zappos knows that people who are happy tend to be more successful, productive, and creative. They know that happiness is contagious and that a happy person has the ability to spread happiness to others, which can have a positive effect on people all over the world. Zappos knows that happiness comes through achieving goals, being kind, helping others, expressing gratitude, enjoying life, and being optimistic. Zappos knows that when coworkers are friends with each other, it can infect the workplace with happiness.

TARA J.

employee since 2007

I love that individuals here are encouraged to pursue their own destiny. Being happy at work is important to everyone here, so we're all encouraged to find what makes us happy and go for it!

TIFFANY G.

employee since 2008

This year, teamwork has been the key takeaway for me. We really know how to come together to get things done!

TIM S.

employee since 2009

Working with a great strong team really gives perspective on what is possible. Tireless testing to become 1% better goes a long way and teaches many lessons. I have been inspired to become better, to try and push harder. When someone can pitch an idea, execute it, and improve the company, it is pretty inspiring to see. I hope to see much more of this in the future.

VARINIA P.

employee since 2012

The Zappos Culture is so much more than having a certain mindset at work. It's coming to work and feeling that every person you meet in the hallway, familiar or not, would lend you a helping hand in anything you need. Feeling the warmth, kindness and fun at work spills over into every other facet of life. Smiling at a stranger in the grocery store, holding the door while leaving a building, giving a kind word, being grateful for everything. It's so much more than a job ... it's life. I've never been happier in my whole life. Working here has made me a better employee, wife, friend and person. The difference between Zappos and other places I have worked is that their final goal is not to make the most money possible, it's to spread happiness to those we come into contact with and better ourselves to better our world. It's a place that has values and actually lives and breathes them every day.

WENDY M.

employee since 2012

The realization of how awesome the Zappos Culture is hit me right in the face while on a visit to another large online company ... literally. I was hit in the face with the door when the person in front of me let it go. That wouldn't happen here at Zappos because we hold the door for each other. Always. It's what we do. We foster a culture of growth, support and success. We help each other help each other ... unless you're trying out for Corporate Challenge; then you'd best come with your game face on! From our pipeline classes to our awesome life coach, we're all happy to help each other succeed. Oh, and we don't do too shabby at Corporate Challenge either!

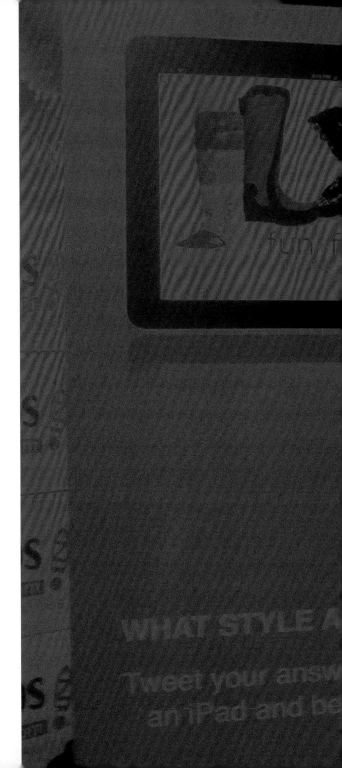

WILLIAM L.

employee since 2010

My second year here at Zappos has been one full of pursuit of growth and learning. I had the honor of being the Z'Apprentice for Brand Marketing and was exposed to yet another department's unique culture.

Through my Z'Apprentice experience, my view of the Zappos Culture has expanded and deepened even further. Instead of the Ten Core Values being an inanimate set of rules that are ignored, I feel that the opportunities I was given are living proof of Zappos' commitment to help cultivate its employees.

I would like to give a shout out to the Brand Marketing team and let them know to Crush it! And don't stop ABC'ing: Always Be Closing!

- LaPoot, a.k.a. Hustler, a.k.a. Will.I.ain't

YEON JIN (AKA ANDREW).

employee since 2011

The Zappos Culture means everything I live for. Since the day I joined the company, every day I felt blessed breathing Zappos air, working with humble, but extremely talented people, always looking for ways to simplify and minimize unnecessary efforts ("doing more with less"). Often we express our kookiness by planning funny birthday celebrations, and bringing smiles to everyone, further expanding the positive vibe.

There is no limit to how much happiness spreads and lives in this community.

I love you, Zappos.

YHAIRA Y.

employee since 2008

I have never felt so proud to work for any other company. It's amazing to see how much emotion I can evoke just by saying, "I work for Zappos." The instant recognition, genuine interest in our company, and support in the downtown movement makes me think that we must be doing right.

Introducing...
Zappos ZN

DIGITAL TABLET
THINGIE
FRONT VIEW

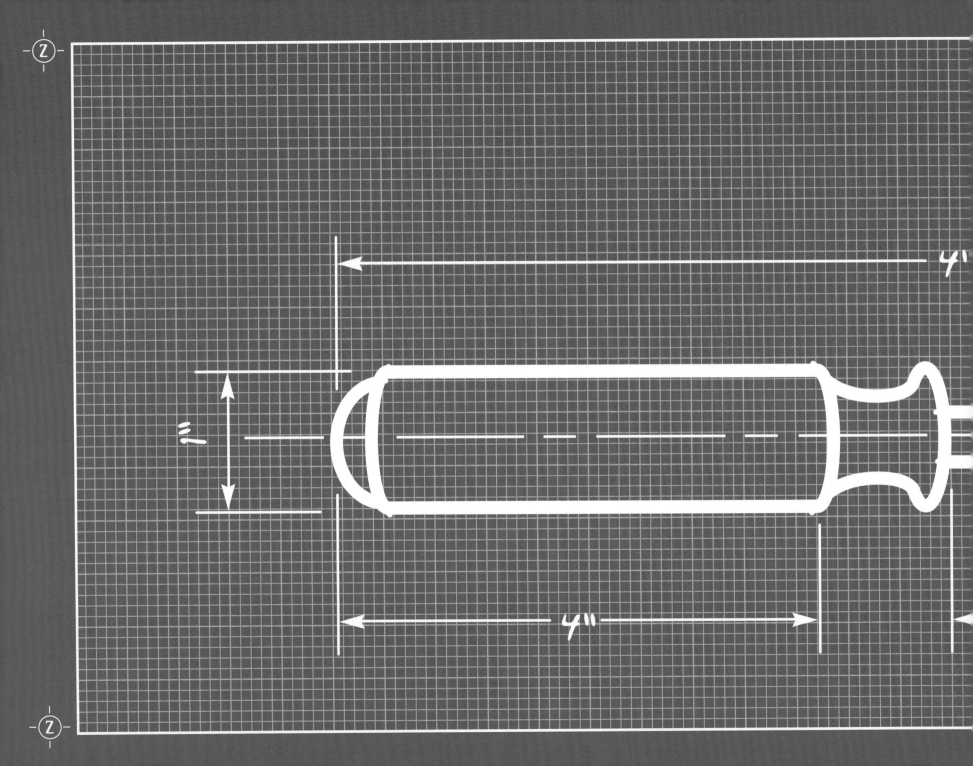

4"

2"

4"

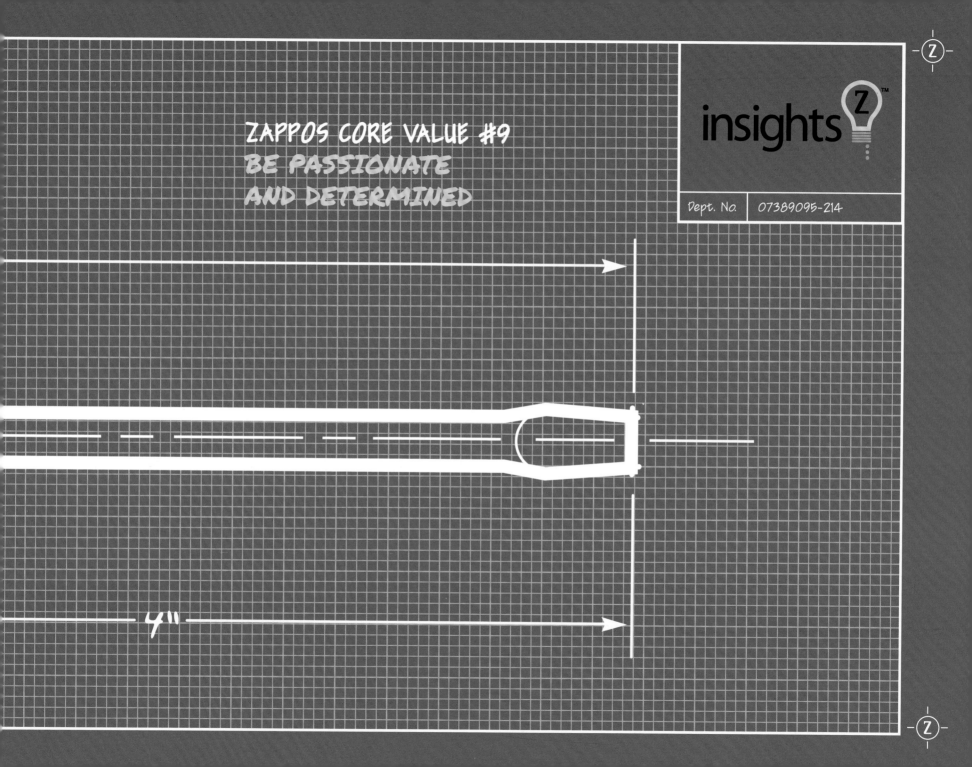

ANDI THE CULTURE SHOWGIRL.

employee since 2009

Today is May 31st, 2012; 963 days have come and gone since I joined the Zappos Family. I heard it was a pretty cool place to work, but honestly, I had heard that all before, many times. Companies had wooed me with promises of advancement and personal freedom, only to have it fade away once my signature had dried on the New Hire paperwork. I wasn't joining the company for those alluring benefits, I simply thought, "Wouldn't it be nice to not be miserable while working in a Call Center?" My first day in training began like all the others. I sat in the back of the classroom, hiding my plethora of tattoos with conventional office casual attire. I stayed interactive but quiet, feeling things out to see what was fluff and what was genuine. As the days continued, I found myself less capable of staying quiet in the back. My arms uncrossed and I felt connected with each person that came to talk with my class, whether it was the legal and marketing sharing their day-to-day tasks, or a presentation and activity to help us learn how each Core Value was truly playing a part in the company. I even found myself with tears in my eyes listening to every person that talked with us about their personal story of how they came to Zappos and how they have thrived. I was sold, but still wondered how long that infatuation and glee would survive past training.

As I spent time in CLT and interacted with more departments, I found how open the opportunities truly were and I genuinely embraced the spirit here at Zappos. I was done wondering when it would stop being wonderful; I was done waiting for things to fade from technicolor to black and white. I was able to quickly become a Mentor and pass on the joy and knowledge I was given and show new

folks that feeling empowered is only scary for a moment, and then it becomes fulfilling. I also was given the chance to showcase my talents (talking and walking at the same time) by moving into a position as a Tour Guide for Insights, a new little team with big dreams. I joined a smaller family within a family. Our entire purpose was to show the outside world that what we had here at Zappos wasn't just hype and was possible in any industry and any country.

I had come full circle, from thinking it's all just a "stage show" to taking folks "backstage" to see that "the show" never ends for us. Sure its great to glitter bomb my manager and go to Happy Hours, but from giving tours to hosting Culture Training events, Insights has given me opportunities and growth that I never thought possible. From strutting my stuff in a showgirl costume on the Garth Brooks stage at the Wynn, to speaking about impacting customers during a Tony Robbins conference at the Bellagio, Zappos has taught me to Dream Big.

I can't wait to see what comes next ...

AUGUSTA S.

employee since 2007

The Zappos CULTURE! It means everything! How we have an amazing environment to work in that doesn't even feel like work. It feels like being with your family every day. You never know what wonderful things will happen that day. And when you work hard and accomplish your goals and tasks, it's such an amazing feeling. Especially if it helps someone else in a positive way. From providing the best possible service to our customers, internal as well as external, to having so much fun. We laugh and smile all the time. We dance and sing. Always knowing that the customer comes first. We work hard and play hard. I have never had this experience before in my life, working at any other company. This is not typical "Corporate America," but then we don't get typical results either. So as I always say, the culture is us. It's me, and every single Zappos family member. It's up to us to make sure it continues to grow with us as we grow and it is alive and well! I love my Zappos family! I love the Zappos Culture and what it stands for! It stands for me! It stands for us! It stands strong!

COREY S.

employee since 2008

To me, the Zappos Culture means turning cynics into optimists.

CRYSTAL S.
employee since 2009

The Zappos Culture, to me, is like music. I'm jammin' out now as I write this, in fact! It's hard for me to find sufficient words to express how much I love music, but I gotta write something, right? It inspires me, drives me, and it brightens my day. It moves me and makes me happy! Like music, our culture just makes me wanna dance!! It's so uniquely wonderful, I can't help but feel motivated and so full of life just being here. Sure, we all have bad days sometimes, but coming to work here makes each day a little better. And being a part of the Zappos Family just makes life overall pretty amazing.

DANI G.
employee since 2010

This place just keeps getting better and better. Here it is, almost two years later, and I am still waiting for the other shoe to drop. I absolutely love this place and I feel so honored, humbled, and blessed to be a part of the awesome culture that we have here. Being a tour guide, I get to share the fabulousness of Zappos with the guests who come through, and it never ceases to amaze me how many people have heard about us and want to come see and learn about us for themselves. The Insights team impacts so many companies and people from around the world and I feel nothing less than blessed to be a part of this team. I am extremely excited about the vision for downtown Las Vegas and I cannot wait to see what unfolds and the impact that it will have on the community, the city, the state, the country, even the world as a whole. My Zapponians have amazed me every day; our Zappos Culture amazes me every day, and I hope that we continue to amaze the world. I love Zappos. <3

ELIA L.
employee since 2009

The Zappos Culture seems to be one of evolution. Our second core value is "Embrace and Drive Change." The world that we live in is constantly changing. Having an entire workforce dedicated to each other and learning from each experience is the key to trailblazing. Our culture is one of taking risks and not being afraid to fail. Failure is the engine of success. I love the quote, "What got you here, won't get you there." We have to consistently change our way of thinking. This leads to innovation and prosperity. This honors our fifth core value of "pursue growth and learning." When people are doing the same thing over and over again, you will find apathy and a sense of entitlement. This simply means that they have stopped learning and growing. Our culture empowers and inspires everyone to make the choice to learn and grow. We value things that we contribute to. When we contribute to our culture, we are also holding ourselves accountable. As we grow and increase in scale, our culture will continue to be our number one focus. If we don't keep it top of our minds it will shift and something else will take its place until it's out of our vision. I am committed to Happiness and Respect. Always remember that it comes down to choice. Happiness is a choice. You can be remarkable or invisible. The choice is yours.

EMAILE H.
employee since 2006

I am quickly approaching my sixth year with the Zappos Family and the Zappos Culture remains true! The past year has been full of new opportunities, stepping out of comfort zones and achieving both personal and professional growth. How lucky am I to be able to share all those moments with people who are more like family than simply coworkers?! The friendships and bonds I've established are sure to last a lifetime!! What does the Zappos Culture mean to me? It means not taking Zappos for granted! Working in Insights and meeting people from all over the world who have less-than-stellar working conditions, I'm constantly reminded that we are a rarity and should appreciate and cherish the Zappos culture daily! Cheers!

JENNA T.
employee since 2008

Zappos has been a big part of my life for over four years now. I've gone through so much personal loss and gain throughout that time that, before my daughter (love you Kaidence!) was born, Zappos was the only thing I could count on. Now that I'm a part of Zappos Insights, my whole perspective has changed! I was in ZCLT for over three years, but never quite grasped the level of epic-ness that is Zappos until now!

Not only am I fortunate enough to be a part of a company that prides itself on breaking the record for largest bar tab at the local restaurant, has toilet races and sumo wrestling in the parking lot, that pays me to attend All-Hands Meetings and the following open-bar Happy Hour, encourages me to Pursue Growth and Learning by offering Pipeline classes for my own personal and professional development and makes sure I'm taken care of in every sense of the phrase, but I get to share that with the world! Through the events we hold at Zappos Insights, I've truly found my passion. Sharing not only our culture, but our business practices with other businesses and seeing the light bulb go on is what makes me love coming to work every day!

To me, Zappos Culture means finding what you're passionate about, doing what it takes to make it happen, and having fun all at the same time!

MARIE M.
employee since 2009

Zappos is my family. It brings a special meaning to who I am and pours over into my personal life. My team has strengthened my personal values and commitment to everything I do.

I wake up each morning knowing I'm playing a part in spreading happiness. Whether I make someone smile or brighten their day, it makes my life better as well.

I have the honor of sharing with the world the amazing things we do here and, hopefully, giving them the tools and "insight" to help play their part to continue to change the world! Peace, Love, and Zappos!

MARISSA J.
employee since 2009

Zappos Culture in two words: Life Changing. It might not always be pretty or neat, but people have always said the right thing isn't always the easiest. And for Zappos it is definitely counter-intuitive to traditional business practices. Every day when I leave the office, I know that I have improved my life, even with the smallest action or conversation. Whether it's through tears, laughter, goofiness, or determination, my life is better because of the Zappos Culture and I am proud to be part of it!

MICHAEL S.
employee since 2010

The Zappos Culture is about making the office a place you look forward to going to. You treat people kindly, be polite, be yourself, and work hard.

MIG P.
employee since 2008

The Zappos Culture has grown, evolved, and strengthened over the past four years I've worked here. We've humanized the workplace. We know our coworkers on a personal and professional level, which makes it easier to relate to and communicate with each other. I appreciate everything Zappos has provided for us. I feel lucky every day!

NATALIE L.
employee since 2010

The Zappos Culture keeps getting better and better! Everyone is encouraged to laugh and play, even at work! I feel appreciated and love that I get to come to work here every day!

RENEA W.
employee since 2007

I've had such an amazing journey! Where else would I have the opportunity to connect with people from around the world and share this unique culture as a tour guide? It's hard to put into words what the Zappos Culture means to me, but this is what comes to mind when I think of Zappos and how our Culture defines us as a family:
C-camaraderie
U-unity
L-loyalty
T-teamwork
U-unabated
R-respect
E-enduring
Thank you, Zappos, for allowing me to live my dream every day!

ROBERT R.

employee since 2009

Zappos goes beyond any traditional definition because it is an idea, a family, a dream, and a people. It's a belief that can be shared across borders and across time. I love telling people I work at Zappos and hearing them say, "I believe in your company." They believe in what can only be described as the paradox – that deep knowing of what's true, despite the contradictions. It's an epic story that keeps evolving ...

First, it was to become the world's largest shoe store, when no one even believed that shoes could be sold online.

Next, it was to create a company whose product itself is customer service. They said it could not be done, and now our products go far beyond shoes because our customers keep coming back for the experience. Next, it was creating one of the best places to work and challenging the idea that you can't constantly have fun and get a lot of work done at the same time.

Next, we turned the culture itself into a product by creating the services of Zappos Insights – a way to share not only culture, but all the tools for any other company to create a strong culture where people love to work.

Now, we are taking what has been widely regarded as a city with no future – Downtown Las Vegas – and we will turn it into a thriving community, and the best place in the world to start a business. The 40 million people who visit Vegas every year will come to see the open, fun and entrepreneurial culture of Zappos, and bring it back with them to their home states and countries.

This is the art and science of doing the impossible, thus changing reality. As said in Delivering Happiness - "Create your own universe, and the universe will form around you." And when that universe is based on the love of serving the rest of the universe ...that's when magic happens.

ROCCO D.

employee since 2010

It is not the streamers, or the tschotchkes, or the shots of delicious Grey Goose that create our culture, it is truly the people. All of the material side effects come as a result of our culture. Take for instance my beautiful inspirational Mariah Carey poster; she provides me with endless happiness, and that is what Zappos is all about – endless happiness.

TRISH B.

employee since 2009

Culture Casserole
Prep time: Ongoing
Cook Time: Infinite
Ready In: Now
Ingredients:
1 cup Zappos CLT, Inc.
1 cup Zappos Merchandising, Inc.
1 cup Zappos IP, Inc.
1 cup Zappos.com, Inc.
1 cup Zappos Retail, Inc.
1 cup Zappos Fulfillment, Inc.
1 cup Zappos Development, Inc.
1 cup Zappos Gift Card, Inc.
1 cup Zappos Insights, Inc.
1 cup 6pm.com
1 splash of Grey Goose
1 dash of Fernet

Directions:
Throw all ingredients together in a large casserole dish. Continuously bake. Culture casserole serves all.

VALERIE S.

employee since 2010

I have learned so much, grown quite a bit as a person, and have had some amazing memories since joining the Zappos Family. My favorite Zappos memory is when I had the opportunity to go on a team-building field trip to San Francisco with Tony, the FACE Team, Mobski and a few others. We took the Delivering Happiness bus for one fun weekend. We visited a worm farm, went to the Outside Lands Music Festival and went to a birthday party for one of the original investors in Zappos. We laughed and created memories that will last a lifetime and for that, I am so grateful for my Zappos Family.

PRETTY
IN PINK
NO SHAME MODEL

2012 ALL HANDS MEETING

SECOND QUARTER

THE
WAAAAASUUUP
DAYTIME MODEL

THE SPOONER
FRONT VIEW

ZAPPOS CULTURE FAIR

APRIL 2012

CONVEYOR
BELT OF
HAPPINESS
TOP VIEW

ZAPPOS FULFILLMENT CENTER

SHIPPING HAPPY BOXES

GOT YER BACK
REAR VIEW

CORPORATE CHALLENGE BIKE RACE

TOUR DE ZAPPS

SUN RACER
5000
SOLAR RECHARGEABLE MODEL

ANONYMOUS

employee since 2010

The longer I work at Zappos, the more subtle I find my understanding of the culture here. I think when one starts at Zappos, one is overwhelmed by the myriad of amazing benefits, great people, fantastic opportunities, and rabid pace of work. It's like stepping from inside a dark room into bright sunlight – it's dazzling and colorful and intense all at once. But spend a little time in that sunlight and you begin to notice the subtle beauty beyond just the bright light.

That's a bit how I feel now, a year and a half into my career at Zappos. Yes, the benefits here are amazing, but it's the small things that really make working here great. No one tells me where I can and can't sit, or what I can and can't sit on. I can wear whatever I want to work. I can work at 2AM or 2PM, if that works best for me. It's these small benefits, these small flexibilities that really engender my loyalty and make it easy to devote long hours to my job. The people ARE great; but spend some time with a Zapponian and one realizes just how intelligent, how talented, how passionate, how special one's coworkers are. There is a youthful hum of new possibility everywhere you walk in the office, and more importantly, a true feeling of closeness and camaraderie in and between each team.

One of the things I like to tell the candidates we interview when they invariably ask, "What do you like best about working at Zappos?" is that, while Zappos is approaching a medium size in terms of employees and revenue, one can still find a true entrepreneurial mindset here. If one is passionate about an idea, if one can flesh it out and make a dedicated effort in pursuing this idea, one can easily find the support to make the idea a reality. I've seen numerous instances of a friend or coworker taking a small idea that was percolating in his or her brain and create an entirely new job or department here at Zappos, something completely different than what they were doing. That's an opportunity many look for their entire lives – the ability to dictate their career, and follow their passions and interest.

Like any organization, however, Zappos has its flaws. The pace of change at Zappos is rapid, and adjusting to these changes can be a challenge, both emotionally and operationally. Because of our collective passion for our community, it often feels like our attention is divided between two responsibilities: our core service business, and our commitment to the transformation of downtown Las Vegas. Describing Zappos as a family is apropos – with all the dysfunction and squabbles and personality wrangling one sees even in the closest of families. And we all struggle with balancing work and life – sometimes it's hard to just find the time to go to sleep! Most importantly, we are reaching a size that makes it a challenge to steward both the culture and business in the same ways we have – or, conversely, sometimes reinforce the importance of the ways we got here. Figuring out this balance is our biggest challenge, and will dictate our ability to evolve.

Yet, as Confucius says, "Better a diamond with a flaw than a pebble without." The defects are our own, and without them, our culture wouldn't be ours. I have no doubt my brilliant coworkers will find new and interesting ways to polish the diamond we've created, and we'll take the Zappos Culture to new and interesting heights. I love it here, and couldn't imagine a better place to work.

MAYRA M.

employee since 2010

My definition of the Zappos Culture is working alongside some of your best friends, getting paid to have fun, travel, and meet new people. Also not being fazed by seeing people in drag, costumes, or wearing silly (or stupid) hats.

ALEX S.

employee since 2010

Zappos is fun.
There's a hole in the bucket, dear Liza, dear Liza,
There's a hole in the bucket, dear Liza,
There's a hole.
Then fix it dear Henry, dear Henry, dear Henry,
Then fix it dear Henry, dear Henry, fix it.
With what should I fix it, dear Liza, dear Liza,
With what should I fix it, dear Liza, with what?
With a straw, dear Henry, dear Henry, dear Henry,
With a straw, dear Henry, dear Henry, with a straw.
But the straw is too long, dear Liza, dear Liza,
The straw is too long, dear Liza, too long.
Then cut it dear Henry, dear Henry, dear Henry,
Then cut it dear Henry, dear Henry, cut it!
With what shall I cut it, dear Liza, dear Liza,
With what shall I cut it, dear Liza, with what?
With an ax, dear Henry, dear Henry, dear Henry,
With an ax, dear Henry, an ax.
But the ax is too dull, dear Liza, dear Liza,
The ax is too dull, dear Liza, too dull.
Then, sharpen it, dear Henry, dear Henry, dear Henry,
Then sharpen it dear Henry, dear Henry, sharpen it!
With what should I sharpen it, dear Liza, dear Liza,
With what should I sharpen, dear Liza, with what?
With a stone, dear Henry, dear Henry, dear Henry,
With a stone, dear Henry, dear Henry, a stone.
But the stone is too dry, dear Liza, dear Liza,
The stone is too dry, dear Liza, too dry.
Then wet it, dear Henry, dear Henry, dear Henry,
Then wet it dear Henry, dear Henry, wet it.
With what should I wet it, dear Liza, dear Liza,
With what should I wet it, dear Liza, with what?
With water, dear Henry, dear Henry, dear Henry,
With water, dear Henry, dear Henry, with water.
But how shall I get it, dear Liza, dear Liza,
But how shall I get it, dear Liza, with what?
In the bucket, dear Henry, dear Henry, dear Henry,
In the bucket, dear Henry, dear Henry, in the bucket!
But there's a hole in the bucket, dear Liza, dear Liza,
There's a hole in the bucket, dear Liza, a hole.
There's a hole.

DESCRIPTION OF
FRUIT LEFT OUTSIDE
TOP VIEW

CHALK DAY

TAKING IT TO THE STREETS

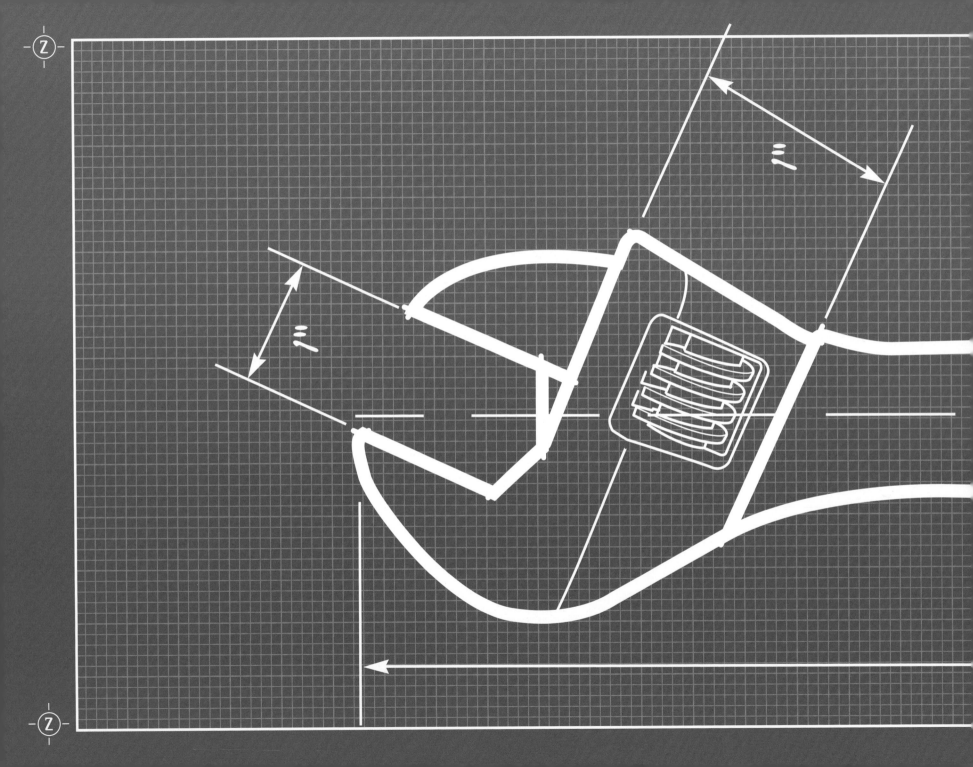

ZAPPOS CORE VALUE #6
BUILD OPEN AND
HONEST RELATIONSHIPS
WITH COMMUNICATION

Dept. No.   6546882-874

7"

ANONYMOUS
employee since 2011

In my first half-year with Zappos, I've come a long way in understanding our culture. It was hard to recognize at first, because everyone here is hired based on it. So, when I was thrown into this fun, crazy and supportive work environment, it was easy to forget how special it was. Little by little, I've begun to realize that our Zappos Culture isn't just about the Ten Core Values. It's about the people. Our teams all seem to love each other and are friends as much as they are co-workers. There isn't a single day where we don't all have a good laugh (or ten) about stuff and I look forward to coming in each day. It's that certain level of appreciation everyone carries for retaining this open and fun environment and a respect for the people who are just a bit crazy and goofy that really lets us all relax and enjoy ourselves just a bit more than I thought possible. So far, I'm really enjoying it.

ANONYMOUS
employee since 2009

The Zappos Culture is a living breathing thing, constantly in flux, and trying to persevere. We are responsible for the culture by being responsible for ourselves. Every day we have decisions we need to make and how and why we make every one of those decisions affects the culture. Nothing is contained or isolated in our cultural system. I hope we can remember this as we go through our work day. We are in it together and no one can elevate it or dismantle it faster than all of us together. Don't rely on HR, execs, your manager, or your teammates. Rely on yourself.

ANONYMOUS
employee since 2011

The Zappos Culture, to me, means working hard and enjoying it; and forming relationships with other people, both at work and outside of work.

ANONYMOUS
employee since 2010

No reason to start a company with your friends because you are working with your friends. You don't have to wait for the weekend to hang out with your friends. A culture fit? Do you think he/she can be your friend? That's what Zappos is. Please let it grow.

ANONYMOUS
employee since 2012

My wife and I packed up our lives four months ago and moved across the country to join the Zappos family. We were greeted at our apartment by my team, who decided they'd come and help me unload my moving truck in their own time. They are people I didn't know four months ago — now I consider them my best friends. The Zappos Culture is being a part of something bigger than yourself, because you know that, in the end, it's not about how many toys you end up with at the end of the day, but the lives you enriched with the toys you had. It's learning how to create more WOW moments, professionally and personally. It's playing pranks on each other knowing that at the end of the day, strangely, it made your connections stronger.

The Zappos Culture is my culture.

ANONYMOUS
employee since 2007

.-- .... .-. / .- .-. / .-- / --. --- .. -. --. ..--..

1.01011101101001E+214

ANONYMOUS
employee since 2010

For me, the Zappos Culture is the invisible, yet powerful force that keeps this highly weird and dysfunctional group of people together. It manifests itself with honest smiles from people you don't know, or sincere greetings when you tell people that you bought your first home or exchanged that car that was giving you a lot of trouble. But it reaches its peak when people get together to participate when somebody needs to be pranked, or helped because they had a life-threatening accident.

It is the sum of all the little things that my Zapponians come up with that makes my workplace an extension of my home.

ANONYMOUS
employee since 2010

It is not what you do, where you go, or when it happens. It is all about who was with you.

ANONYMOUS
employee since 2010

The Zappos Culture has a couple meanings to me. First, it is the life blood of the company. The things that the company sets out to do and achieves are heavily influenced by the culture. Think of it as the DNA of an organism. The culture is also a guide book. When we fall out of place or get lost along the way, the Zappos Culture is always a reference to get us back on our feet!

ADAM G.

employee since 2005

Having been at Zappos for seven and a half years, I can still say that it is a great place to work. Every day is exciting and brings new challenges and learning opportunities. I've met some of my closest friends at Zappos, and continue to meet more. Most of all ... I'm still a man of few words. ;-)

ADAM W.

employee since 2012

The Zappos Culture, to me, means:
Being able to focus when you need to, and be distracted when you need a break.
Being able to be yourself around your coworkers without (much) peer pressure.
Making friends among your coworkers and hanging out with them outside of work.
Looking forward to the various events held at HQ.

ALEC F.

employee since 2009

"Ever-newer waters flow on those who step into the same rivers." – Heraclitus

ALEX E.

employee since 2012

To me, the Zappos Culture is ... being yourself for the betterment of the company and not having to fear being judged for doing so. One of the few places where work can be fun and productive, Zappos provides a safe environment for us to truly be passionate. (Side note: true story)

ALICE H.

employee since 2011

A year prior to joining Zappos, I was on a mission to find inner happiness. I read self-help books, joined yoga retreats, tried hypnotherapy, but nothing worked. Then I found out that Zappos was opening a back-up office in San Francisco and I knew the mother ship was calling me home. Countless friends emailed me to let me know, as I have preached my love for Zappos since the beginning of time. (I may or may not have exited my mother's womb waving an "I <3 Zappos" flag).

ALISTAIR P.

employee since 2012

I believe that the Zappos Culture is our sustainable competitive advantage! Our success is an emerging phenomenon; simply by living our core values, we've created an amazing company. Our culture is what makes Zappos such a happy place, and our culture is what makes Zappos such a successful place!

AMARA S.

employee since 2005

The Zappos Culture is all about the amazing folks who are incredibly smart, hardworking and so much fun to be around. I look forward to interacting with them personally and professionally. Those are the people that are the heart of Zappos – the ones who continue to motivate and inspire everyone.

AUSTIN K.

employee since 2008

The Zappos Culture means that my coworkers are my friends and that I can safely assume that people at work whom I do not yet know are not jerks.

BARRY VAN B.

employee since 2009

The Zappos Culture allows individuals to truly define the role they play within the organization, while providing the flexibility to experiment with other career opportunities via cross-departmental internships, etc. It is unlike anything I experienced in my pre-Zappos life.

BILL W.

employee since 2007

Nsgre 5 lrnef, fgvyy cnffvbangr naq qrgrezvarq!

BOB S.

employee since 2010

The Zappos Culture ... I think the best way to describe it is "WOW!" Every single day is filled with fun, excitement and challenge. The days literally fly by, and when you look back it's hard to believe how much time has passed. Everyone is so eager to help and make things happen. Friends, smiles, good times and fun – that about sums it up!

BRENT C.

employee since 2007

Just a spoonful of culture helps the medicine go down.

BRIAN E.

employee since 2011

I love the people, friends, coworkers, customers, everyone. They make me laugh, spark my imagination, and genuinely make me a better person.

BRIAN K.

employee since 2010

The Zappos Culture is an environment that produces an opportunity to learn and grow with people who are interested in helping you do so. It's also an opportunity to help those around you do the same. I've long felt that proper leadership is an opportunity to serve those whom you lead and Zappos seems to exemplify this principle.

BRYCE M.

employee since 2009

Everywhere I've worked, there have been good days and bad days. At Zappos, I've never had a boring day. It's unlike anywhere else I've worked; I'm constantly being challenged to learn new things and to grow.

CARRIE W.

employee since 2012

The Zappos Culture is a collective passion for making all things exciting, inspirational, and delightful.

CHERYL ANNE F.

employee since 2006

What would you do if I sang out tune? Would you stand up and walk out on me?
(I'd like to think no; you'd let me sing at the top of my lungs, and then whisper in my ear that maybe I should check what key I should be in ... and we'll sing the whole song again together!)
Lend me your ears and I'll sing you a song

I will try not to sing out of key.
(Because I trust you'll tolerate mistakes and let me take risks, so I want to give you the very best performance I can.)
Oh, baby, I get by with a little help from my friends.
All I need is my buddies.
(To back me up when stuff doesn't work, when things get completed slower than expected, when we change our minds and decide we want not X, but the exact opposite of X.)
Said I don't know if that's what I'm sure to do
(I'm not in a self-actualized/this-is-my-calling-and-passion moment as I write this, but that's okay. The world is not ending because I'm not delivering maximum happiness; it is better because I'm trying my best to.)
Said I'm gonna make it with my friends
Get by with a little help from my friends
Said I'm gonna keep on trying.

CHRISTOPHER W.

employee since 2008

Here be I. Rock you like a gentle rain.

COREY B.

employee since 2011

It's quite interesting ... When I started with the company, I thought the Zappos Culture was set, that the leadership team had "gotten it right," and as a company we were "in the clear," so to speak. Over the time I've been here, I've realized how dynamic and fluid the culture is, how important it is that we care for it, and how easily it can be destroyed if the right attention isn't paid to it.

I love the Zappos Culture ... I think it's one of the great things I've experienced in my professional life. I also realize the true impact one person can have on both our culture, and our experience here at Zappos. It's wonderful to be a part of something bigger than yourself ... but it's even better to realize the positive impact you can have on the lives of others (and the positive impact they in turn have on you)! Slightly introspective ... but for the difference it's had on my life, extremely profound!

CRYSTAL T.

employee since 2012

I'm so grateful that I work in a place where I'm accepted and all my ideas are accepted and considered. Where I'm expected to WOW every day! WOW ... that's all I can say ...

DANIELLE C.

employee since 2010

The best thing about the Zappos Culture is that you can pursue any interests you have and make them come to life. Helping establish a sustainability program here has been incredibly rewarding! Everyone has been super-encouraging and supportive to help make the program even better than I imagined. Not many companies promote people to follow their passions and make a difference. This is why I love Zappos!

DANNY S.
employee since 2010

Zappos is an amazing company. I am excited to come in to work and see everyone so happy to be doing good for the company. It is hard to effectively balance staying comfortable, being motivated, and producing results. And it's not only at work for us. It carries over even at other events, such as the Corporate Challenge! Zappos really does it all!

DARSHAN B.
employee since 2010

The Zappos Culture is about truly feeling like you are part of a family. You get to work with close friends, not just coworkers.

DAVE F.
employee since 2010

Some people say Zappos is like college. Except you have responsibility. And you get paid. And there are no keg parties ... Wait, scratch the last one! I think people compare Zappos to college because there is a sense of living in a bubble. It is a bubble, because people are in disbelief that one could have this work environment. We work and party hard. C'mon, we're in Vegas, baby!!!

And that is it. I go to work and hang out with friends. I go to hang out with friends and get work done. There have been work calls at 3 a.m., and there have been drinks at 10 a.m.

So where's the work-life balance? Who cares!?!? Some call it culture ... I think it's a lifestyle I share with friends choosing to pursue happiness at work and at play.

I like you, I love you, I thank you.

DAVID H.
employee since 2009

The Zappos Culture, to me, is about being part of something that encourages you to be the best version of yourself. We work hard, we play hard, and we make sure that everyone we interact with – either at work or just out there in the world – gets to enjoy that feeling right along with us! And with any luck, it makes them a little happier.

ED L.
employee since 2005

Another year has passed, and ever since day one it's been an amazing ride. I'm looking forward to the next seven years and what we make out of it.

ELAINE Z.
employee since 2011

The Zappos Culture means working hard to do a good job because you genuinely want the best results for your coworkers, for the company, and for your customers.

It means being surrounded by friendly, positive and considerate coworkers.

It means realizing that at Zappos, change is constant, growing pains exist and it's okay.

It's finding great friends, bonding through difficult times and being your true self throughout the journey.

ELISABETH (LIZZY) B.
employee since 2010

Zappos is like no other company. I absolutely love my job and also love being at work with amazing people who are genuinely kind and happy. We work hard and still have fun. I also appreciate our relationships with other departments here at Zappos. Being in the Retail Operations/ EDI team allows me to connect with a lot of employees around the company and meet new people regularly. The culture here is like no other. I am proud to wear my Zappos badge wherever I go! I have lots of pride in this company and have high expectations. I think a lot of people feel the same way too, even our customers! YAY for the existence of Zappos!! <3

EMMANUEL M.
employee since 2010

Zappos Culture is amazing. Astonishing. Fantastic. Friendly. Incredible. Invincible. Mighty. Sensational. Spectacular. Strange. Uncanny. An uncle once said "With great power comes great responsibility" but I say "With great coworkers comes great culture." It is a privilege to be part of this one-of-a-kind culture that is Zappos. Zappos, Assemble!

HEMA A.

employee since 2012

This is my first month at Zappos, and so far the culture has been very a refreshing change for me. I love how everyone is very friendly and relaxed.

IAN CHRISTIAN M.

employee since 2008

The earth's inner core is a solid ball, composed mainly of iron, with a radius of about 1,220 km, and a density of approximately 13 grams per cubic centimeter. Therefore, the Earth's Core Value, as of Q2 2012, is around $146,200,000,000,000,000,000,000 USD. However, because the inner core is found 5,150 km below the Earth's surface, where temperatures reach 9,800 degrees Fahrenheit, I imagine the culture isn't particularly fun. So, that's something to think about.

JAMIE W.

employee since 2007

To me, the Zappos Culture is how we are represented as a brand. Everything from our speedy delivery, excellent customer service, passionate and talented employees, and most of all, our Ten Core Values.

JEFFREY S.

employee since 2010

It's been two years since I started at Zappos and I feel like I am really starting to enjoy it even more. Definitely there have been some ups and downs through the year, so it's not all fun and games all the time, like everyone thinks it is. We get real work done here and sometimes that work isn't glamorous, fun or rewarding — but the people you work with definitely make it worthwhile. I guess no matter how mundane a thing you have to do here, there is some comfort knowing that it is necessary and it will help your family – the Zappos Family, that is – grow stronger. I think that is the culture. We are about fun – we have tons of it – but we also accept the bad with the good. We know that we have to go through some hard times to get to the really good stuff and we have each other to rely on as we go through those hard times. Going downtown in the coming year is going to be another challenge for us, and one I think we are ready to accept. Our culture is continuing to grow and change as we speak, but the core of it is still there. So until next year's Culture Book, I like you, I love you, thank you!

JESSE C.

employee since 2005

After nearly seven years with Zappos, I've had the pleasure of watching our culture grow and evolve. The one thing that never changes, though, is just how much I love working with these great people. Culture without people is like dividing by zero. The concept doesn't even make sense. Zappos is not a building or a website; it is a collection of people hell bent on doing something meaningful in an arena where meaning is barely an afterthought. What an experience! What a great way to have spent these last seven years. Bravo, everyone. Bravo!

JESSICA R.

employee since 2011

Zappos is the last place I ever want to work! Period. I wake up every day, excited to work with amazingly talented people. Oh yeah, and did I mention that we're all friends and enjoy spending time together, AND we have a lot of fun while accomplishing a ton of work? It's true! At Zappos, I feel empowered to get involved, to push projects forward and to make decisions while creating fun and a little weirdness. How great is that? It's truly a magical company. Thank you, Zappos, for being my home and my family!

JIA T.

employee since 2010

I've been here for a few years now and the Zappos Culture seems to be getting better and better every year. There are so many activities going on and lots of fun people to hang out with. There are always learning opportunities and lots of open doors for trying new things. I always seem to be able to keep myself busy and be engaged with the Zappos Culture. It is fueled by us employees and its potential is limitless.

JIM D.

employee since 2012

Coming to the Zappos Culture from the military has been a breath of fresh air. When my family and I made the move to Vegas, we knew we were in for an exciting time. What we didn't know was that we would find a family that would adopt us wholeheartedly, in the way that Zappos has. I could never have imagined looking forward to Mondays, or wanting to spend Friday afternoon at the office hanging out with the same people I've been working with all week. Everything is different here, and that's a good thing! In my short time, I've seen Zappos employees pull together to work for the good of the company in times of distress, not because it was the right thing to do, but because they believe in Zappos and want the business to succeed. I am continually amazed by the culture of openness and the opportunities for learning here at Zappos. It's my hope that in the coming years I'll be able to contribute and enhance the unique culture and environment we have here.

JOHN B.

employee since 2009

The Zappos Culture, to me, means being a family with your coworkers. Having a company where people often interact with each other outside of work, allows everyone to grow close. In turn, this allows interactions at work to be very cooperative.

JOHN H.

employee since 2008

The culture at Zappos is constantly moving and changing. There is always something new happening and something to be passionate about. It makes each day new and interesting. This year has been tough ... Zappos has been a foundation for me.

Through thick or thin, blood or tears, people here will help you.

That's what the Zappos Culture really means to me.

JOHNNY P.

employee since 2007

The Zappos Culture is what makes it a pleasure to come to work in the morning. Work doesn't really feel so much like work when you are around friends and accomplishing amazing things that will make our customers happy and make this a stronger, better company. It also means building lasting relationship with your colleagues because they are great people.

The culture also means not taking this company or its culture for granted. It is hard work to maintain such an open, honest, fun, hard-working environment. It means coming in every day and trying to make the culture 1% better.

KEDAR D.

employee since 2011

Working on a new quest along with fun-loving people.

KEITH T.

employee since 2011

Opportunity abounds! The open-minded, sharing approach of the business and tech teams allow me to stretch my skill sets in ways I've never experienced in other organizations. "Not my/your job" isn't in the vocabulary or part of the approach our teams take to finding solutions for our customers. Our culture provides an outline and framework for growth extending far beyond the traditional, structured career path.

KEN K.

employee since 2011

One of the things that really inspires me about Zappos is its culture. I know that every day, regardless of whatever else is going on, I will walk into a supportive work environment where I not only like the people I work with, but also look forward to coming to work every day! I do not sense the overt political agendas I've encountered elsewhere, and there is a real sense of coming together for the common good that I've not encountered elsewhere. That is what I think is the real edge Zappos has – we are always there for one another.

KEVIN L.
employee since 2012

I really enjoy coming to work. Sure, there are things that are difficult, but on the whole, I feel blessed to be part of this company. I've made so many good friends here that I hang out with them on the weekends and after work. I also love what I do! I think the strong relationships that I have at work are a direct result of Zappos' conscious effort to balance social activities with work. The company also seems to have a good sense of balancing efficiency with quality; at other companies I've seen products rushed out the door while developers are under pressure, and that's never fun. Zappos does a lot of little things that really make you feel like the company wants its workers to be happy!

KRISTIE L.
employee since 2011

I've been at Zappos for about seven months and it's everything I was afraid it wouldn't be. I didn't think working here could possibly be as awesome as it was portrayed, but it is. My coworkers really care about what they do here. They work hard and are positive people. I've become more positive as a result. I've been encouraged to grow, and recognized for my work. Anyone who comes from less-than-ideal working conditions would really appreciate these things. In addition, there is so much happy energy here. People smile, greet each other and chat, even when they don't know each other. I really intend this to be the last company I work for. I doubt there is anywhere better.

LENNY B.
employee since 2011

The memories lost in the last year would make for a great Culture Book entry!

LYNN W.
employee since 2008

Zappos, to me, is about family. We celebrate each other's successes and help each other in times of need. I am amazed by the amount of caring that Zappos employees have for each other.

MANUJ M.
employee since 2012

Hi there!!

This is my first Culture Book entry. I just started at Zappos four weeks ago!!

I love being here. The part I like best about working at Zappos is that you can be yourself and still get the work done.

Before joining Zappos I always thought, "How can it be done?" But I can say now, you can have fun while working very hard (or hardly working)!! I am sure I am going to enjoy my stay here and will be here 4ever!!

MARK J.
employee since 2011

The Zappos Culture means having a place that I look forward to coming to every day. It creates a place that you want to be a part of instead of feeling like you have to be there. I'm so grateful for the culture we have and wouldn't trade it for anything.

MARK M.
employee since 2008

Zappos is awesome! I love Zappos!
This is actually somewhat of a test entry ... I'm debugging the Culture Book submission page live right now. (Some questions regarding newline characters; trying to fix that as we speak. Do more with less, right? :-) Zappos Development is the best!

MATT K.
employee since 2012

I've been with Zappos for about a month now and I still can't believe what an amazing company it is and how awesome the people that work here are. It is so awesome how much we care about our customers and what we are willing to do to WOW them. I never in my life would have imagined I would get an opportunity to have so much fun at work and enjoy what I was doing so much, and I feel I am one of the luckiest people to get the chance to work here. I am super-excited to bring new ideas and a fresh perspective to Zappos and look forward to a long, rewarding career working for a company I can truly be proud of!

MATTHEW R.

employee since 2006

Six years ago I applied to Zappos, looking for a job right out of college. I had a film degree and a bachelor of arts degree. Not exactly the perfect training for a programmer, but Zappos gave me a chance. From learning Perl, to writing whole sites in a few weeks (Canada!), to writing whole sites in a few months (6pm!), to learning Java and rewriting the site in it, to search code, to Android code – I've done quite a bit over my six years here. So many people at Zappos have taught me so much, and never has anyone told me what I can't do. At Zappos, you really can do what you want – if you're willing to stick with it and just make sure it happens.

So much after only six years – film major to computer science type. Who would have thought? What amazing things will I be doing in 2018?

MEG M.

employee since 2007

The Zappos Culture = Choices, Chances, Changes, Celebrations. Repeat daily as needed.

MELISSA M.

employee since 2010

Brohoof /]

MICHAEL R.

employee since 2011

Zappos is a place where I actually look forward to the workday. Never have I been part of a work environment where coworkers are so friendly and consistently maintain great attitudes. More so, I wouldn't have anticipated having so many new people become my close friends in such a short period of time. Here, we work hard but we also know how to have fun. It's brilliant that a company will let us regulate ourselves and I believe that it's a big part of how we don't burn out!

MICHAEL S.

employee since 2010

Each one of Zappos' Ten Core Values has real meaning, and that's awesome. Being at this company has given me both the drive and the opportunities I need to create change, not only in my work life, but in my other lives as well. I like that. No, I LOVE that. Thank you.

"Only a ginger can call another ginger, Ginger." – Tim Minchin

… just like only a ninja can sneak up on another ninja."

To Brandon: "What's up, my ginga!?"

MIKE O.

employee since 2010

The main way the Zappos Culture manifests itself for me is in how everyone treats everyone else: Zappos employees are universally nice. There's an underlying assumption that everyone is operating from pure intentions and will go out of their way to help you if they can. When you consider that we spend one third of our life at work, working in an environment like this really enhances our lives.

NICK P.

employee since 2006

After six years, I feel as if our Zappos Culture is at a turning point; we've become a really big company now and I'm always wondering what the next big thing will be. I feel like we're on the verge of it with the move to downtown. I can't wait to see what it grows into next!

PAMELA J.

employee since 2011

The Zappos Culture is success! As an experienced professional who has worked for other major corporations, I'm aware that the culture of a company plays a significant role in its successes and failures. Companies that take their culture seriously routinely outperform their competition. For me, while working for companies that seriously embrace their culture, I was/am able to achieve so much more personally and professionally. My quality of life is much better, I am excited to be at work, and am able to push myself to achieve things I never thought possible. Zappos has changed my life and raised my bar of expectations of what companies today should offer!

PATRICE L.

employee since 2009

I am overwhelmed with excitement every day when I come to work and get to see the lovely faces of Stephanie, Dave, Trish, Rachel, Rebecca, Meg, Vanessa, Vita, Tricia, Hema, Natasha, Lizzy, Bernie and Thomas! I love those crazy kids. =)

PATRICK G.

employee since 2011

We recently got three interns on the website systems team. In order to welcome them we decided to decorate their desks. My intern's desk was covered with ten bags of Swedish fish, a display case of energy drinks, and a pile of quarters for the vending machine. When he came in and saw it, he couldn't help but take a picture and send it to his aunt who works for a typical corporate company. Her reply makes it clear what Zappos is all about. She said, "Are you joking? You can't be serious … Can they even legally do that?!" The interns are going to really enjoy finding out what it is like to work at a job you love coming to because you can be yourself, be happy, and have fun. That is what the Zappos Culture is all about :)

PAWEL S.

employee since 2007

This marks my fifth year at Zappos, and despite all of the changes going on, it has been one of the best years so far. I've transferred to the San Francisco development team while living in Vegas, and I get to work with some really wonderful people in both places. In November of last year, with the help of awesome people and funding from Zappos and Downtown Project, we opened /usr/lib to the public. Today (March 31st) I'm excited to hear back about a proposal for an even more ambitious project.

It's all about the people … and I've been lucky enough to meet some fantastic ones here.

PHOEBE C.

employee since 2012

This is my first year at Zappos and I'm amazed at the investment they have already made in me — from getting a water bottle in a shoebox with my offer letter to investing in a one-month training to learn the Culture and CLT processes and tools before starting my actual job. It's been great! I look forward to continued learning and giving back to Zappos!

RACHEL A.

employee since 2011

The Zappos Culture is a fun adventure of balance. On one side, you're encouraged to have fun, chat and connect with your team members (as well as integrate with other teams), and be goofy, but on the other side there's also always a ton of work to do, deadlines to meet, and broken stuff that needs fixing. I love challenging myself to have at least one 5-10 minute conversation a day that's not about work (and I love that that challenge is fully supported by my managers).

RACHEL L.

employee since 2011

As I write this entry, the entire tech area has just finished a gigantic Nerf™ war to welcome the New Hire class. This is just one example of the unique Zappos Culture that I've never seen replicated in another work environment. I started at Zappos as an intern two months after I graduated college, and now I've been working here for about 11 months. In those 11 months I've worked as a technical writer, I've been to countless team lunches, boating on Lake Mead, haunted houses, happy hours, a team pool day at the M, and many fun parties. The Zappos Culture is like a lifestyle. To me, it's not about balancing work and play, but to work hard, have fun, and build relationships while doing so!

RACHEL M.

employee since 2010

The culture at Zappos is the kind of thing that is hard to put into words, but to me, it means a place where I get to be myself. We get to live and be a part of the culture instead of having to conform to it.

RIAN S.

employee since 2012

As a relatively new employee, I am most impressed with the willingness of everyone to participate – whether it's in an impromptu conversation or some crazy volunteer hike across mountains. I've yet to see much of the typical technical or management defense of turf that stifles conversation at many companies. It's nice to know that I can ask anyone a question, and they'll (almost) always happily take the time to answer. That said, I'd love to see the Heart Attack Grill flattened by a front-end loader. I think that's about it.

RICH H.

employee since 2011

Culture defines the character of Zappos as if it were a human being. The Core Values map how customers, community and "family members" are dealt with at every level. The culture is constant and can be applied across the business in any situation (growth, planning, performance, etc.).

Tying human elements to how the company operates makes this place fun, engaging, and different from any other organization that I know of.

RICH J.
employee since 2011

Zappos Culture to me means that everyone in Zappos has the same goal, which is why we are successful, and that everyone has a hand in this success no matter what their role within the company. Our culture is about service... and that's not just service to the end customers, but also our internal customers.

RICHARD H.
employee since 2011

For me, the Zappos Culture means being a part of something bigger than myself. It's about making a difference.

RICK D.
employee since 2011

I truly believe the Zappos approach to culture is transformative to running a company. Being part of what is probably the world's largest experiment of its kind is both exciting and humbling. Seeing how a company driven by its culture continues to evolve as it grows shows that there can be a focus on people and their well-being, yet such a company can still be financially successful.

RITA R.
employee since 2010

Happy to be part of the Zappos Family! Zappos is known for its rich culture! :)

RYAN A.
employee since 2007

Just as I've got it all figured out, they switch it on me. It's amazing how much my job description and responsibilities have changed since I started almost five years ago. I love facing the constant challenges and the continued learning, technically, professionally, and personally. And the wonderful people around me make it worthwhile and fulfilling to keep doing it every day.

SEAN M.
employee since 2005

Apparently, it is illegal to ride a camel on the highway in Nevada. Please keep that in mind in 2013 when determining transportation to the new downtown offices.

SHANNON G.
employee since 2010

To me, the Zappos Culture means having the ability to make quick decisions without fear of reprisal and adjust as needed, learning along the way. A supportive environment lets us create, grow, learn, and adapt on a daily basis!

SHARON S.
employee since 2011

Every day I learn a little more about what the Zappos Culture is, but for now it's working with friends, having fun, being weird, being passionate, trying new things, wearing what you want to work (i.e., no suits!), hackathons, and so much more!

SHAUN H.
employee since 2011

Here are some fun stats about our Core Values:
Number of core values: 10
Total words: 47
Total characters: 261
Average number of words: 4.7
Average number of characters: 26.1
Average number of characters per word: 5.55
Shortest core value: 2 words, 8 characters
Longest core value: 7 words, 48 characters
Most common word: "and" (7 times)
Most common letter: "e" (35 times)
Look out for more fun stats in the next issue!

SHAWN L.
employee since 2010

I've been here almost two years, and I still wake up every morning looking forward to coming into work. I love my coworkers and love my job.

SHELDON S.
employee since 2007

One thing I like about Zappos is the quarterly "All Hands" meetings — to me, a fairly recent addition, since I've been here five years now. These are an awesome way for the company to come together and feel like one big team instead of a lot of scattered small groups. The different locations for these events and the happy hour afterwards are a fun way to meet new people and also reconnect with people that I no longer work closely with. The guest speakers are a good way for us to think and learn about something new. Even if I am not interested in their topics, I can almost always get a new or different perspective on whatever they are discussing. The financial updates and QA sessions are a good way to keep everyone focused on how the company is doing and what the hot-button issues are. There are lots of Core Values being exercised by having these All Hands meetings.

SOTHEAVY O.

The culture at Zappos is one where you can break down walls between cubicles, but still hang a piece of paper up to block a coworker's direct stare without offending them. I'm (not) looking at you, Brian and Susan.

STEPHANIE S.
employee since 2006

What does the Zappos Culture mean to me? Happiness. At the end of the day I'm happy, happy to have come to work, happy to hang out with my coworkers, happy to be a part of such an amazing company!

STEPHEN H.
employee since 2005

The Zappos Culture, to me, is this intangible thing that everyone fosters. Without buy-in, it just doesn't work, but surrounded by those who believe in and perpetuate our Core Values and embrace the culture of the company, it feels just like being around family.

STEVE L.
employee since 2009

The best part of the Zappos Culture has always been the friendly and honest people we work with and interact with on a daily basis. Regardless of what you're doing, good friends and coworkers make it better.

STEVEN A.
employee since 2011

I have been at Zappos for about a year and half now and I still think it is one of the best companies to work for. One of the things I love most about the Zappos Culture is that we are encouraged to be ourselves while being challenged to be our best (and to have a little bit of fun while we are at it). Zappos' culture is certainly unique, but that is what makes it so great.

SUSAN A.

employee since 2007

Five years and two and a half babies later, I'm still at Zappos and still loving it! Zappos keeps me on my toes and entertained, to say the least. I'm excited about what has happened in tech the last year and am very excited for the upcoming year. Plus, I can't wait to see what Zappos has in store for us with the move downtown! :)

SUSAN H.
employee since 2011

I thought my stay in Nevada was going to be a short one, but when I found Zappos everything changed. Las Vegas stole my heart and Zappos has played such a big part in that. I've improved so much as a person during my first year here, and have had many positive life lessons along the way. I arrive at work each day knowing I can be myself in such a fun and supportive environment. It's so humbling to finally feel that I belong somewhere, and I hope I'm still part of the family here for years to come.

TRICIA O.
employee since 2010

When you go to an "All Hands" meeting and get GOOSE BUMPS from all the exciting updates, progress reports, entertainment, collaboration, creativity and touching stories that YOU have witnessed, you know you're in the right place. And I'm talking about the goose bumps like reality show judges get when they find "the one!" I'm blessed to be a part of a group of people that are changing the way we work in the workplace.

TRISH C.
employee since 2011

I haven't been speechless very many times in my life, but when I walked into Zappos for the very first time, it literally took my breath away. I felt like Alice when she fell down the rabbit hole! Mind you, this was a GOOD thing! Finally, after all my years of working, I had found my home. The zany, the crazy, the laughing and the politeness of everyone washed over me like baptismal water. I was reborn as a Zappos employee! They say it's tough to teach an old dog new tricks, but it can be done. Look at me – I've learned to relax, to enjoy each and every day, to reach out to strangers, to embrace my fellow Zapponians as friends AND family. I LOVE the Ten Core Values and have been working to incorporate them into both my work and home life.

I will never stop singing the praises of Zappos to people I talk to casually on the street, to my family and to my Facebook friends. I truly have arrived!

UJWALA B.

employee since 2010

Love it being here at Zappos! Everyone around here is nice and helpful. There is always a smiling face. :)

VANESSA S.
employee since 2005

I think that it makes PERFECT sense that we call ourselves the Zappos Family because, in a family, you get to see each other develop, face challenges, succeed, and fail, while always providing encouragement and support. I feel very fortunate to be a part of this family and can't wait to see what we do together next!

VINCENT S.
employee since 2010

I believe there is one main thing that separates people who hate going to work and those who actually enjoy it: Individual freedom.

It isn't about perks, comforts or luxurious bonuses, although all those things are welcome if the company has the resources. But there are certainly high-compensating companies that have extremely unhappy employees and high turnover. Strangely, it isn't even about loving what you do. It's a great thing when you do and it is something to work towards, but we all know people who love what they do, just not where and who they work with. So just what is the one thing that I feel leads to the best chance of happiness at work?

Creating an environment where people have the freedom to be themselves and pursue their passions.

I've never felt so comfortable in the relationship between my personality and my employer as well as my coworkers. I know I can go to work and be myself so I can actually focus on work while having a great time. Credit this to hiring like-minded individuals who can work and play together, yet bring their unique personalities, perspectives, and skills to their teams. My coworkers are more like friends, motivating me to work with them and for them.

Zappos is not a perfect place. No workplace is. But what has been built and what it is constantly evolving into is a company where, as a whole, everyone is happy and proud to be working. Because we are given the individual freedom to instill changes and be ourselves, it really is ultimately our responsibility to make the culture and the company what we want it to be. So far, as long as I have been here, I have been nothing less than awed and impressed by the contributions I'm seeing everyone make to transforming Zappos into the perfect place to work. We may never get there, but we'll have the best time we can possibly have in our journey towards it. And who knows ... they also said an internet shoe store would never work. Go, Zappos, go!

VIRGINIA R.
employee since 2010

I couldn't be happier working at Zappos. This past year I had the opportunity to move from the headquarters in Las Vegas to the new San Francisco office, and the journey has pointed me in a really exciting career direction. The San Francisco office has the same joy and enthusiasm of HQ, with the fun twist of being in a startup-like environment. I can't imagine being anywhere else!

WILL Y.
employee since 2010

Our culture means it's okay to realize that we sometimes have no idea what we are doing. But we've got amazing people around us to help us learn, change, grow, and push up to be the best at what we do. That's pretty damn special.

YOANDY T.
employee since 2010

The Zappos Culture means the freedom to be myself around others. When I go to work, I am also going home. It feels good to be around other crazy people.

YOUNG T.
employee since 2010

Compared to a traditional corporate environment, Zappos is like a theme park. You continue to discover new adventures and interesting/fun people. Sometime they make you become a kid again.

THE Z-BALL
PITCH DEMONSTRATION

51s ZAPPOS NIGHT

BATTER UP

BUBBLE GENERATORS GROUPED VIEW

2012 BALD AND BLUE

TWO SNAPS IN A Z-FORMATION

LEPRECHAUNS IN THE OVEN
FRONT VIEW

LUCKY CHARM LADS
DEMO MODE

2011 ZCON

ST. PATRICK'S EDITION

GREEN
GLASSES
GIANT
IRISH EDITION

LADIES IN
THE WATER
FRONT VIEW

ZCLT MIXER

JUNE 2012

RECYCLING
QUEEN
ACTION MODE

EARTH DAY

BECAUSE WE ONLY HAVE ONE

STREET BIKE
2000 X320
SIDE VIEW

ZAPPOS...POWERED BY PEOPLE

COUPLE
MCMUFFIN
FRONT VIEW

CIRQUE DU
ZAPPOLEIL
FRONT VIEW

ZAPPOS...POWERED BY PEOPLE

THE
BABY BOX
SPECIAL
TOP VIEW

BEAR HEADSET
FRONT VIEW

ZAPPOS...POWERED BY PEOPLE

THE DOUBLE
DOUBLE DOUBLE
RAINBOWS
FRONT VIEW

ZAPPOS...POWERED BY PEOPLE

AUDREA H.
employee since 2011

Our culture is about family first and foremost! The culture is like no other that I've seen, and is very unique & special to me. We have such a diverse group of people that bring VALUE to our company daily by bringing their "real" selves to work. It's the Zappos Family Circus staring people that are genuine, highly motivated, goal orientated, fun, and passionate people. We have some class acts, dare devils, and clowns! I love cultivating our culture amongst them!

BOBBI K.
employee since 2008

After four years, I still absolutely love coming to work every day! This is the most awesome place to work! There is fun incorporated in our work and we are all family, not just friends! I love my job ... REALLY I DO.

BRIAN F.
employee since 2010

I am as happy as I've ever been in my life. This is due in part to the fact that I spend the majority of my time with Zappos people. 40+ hours a week, most Holidays, and a lot of my free time. If that's not emblematic of "Family," I don't know what is.

JANELL G.
employee since 2011

The Zappos Culture, to me, means the ability to be myself. It's an atmosphere where you can express yourself and not be judged by your appearance, but on your performance. Zappos is a very fun atmosphere, geared more for the young and eccentric, but it caters to older folks as well. I wish more employers were like Zappos. The morale of people would be so much higher and more functional if more employers stressed performance over appearance.

JOSHUA G.
employee since 2011

Right on! Peace!

KRISTEN K.
employee since 2010

The Zappos Culture is unlike anything I have experienced, even after two years of working here in Kentucky. When I share how I spend my days at Zappos with my friends and family, they are in awe of the stories of the family-type environment that exists within the walls of Zappos. What's even more brilliant is that the family doesn't exist only within the walls, but follows into your personal life. Our culture is an opportunity to develop a second family to celebrate with, to cry with, to laugh with, and to have a drink with. I could not be more thankful for the opportunity to experience a family like my Zappos Family. I have personally changed for the better because of the experience and relationships that Zappos has introduced to my life and my world. I am so grateful, thankful and blessed.

PEEJAY L.
employee since 2012

My first year with Zappos!! Never leaving. I'm here for life!!!!

AUDREA H.
employee since 2011

Our culture is about family first and foremost! The culture is like no other that I've seen, and is very unique & special to me. We have such a diverse group of people that bring VALUE to our company daily by bringing their "real" selves to work. It's the Zappos Family Circus staring people that are genuine, highly motivated, goal orientated, fun, and passionate people. We have some class acts, dare devils, and clowns! I love cultivating our culture amongst them!

BOBBI K.
employee since 2008

After four years, I still absolutely love coming to work every day! This is the most awesome place to work! There is fun incorporated in our work and we are all family, not just friends! I love my job ... REALLY I DO.

BRIAN F.
employee since 2010

I am as happy as I've ever been in my life. This is due in part to the fact that I spend the majority of my time with Zappos people. 40+ hours a week, most Holidays, and a lot of my free time. If that's not emblematic of "Family," I don't know what is.

JANELL G.
employee since 2011

The Zappos Culture, to me, means the ability to be myself. It's an atmosphere where you can express yourself and not be judged by your appearance, but on your performance. Zappos is a very fun atmosphere, geared more for the young and eccentric, but it caters to older folks as well. I wish more employers were like Zappos. The morale of people would be so much higher and more functional if more employers stressed performance over appearance.

JOSHUA G.
employee since 2011

Right on! Peace!

KRISTEN K.
employee since 2010

The Zappos Culture is unlike anything I have experienced, even after two years of working here in Kentucky. When I share how I spend my days at Zappos with my friends and family, they are in awe of the stories of the family-type environment that exists within the walls of Zappos. What's even more brilliant is that the family doesn't exist only within the walls, but follows into your personal life. Our culture is an opportunity to develop a second family to celebrate with, to cry with, to laugh with, and to have a drink with. I could not be more thankful for the opportunity to experience a family like my Zappos Family. I have personally changed for the better because of the experience and relationships that Zappos has introduced to my life and my world. I am so grateful, thankful and blessed.

PEEJAY L.
employee since 2012

My first year with Zappos!! Never leaving. I'm here for life!!!!

FROM THE CEO AND CHIEF HAPPINESS
OFFICER OF DELIVERING HAPPINESS, LLC

A Year in Delivering Happiness

Change the world with happiness? If I said that was a remote possibility fifty years ago, I would've gotten a pat on my head and a one-way ticket to the cuckoo's nest. Thirty years ago, I would've been labeled a Haight Street hippie. Ten years ago, I would've heard, "Talk to me about the economy first, then we can talk about happy."

But there were those along the way that always believed in happiness. Just like those just accepted that the Golden Rule is the right thing to do, more or less in blind faith.

If you've been one of those believers, these kind of experiences are probably familiar: when you smile to a stranger without knowing you'd get one back, or you had a rough day at work but you still paid toll for the car behind you. Because of some fundamental belief that putting happiness out there will do more good than harm.

One of the most ironic things is that growing up, I wasn't that person. Listening to the (early) Cure and reading *The Stranger* in high school didn't lend to a happy-go-lucky childhood. I was a thinker, not a believer. But seeing that I have faith in happiness today, it's safe to say a lot has changed.

An act of happiness might've seemed to be a small thing in a big world. But now, happiness is making a difference so that even the biggest naysayer really can't say nay anymore.

TIPPING POINT

After the book *Delivering Happiness* came out in 2010, we experienced a shift not just here in the US, but around the world. People resonated with our message and raised their hands to be a part of the belief – not just to talk about happiness in their lives, but to DO something real about it. To change the world.

Truth is, all this talk about happiness isn't new. Whether it's America's founding fathers that inked the "the pursuit" of it, or Aristotle's philosophy that it's a central purpose of life, or Buddhism's ideal Middle Path between the extremes of life...it's been around.

The difference is that the world has access to the scientific data backing what felt like "the right thing to do". Research shows that, as humans, we're terrible at predicting what makes us happy. But we now know there are tangible, everyday things we can change that...to make it last. In this past year, I've seen people come out of the woodwork to share their own ways of increasing happiness. Other companies outside of Zappos validating that focusing on culture and higher purpose have a higher chance of creating long-term sustainable brands. Books like *The Happiness Advantage* by Shawn Achor scientifically show success doesn't create happiness...happiness creates success. The UN releasing its first Human Happiness Report on the world, following Bhutan's lead that happiness should be considered as important as the economy/GDP of a nation. Articles on the value of happiness have splashed the front pages of *The Harvard Business Review*, *The Economist* and *USA Today*.

And all of this, in the last year alone.

THE MOVEMENT TODAY

So what does this mean for us, Delivering Happiness? Well, everything and absolutely nothing at the same time :]

Everything because we're now able to connect all the other dots in the world that know that together we can change the world with happiness.

Nothing because – for better or for worse – we were set to go down this path of what we've learned to be true.

INSPIRE AND BE INSPIRED has been our mantra and it continues to be today. Why?

Our movement is now represented from people in 110 countries (that's over 50% of the world! A factoid that still befuddles my mind). EVERY story I hear – from people quitting their jobs, to pursuing their passion, to realizing that smiling to a stranger is creating more happiness in the world – Delivering Happiness still stays true to the reason for existing. People. And this is how:

THE 3C's

Our 3C's = Company/Community/City
 (No, not the Zappos 3 C's of Clothing, Culture and Customer Service – who knew there would be so many C's of importance;)

Our belief is that the more we make companies, communities and cities happier, the more we're creating a happier world.

COMPANY

With our DH@work team, we've been consulting with companies to figure out ways that happiness can be a more engaging, productive and profitable business model.

COMMUNITY

With our DH Collection apparel line (just launching on Zappos as I type!), we're giving back 100% of our net profits back to providing tools, classes and events so people can learn ways to create more happiness in their lives.

CITY

If the science of happiness can be applied to a person's life and companies, we believe the same things can work for a city too. So we're building the tools to measure and help other cities learn from all that's to happen in downtown Vegas.

This has been an incredible year of evolution for us – taking DH beyond the book and bus tour has given us this amazing foundation of what we can do from here. No doubt, it's been challenging (like any startup environment can be) but by staying true to our values and people that inspire us every day, the more we know we're changing the world, one company/community/city at a time.

Here's to changing the world with happiness!

-Jenn Lim
CEO and Chief Happiness Officer – Delivering Happiness, LLC

DELIVERING HAPPINESS

...THROUGH THE YEAR

VERY
HAPPY PIZZA
VEGGIE COMBINATION

BURGER
CONSTRUCTION
SIDE VIEW

2012 CORPORATE CHALLENGE

DOWNTOWN LAS VEGAS

FOUR PEACE, ONE THUMB
FRONT VIEW

3,504 NEW WORLD RECORD
zappos.com
MOST SIMULTANEOUS HIGH FIVES

MOST SIMULTANEOUS HIGH FIVES

WORLD RECORD

A GOOD SIGN
WIDE VIEW

WRECKING
CREW
GROUP VIEW

CITY HALL DEMOLITION

BREAKING DOWN WALLS

BOYZ III MEN
SIDE VIEW

2012 ALL HANDS MEETING

THIRD QUARTER

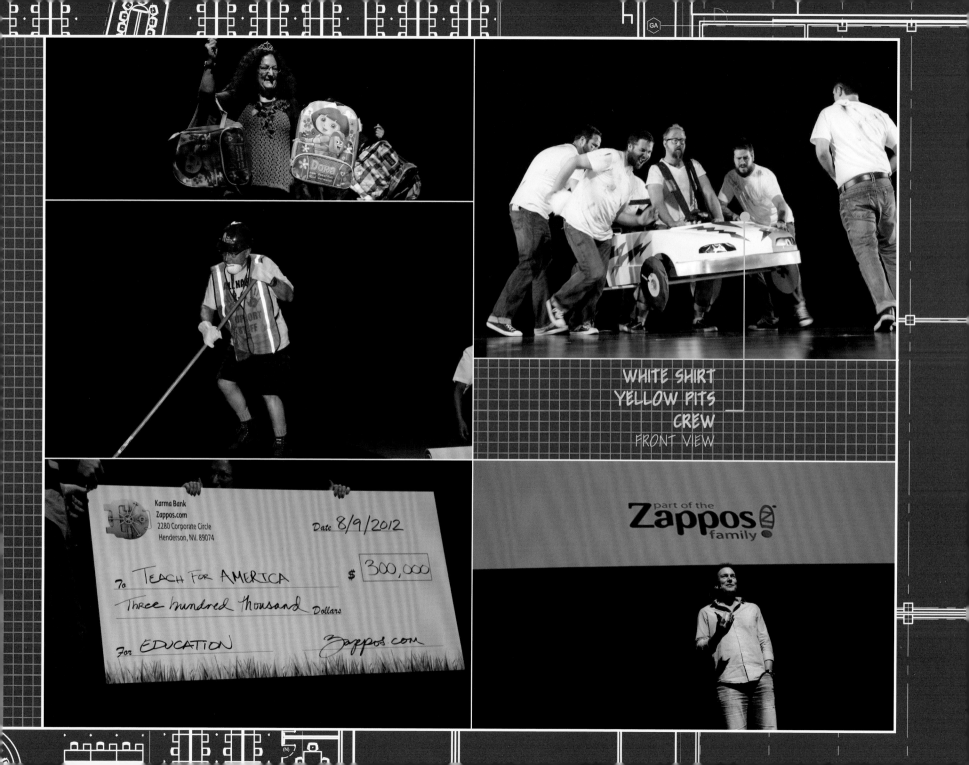

WHITE SHIRT
YELLOW PITS
CREW
FRONT VIEW

Karma Bank
Zappos.com
2280 Corporate Circle
Henderson, NV. 89074

Date 8/9/2012

To Teach For America $ 300,000

Three hundred thousand Dollars

For EDUCATION   Zappos.com

part of the
Zappos
family

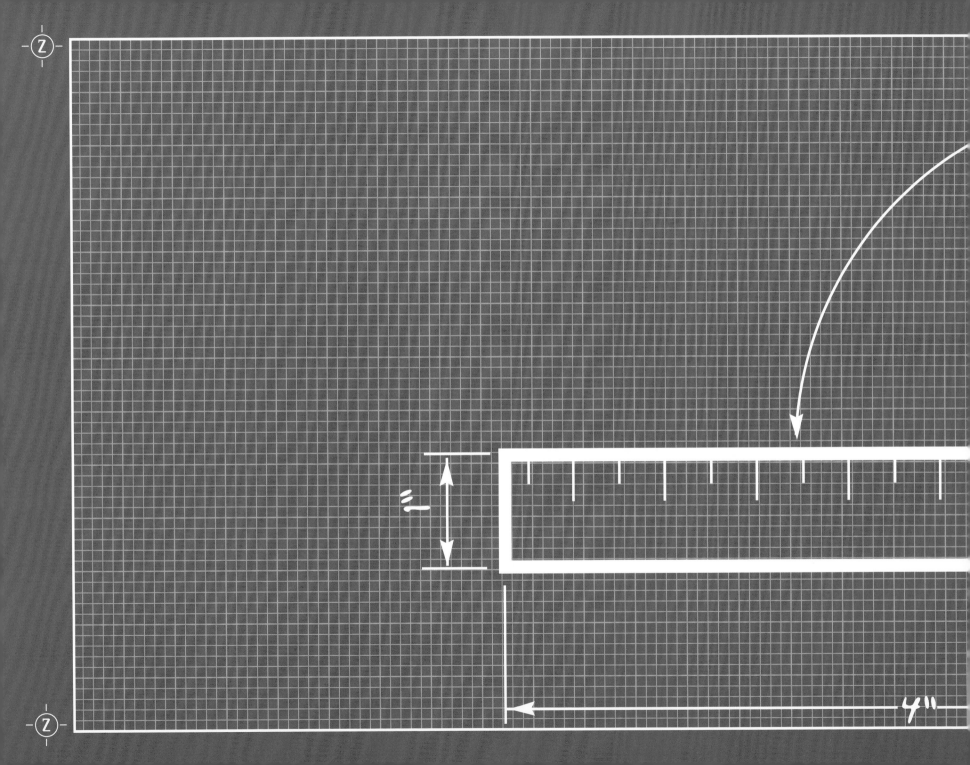

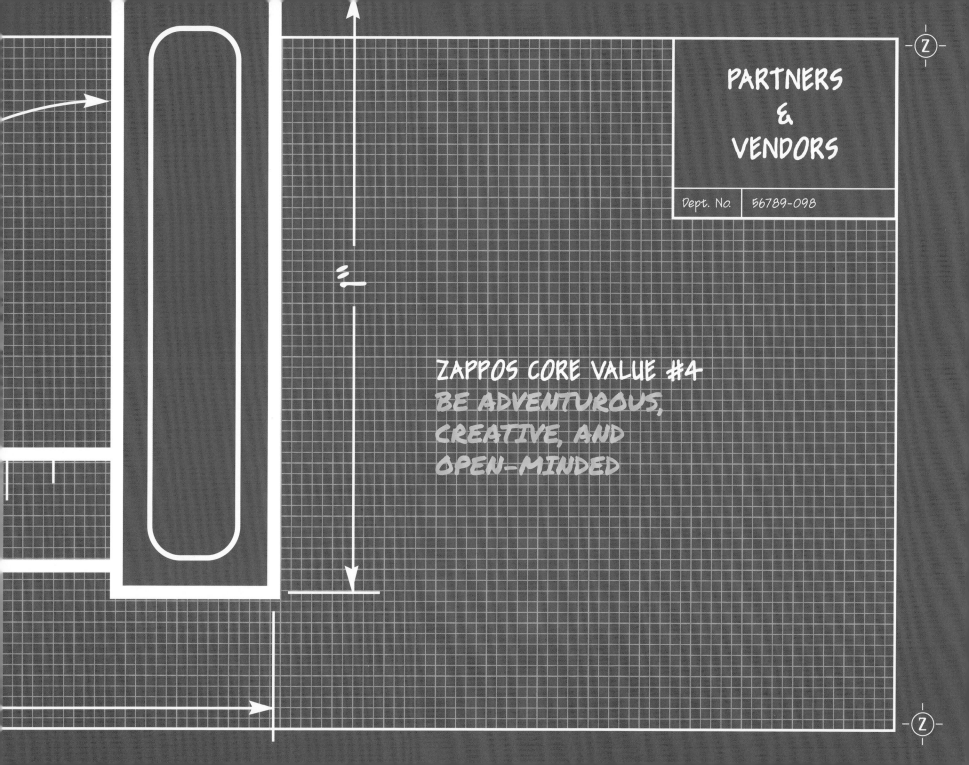

PARTNERS
&
VENDORS

Dept. No. | 56789-098

ZAPPOS CORE VALUE #4
BE ADVENTUROUS,
CREATIVE, AND
OPEN-MINDED

MOLLY D.
contractor since 2009

The Zappos Culture is a living, breathing thing that takes care and feeding to come to life every day. I can't think of a day where I haven't thought or spoken one of the Ten Core Values as it relates to my day-to-day work. I've never worked in a place that truly lives and breathes its core values – Zappos rocks!!

JESSE K.
contractor since 2012

They were wrong about what they said of human intelligence--that our mental superiority alone enabled humans, but not other apes, to conquer the earth. It was not just smart or fit individuals that propagated and flourished, but humans in groups too. Cultures, more than brains or brawn, determine the success or failure of human groups, ancient or contemporary. But what is culture?

Culture is what happens when thoughts, feelings, and behaviors instantiate themselves in the physical or social environment. When the instantiation is physical, it is obvious to anyone with eyes; when it is social, it becomes visible only to the initiated and invisible to the outside world. And this is how culture becomes a superpower for groups. Culture, done right, can open the heart, minimize self consciousness, maximize the interests of the group, and infuse missions with purpose and meaning.

Zappos' culture does not exist independent of us, it is a product of us. It will live on after we're gone. It is the thing that creates the context for our success. Contribute to it, and guard it as if your life depended on it, after all--it IS why we're here.

CONTRACTOR UNDER ZAPPOS.COM
partner since 2010

My best friend once told me that her boss doesn't allow microwaves in the office because he doesn't like the smell of other people's food. She is forced to buy lunch every day and she is so busy some days that she doesn't have time to get lunch and thus, doesn't eat until she gets home from work. I have never felt more fortunate to work at a place where employees' needs come first. In the end, it's not so much what you're doing, it's who you are doing it with, and I get to work with some of the smartest, most generous and kind people in the world. I wish I could get all of my friends a job at Zappos.

CORINA C.
partner since 2011

This past year has been amazing. From team buildings and one-on- ones, the people within this company have helped to make my life as great as it is! I'm surrounded by people who mean so much to me. Not to mention, Zappos brought me my best friend, albeit unintentionally. How great is that!? Uhmayzing!

JUICY COUTURE CLOTHING
partner since 2009

While working with the Zappos team (and God knows Juicy Couture has worked with many of them), a word sticks out in my mind and that word is Partnership. There is no other retail partner in this industry who that truly cares for their vendors like the Zappos team. No matter the employee, their level, or their team while on any coast, which ever home front or bar you may be in, you will always feel the partnership between you and your Zappos team.

NYDJ
partner since 2007

I am the sales representative for NYDJ and have been working closely with members of the Clothing Team for five years. I can't say enough about what a terrific experience it has been to work with each and every one of this wonderful group. The attribute of the Zappos Culture that hit me first, and has been consistent throughout the years, is that all of the buyers truly treat you as a partner in growing the business. It is an open line of communication, an ongoing exchange of ideas, and just plain working together to have the product succeed.

REBECCA TAYLOR CLOTHING

partner since 2010

Zappos delivers a feeling that is uncomplicated, pure, and bursting with energy! The environment is something that you have never discovered before. You must see it for yourself.

TOMMY BAHAMA

partner since 2007

HOPE... at a period when the world was upside down and everyone feared the worst, Zappos and team Hardy always asked "how high," how much can we do?... the glass was always half full. The players all worked hard and played hard and the numbers proved it to be a winning formula. Anything is possible. I love working with people that believe "yes, we can." Good Times.

TWIG FOOTWEAR, LLC

partner since 2003

There are so many ways Zappos impresses their vendors. Without fail, the one work group of employees who always amaze me are the folks that drive the shuttles. I refer to this group as the "ambassadors of rides," They are always on time, but also this dedicated group of guys and gals are unanimously upbeat, positive and go out of their way to ensure that your first and last contact with Zappos HQ is positive. They are apostles for the brand, stewards for the company, and just all around good guys. On my last visit, when I thanked Zack for giving me a ride to the airport, he replied, "thank you for letting me take you."

UNITRENDS USA, INC.

partner since 2004

We are now in our eighth year as aof partnernering with Zappos, and the Zappos Culture remains as solid as it was on our first tour of those crazy offices. Earlier this year, when Zappos was hacked, I remember seeing it all over the media and thinking oh man, this is going to be bad. Although business may have been affected in the short term, the way Zappos handled itself was very commendable. As a vendor and as a customer (of course), I immediately received an email from Tony explaining the situation, and how to quickly resolve it. So I resolved it, and spread the word out to friends and family who are also customers. I don't remember any other companies coming out and being so honest about the situation after being hacked. This just solidified my thoughts about how awesome Zappos is regardless of the circumstance. Open and honest communication – in this case you guys nailed it. It was also great to see how all Zappos employees switched their focus on taking care of customers throughout the whole process, because that's what it's all about anyway! Don't ever lose the focus on your culture; it's enviable in so many ways.

Zappos sandals and Zappos crops on a New York City street :-)
-Kristie Kistner

"OUR HOUSE" :)
ICA APOSTOL

WEDDING KICKS
VANESSA POTTS

This backpack was bought for me, and my first question was, "It's from Zappos right? You know they have the best deals." It stuck by my side through walking across TN.

Thanks Zappos for being SO awesome!
-Jenni Siegel

We are cheesemongers!
-Barbara Garcia

CUSTOMER APPRECIATION

CUSTOMERS AROUND THE WORLD

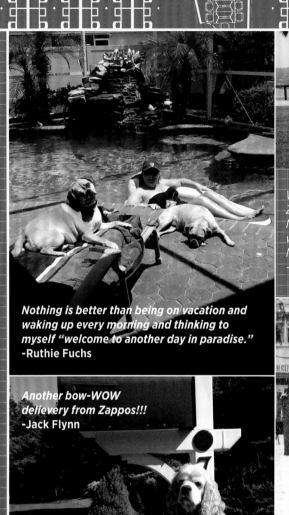

Nothing is better than being on vacation and waking up every morning and thinking to myself "welcome to another day in paradise."
-Ruthie Fuchs

Another bow-WOW delievery from Zappos!!!
-Jack Flynn

What makes you happy & Favorite Zappos item (all in one photo!) Marrying my best friend in Jamaica while wearing my purple rsvp: Michaela shoes from Zappos.com!!!!
-Melissa Hiester

My name is Oleksii, i'm from Kharkiv, Ukraine. Let me provide you with my image which shows how much i love and enjoy every moment of my life:))))
-Oleksii Volkov

Keep up the magic -- we're happy to be a part of it on the other side of the world!
-Adrienne A. Isakovic

"This is what makes me smile" Hi this is a picture of my almost 2 year old daughter and our dog Lola....oh and wearing her Stride Rite shoes from Zappos too :)
-Coll S

Here is a beautiful pic of my grandaughter at her school carnival getting a heart painted on her face. Perfect for anything to do with family and love. :)

PS - love Zappos and Tony. XOXO
-Susan Kemp

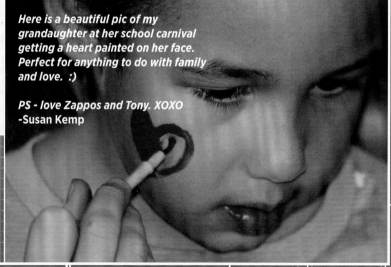

Welcome Home 😃

SEPTEMBER 6, 2012
DOWNTOWN HERE WE GO...